THE MARKETING O

THE MARKETING OF INDUSTRIAL PRODUCTS

SECOND EDITION

Edited by
Norman Hart

McGRAW-HILL Book Company (UK) Limited

London · New York · St Louis · San Francisco · Auckland
Bogotá · Guatemala · Hamburg · Johannesburg · Lisbon · Madrid
Mexico · Montreal · New Delhi · Panama · Paris · San Juan
São Paulo · Singapore · Sydney · Tokyo · Toronto

Published by
McGRAW-HILL Book Company (UK) Limited
MAIDENHEAD · BERKSHIRE · ENGLAND

British Library Cataloguing in Publication Data

The marketing of industrial products.—2nd ed.
  1. Marketing
  I. Hart, Norman A.   II. Wilson, Aubrey.
  Marketing of industrial products

658.8   HF5415

ISBN 0-07-084767-3

Library of Congress Cataloging in Publication Data

Main entry under title:

The Marketing of industrial products.
  Rev. ed. of: The marketing of industrial products /
  edited by Aubrey Willson. 1966, c1965.
  Bibliography: p.
  Includes index.
  1. Industrial marketing—Addresses, essays, lectures.
  I. Hart, Norman A.

HF5415.M3165   1984   658.8   84-15757

ISBN 0-07-084767-3

12345WC   87654

Typeset by Eta Services (Typesetters) Ltd, Beccles, Suffolk, and printed and bound in Great Britain by William Clowes Limited, Beccles, Suffolk

CONTENTS

THE AUTHORS

Alfred Alles, DIC, Dipl.Ing., C.Eng., M.I.Mech.E., is an industrial consultant who, after 20 years of engineering R & D, production and export sales experience has applied his extensive knowledge of the European industrial scene of action to international marketing of industrial products generally and to the use of exhibitions as marketing tools particularly.

Peter L. Beddowes B.A.(Econ.), M.A., M.Inst.M., is a Director of Ashridge Management College and specializes in marketing consultancy and training work.

Peter studied at the then newly founded University of Lancaster and returned a few years later to complete an MA in Marketing.

Peter's business career spanned seven years in two marketing management positions prior to consultancy experience at a business school in New Zealand.

Since joining Ashridge in 1977 he has developed long-term advisory relationships with a number of medium size companies in marketing and business development.

Gordon Brand, B.Sc.(Econ.), M.Sc., Cert. ITP(Harvard), M.Inst.M., is Head of the Business Studies Department, Roehampton Institute of Higher Education. He was formerly Principal Lecturer and Subject Chairman for Marketing at the South West Regional Management Centre, Bristol Polytechnic. His experience has included sales and marketing research with Standard Telephones and Cables. He was at one time Head of Research at Industrial Market Research Ltd and is the author of *The Industrial Buying Decision* and co-author of *How British Industry Sells.*

Martyn R. Brown, B.A., Dip.M., A.Inst.M., M.CAM., is Director of Marketing and Sales Management Programmes at Ashridge Management College.

For many years he worked in marketing, planning and sales in the automotive industry, first with Ford Motor Company and later with Lex and Heron. He then moved into marketing consultancy and training with Marketing Improvements Ltd before moving to Ashridge. His wide consulting experience ranges across different company sizes, types and industries, particularly in developing and implementing industrial marketing strategies.

E. J. Davis, B.Sc.(Econ.), FIS, FMS, is a member of the Senior Faculty at Henley: The Management College. Before joining the College in 1975 he had worked with Gillette, British Overseas Airways, the Attwood Group, the British Market Research Bureau and the J. Walter Thompson Company. He is a Fellow of the Marketing Society and of the Institute of Statisticians, and member of the Market Research Society. He is the author of *Experimental Marketing* and numerous papers, and was awarded the Gold Medal of the Market Research Society for his work on test marketing.

Norman A. Hart, M.Sc., F.CAM, FIPR, Dip.M., has been Director of the CAM Foundation from 1972 to 1984, and is a director of the well-established business-to-business advertising agency, Carter Matanle Southern, and of Interact Communications Ltd, London. He was previously Chief Marketing Executive of IAB Marketing, a government-sponsored management consultancy.

He joined Roles & Parker in 1957 and was a Group Chief Executive when he left to become Publicity Manager of a Unilever company, Thames Board Mills. He subsequently became Marketing Manager and finally went into publishing with Morgan Grampian where he was Divisional General Manager.

A frequent speaker on advertising, public relations and marketing both in the UK and overseas, Mr Hart is the author and editor of a number of books including *Business to Business Advertising*. He is a Visiting Fellow of the University of Bradford, a Visiting Associate of Ashridge Management College and holds a Master's Degree in Business Administration.

John Leach is Principal of the marketing consultancy, Marketing Support Services, based in Northampton. His main areas of specialization are in the fields of strategic market planning and new product development, and he practises these through traditional consultancy assignments and through the medium of marketing training for a number of well-known companies and as a visiting lecturer at the College of the Institute of Marketing. He is an economics graduate of the University of Kent and has a master's degree in marketing from Bradford University Management Centre.

Theodore Levitt, Edward W. Carter Professor of Business Administration, Harvard University Graduate School of Business Administration, is the author of numerous articles on economic, political, management, and marketing subjects, including the prize-winning article 'Marketing myopia' in the *Harvard Business Review*; a four-times winner of McKinsey Awards competitions for articles in the *Harvard Business Review*; winner of Academy of Management Award for one of the outstanding business books of the year, 1962, for *Innovation in Marketing*; winner of John Hancock Award for Excellence in Business Journalism in 1969; recipient of Charles Coolidge Parlin Award as 'Marketing man of the year', 1970; recipient of the George Gallup Award for Marketing Excellence, 1976; recipient of the 1978 Paul D. Converse Award of the American Marketing Association for major contributions to marketing.

Theodore Levitt is author of *Innovation in Marketing*; *Industrial Purchasing Behavior: A Study in Communications Effects*; *The Marketing Mode: Pathways to Corporate Growth*; *The Third Sector: New Tactics for a Responsive Society*; *Marketing for Business Growth*; *Marketing: A Contemporary Analysis* and *The Marketing Imagination*.

The author is on the board of directors of Consolidated Natural Gas Company, GCA Corporation, the Gintel Fund Inc. and Gintel ERISA Fund Inc. He is a Trustee of the Marketing Science Institute and Consultant to a large number of major international corporations in manufacturing, finance, natural resources and trade.

William Paterson, F.CAM, F.IPA. After training in personnel and sales management, Bill Paterson spent some 30 years in corporate public affairs work with the last 20 years as Director of Public Relations with the TI Group and since 1979 as Specialist Director Public Relations with Whitbread.

He is a Fellow of the Institute of Public Relations and a Fellow of the CAM Foundation in addition to being Chairman of the CAM Development Committee and on the ISBA Finance Committee. He is a contributor to management journals and a speaker on public affairs.

*Professor Leslie W. Rodger, B.Sc.(Econ.), FBIM, F.Inst.M., FMS, M.CAM,*was Head of the Department of Business Organization at Heriot-Watt University, Edinburgh from 1974 to 1983, following a career of 25 years in business.

A graduate of London University, he took his first job with Tube Investments as market research executive. He subsequently became a member of the Economist Intelligence Unit and an editorial assistant with *The Economist*. Between 1951 and 1955 he was market research executive and later marketing executive with Young and Rubican Advertising Ltd, and from 1955 to 1965 he was Marketing Manager and later Director of Marketing, European Marketing Co-ordinator and member of the board of McCann-Erickson Advertising, and travelled extensively in Europe, Scandinavia and the USA on marketing assignments. He was appointed General Manager of the Central Marketing Services Division of Mullard Ltd, part of the Dutch-owned international Philips concern, in 1969.

Professor Rodger is author of *Marketing in a Competitive Economy*. Also for Associated Business Programmes in 1974 he edited *Marketing Concepts and Strategies in the Next Decade*. He has been a contributor to *Marketing and The Consumer Movement*, ed. J. Mitchell, McGraw-Hill, 1978 and *Marketing Handbook*, ed. M. Rines, Gower Press and Institute of Marketing (to be published shortly). His latest book *Statistics for Marketing* is published by McGraw-Hill.

Professor Rodger is a Fellow of the British Institute of Marketing and was Chairman of its Edinburgh branch, 1981–83. He is also a Fellow and former Chairman (1971–72) of the British Marketing Society, a Fellow of the British Institute of Management, and a member of the CAM Foundation. Among his many responsibilities within Heriot-Watt University, he was Chairman of the Management Studies Board and a member of the board of Unilink, the University's business consultancy division. He was appointed Dean of the Faculty of Economic and Social Studies, a post he held from 1977–80.

John Samuel is a Fellow of both CAM and IPA. His career in advertising has been spent in London agencies with a switch halfway from orthodox 'consumer' markets to the emerging business or industrial sector. From 1962, he led Roles & Parker's drive for the higher standards of advice, creativity and planning in industrial promotion—the success of that initiative can be judged by R & P's own marked progress, its reputation in the agency business and the number of agencies which have embraced business and industrial clients with a new enthusiasm. John is an ex-Chairman of the IPA Industrial Committee and, currently, Chairman of the CAM Graduate Committee.

Richard N. Skinner, B.A., F.Inst.M., was educated at Brentwood School and University College, London, where he read classics. Richard Skinner spent his first 10 years in marketing with Remington Rand Ltd, moving from direct selling, through sales training and field management, to product management and market research. He joined Reliance Systems Ltd as Sales Manager in 1964 and is now Deputy Managing Director. His publications include *Launching New Products in Competitive Markets, Organizing for Marketing on a Small Budget, How British Industry Prices* and *Pricing Strategies to Cope with Inflation*. He has lectured on selling and marketing topics to a variety of organizations including BIM, IEE, the Japanese Marketing Association, CAM and the Institute of Marketing, of which he is a Fellow.

Hugh Walker, M.A., M.CAM, is an independent management consultant practising as Hugh Walker & Associates, a firm he started in 1971. After war service in the RNVR, he graduated in Politics, Philosophy and Economics at Hertford College, Oxford. He started his business career in the International Department of J. Walter Thompson's London Office. He has run sales and strategic marketing training courses for a wide range of industrial clients and, for the past five years, he has directed the Marketing Industrial Products course at the College of the Institute of Marketing.

Christopher West, B.Sc.(Econ.), is a graduate of the London School of Economics with an honours degree in geography. He subsequently obtained a wide range of experience in marketing and planning through appointments held in London and Paris.

He was with Industrial Marketing Research Ltd until 1984 and is now Managing Director of Business Marketing Services Ltd. Prior to joining IMR he worked in the Economics and Supply and Planning Departments of Shell International Petroleum Company where he carried out a number of studies on the oil and energy industries. He subsequently served as an economist with Eurofinance, a Paris based financial and economic consultancy where he carried out a number of European-wide industry studies and short-term economic forecasts for a group of leading European and American banks. He was also engaged on projects for the EEC and OECD.

Christopher West has edited two books: *Marketing on a Small Budget* and *Inflation— A Management Guide to Survival*. He has lectured extensively for management organizations in the United Kingdom, Scandinavia, the Netherlands and Spain and has broadcast on the BBC.

His project experience at IMR covers a wide range of product and service businesses and he has specialized in the use of market research for corporate planning applications.

Ray Willsmer, B.A., F.CAM, FMS, M.Inst.M., is one of the few men to have held board level appointments in manufacturing, marketing and advertising. He now has his own group of companies involved in advertising, marketing consultancy and training and retailing. He is the author of *Directing the Marketing Effort* and *Basic Arts of Marketing* as well as having contributed to several books. He is actively involved in marketing education as Chairman of the Governing Body of the College for the Distributive Trades and as a specialist member of the Council for National Academic Awards.

Aubrey Wilson, who after a long and very successful business career is now an independent consultant, is acknowledged internationally as one of the pioneers of industrial marketing. Many of the techniques in use today were devised by him and he continues to develop new practical approaches for improving productivity in marketing. It was Aubrey Wilson who originally conceived the idea of this book when industrial marketing was in its infancy in Europe and when he felt a truly relevant text was, at that time, beyond the capability and experience of any one person.

He has now published nine books on marketing subjects. A survey of British universities and business schools revealed that two of his books are listed in the 20 most highly recommended texts for marketing courses. He is also a frequent contributor on marketing subjects to the *Financial Times, Harvard Business Review, Management Today* and many other publications. Mr Wilson was recently awarded the annual prize of the European Association of Marketing Consultants for his contribution to the practice of marketing.

R. M. S. Wilson, M.Sc., B.Phil., B.A., B.Com., FCMA, FCCA, Dip.M., M.Inst.M., M.CAM., is a non-executive director of a number of companies; a consultant (on marketing and distribution) to the World Bank, and (on economics, financial control and marketing) to Harbridge House (Europe). He has had commercial experience in a number of industries (covering industrial and consumer goods and services), as well as having been a Research Associate of Roles & Parker Ltd, the industrial advertising agency.

Among the publications he has produced are *Financial Dimensions of Marketing* (Macmillan); *Management Controls & Marketing Planning* (Heinemann); *The Marketing of Financial Services* (MCB); *Cost Control Handbook* (Gower); *Technological Forecasting* (Penguin); and *Financial Control* (McGraw-Hill). He is currently active as an Associate Editor of *Management Monitor* and *Journal of Enterprise Management*.

PREFACE

The first edition of *The Marketing of Industrial Products* was a pioneering, innovative, almost revolutionary text which put industrial marketing firmly on the map. Its authors were authoritative and its editor, Aubrey Wilson, outstandingly talented in orchestrating a very wide range of disparate inputs into a cohesive whole. Much was the acclaim given to the first edition by businessmen, academics, students and the management press.

Twenty years later much has changed: indeed the change is due in no little measure to the impact which the book had upon British Industry. A 'second generation' of the text was therefore called for, and for the most part that is what the second edition comprises. With a number of the original contributors, and a whole list of new ones, the latest offering attempts to bring to those responsible for directing and executing business-to-business marketing a comprehensive survey of the latest principles and practices that lead to the successful operation of a company.

One chapter only has been retained in its original form, Levitt's Marketing Myopia. This has become the great classical statement on marketing philosophy, and its authority remains as soundly based as ever, notwithstanding it being twenty years old.

This book is dedicated to the thousands of managers who conduct industrial marketing operations still in the face of uncertainty, ignorance and even opposition from their colleagues in other functional areas. It is commended to such managers and indeed to chief executives who may be struck by the emphasis given to the vital role of marketing within the corporate strategy. At the other end of the scale, students will stand to benefit from a text which bridges the gap between concepts and real life practice. The book will be relevant especially to CAM, Institute of Marketing, and Business Studies students.

A final tribute must be paid to Aubrey Wilson for collaborating in this project with his usual dynamic enthusiasm, even to the extent of contributing the final chapter.

Norman A. Hart

INTRODUCTION

Norman Hart, the editor of this book, was always the most enthusiastic supporter of its previous version, sometimes, both the original editor and contributors felt, more than it deserved. For many years after the last of the several impressions and the paperback edition of the book went out of print, he had urged me to revise and update it—a suggestion which I found by no means tempting. I had learned that to edit a book is infinitely more difficult than to write one, and that it calls for skills which I had difficulty in acquiring and no ability at all to retain—diplomacy, tact, patience, persistence and self-discipline. It was natural, therefore, when the pressure for a new book really mounted that Norman Hart should undertake the task and, in any event, my own interests some seven books further on, had changed. I was thus delighted to hand the mantle and title to Norman Hart, confident that he would vastly improve the approach and contents and introduce a fresh and exhilarating new editorial style. I am indeed happy that he should have felt the subjects and ordering of the original book were sufficiently relevant to retain them with little alteration and to find new contributors to fit the subjects. My confidence was well placed and it is neither patronizing nor false humility to say the task has been well done, and better done than by his predecessor.

The 16 authors of the 1963 version of this book were all my friends. Those whom the two decades have spared are still so. Indeed, exactly half of the authors contributing to this book continue to be active in marketing and remain close personal friends although only three of the original contributors are now included. Retirement, changes of activity and interests and the emergence of new responsibilities and pressures are among the reasons for their being either unable to revise their original chapters or for feeling they were no longer sufficiently involved in the areas and subjects they discussed, to justify their re-inclusion.

If it served no other purpose I am convinced that all the contributors, like myself, in re-reading the original chapters which they either wrote or which they are now replacing will have been as astonished and delighted as I am at how much industrial marketing has changed for the better in the two decades which have passed. Obviously not everything has advanced as far or as well as it might have been hoped, but overall, without being complacent, practical industrial marketers and teachers have much to congratulate themselves on. This book, it is hoped, will give impetus to the process of taking industrial marketing further forward and perhaps, when the third edition is prepared in the year 2000, the new authors will deal kindly with us all.

Aubrey Wilson
London 1984

ONE

THE MARKETING CONCEPT

Leslie Rodger

WHAT IS IT?

It is *not* a panacea for all your business problems.

It is *not* a re-labelling exercise, e.g., for 'sales manager' read 'marketing manager'.

It is *not* a case of 'tried it, old boy' like some companies have 'tried' advertising or 'tried' management by objectives.

It is *not* something to which you only pay lip service to show that you are 'with it'. Lip service is the kiss of death for marketing or anything else in business.

It is *not* just another reorganization.

It is *not* a sort of philosopher's stone that will turn base products into gold.

It is, none the less, a philosophy and an attitude of mind towards the way you run your business. It is a philosophy founded on the belief that profitable sales and satisfactory returns on investment are best achieved by identifying, anticipating and solving customers' problems. It is an attitude of mind which places the customer at the forefront of the business and orients the firm towards its markets and customers rather than towards its factories and laboratories.

It is both a way of thinking about the purpose of the business (why are we here?) and a way of doing business (how do we intend to operate?). According to the marketing concept a business firm exists to achieve 'the most profitable match between the firm's resources and capabilities and the requirements of the customer'.[1] It will seek to do this through 'the identification, creation and profitable delivery of optimum customer values, i.e., maximum values at minimum costs'.[2] A firm has neither a moral nor a social responsibility to provide customer value at any cost, irrespective of what the customer is able or willing to pay. To survive and grow, a firm must earn a satisfactory long-run rate of profit if it is to continue to serve its customers over the long term.

ENTREPRENEURSHIP AND COMPETITION

None of this, of course, is new. The old style entrepreneur knew quite a lot about marketing. Maybe he did not call it that, but that is what it was. An entrepreneur is someone who identifies and anticipates a market need and then marshals and organizes resources to satisfy that need.

Since the Industrial Revolution, the structure of organization has changed and managerial functions have become more specialized in order to cope with the growing complexity, diversity

1

and volatility of markets and greater sophistication of customers' wants. The emergence of the multi-business, multi-product and multi-national organization has been a response to these developments.

The management of a business, even of the big multi-national companies, starts out being entrepreneurial. All businesses initially develop around a narrow product/service base. As the business grows, management has less time to devote to the entrepreneurial role. It gets bogged down in operational details and administration. One hopeful way of counteracting this trend has been by divisionalization or breaking down the total business into product divisions, strategic business units or profit centres.

Since the 1950s, there have been indications that the initial entrepreneurial thrust of many businesses, sparked off by the Industrial Revolution, has begun to run out of steam, at least so far as their strategic core activity is concerned. So we find managements moving into other businesses—businesses that they know little about or, at any rate, don't always know as well as their original businesses—and using diversification as a vehicle for sustaining growth. The late 1950s and the 1960s witnessed a diversification boom as organizations sought to acquire counter-cyclical businesses and to make themselves less dependent on one product, one market, one industry or one country.

However, complexity rather than sheer size is the source of many of our business problems. When the scale and the physical dispersion of operations increase beyond the control of one man or of a small, close-knit founder group, a proliferation of functional specialisms develop. Greater product and service complexity, greater distribution complexity and wider geographical dispersion of operations, inevitably introduce difficulties of coordination and integration.

Running parallel to this growing organizational complexity, since the mid-1950s, many traditional markets have shown signs of instability and, in some cases, decline, brought on by heightening international competition; political, social, economic and technological changes; and the emergence of new products based on newer technologies.

One consequence of all of this has been that entrepreneurial managers have had to cede much of the corporate high ground to the administrators and operating managers preoccupied with the day-to-day problems of running a competitive business. The entrepreneurial mode of behaviour of the firm ('what should we be making that can be profitably sold?') has taken second place to an aggressive, competitive mode of behaviour ('how can we dispose of what the factory makes?') involving rationalization, cost pruning and price cutting. This latter remains the typical mode of behaviour in most industrial firms.

THE MARKETING LINK

Marketing, if implemented in both the spirit and the letter, can be the linking concept that helps to bring these two modes of behaviour into better balance—on the other hand, innovative, creative, future-oriented entrepreneurial activity and, on the other hand, customer-centred, problem-solving, competitive activity. Entrepreneurial activity is concerned with identifying market opportunities and developing new, future profit generating links with the environment. Competitive activity is concerned with exploiting and extracting profit from existing links with the environment.

The rationale for the marketing concept is to provide a working philosophy that will enable the firm to marshal its efforts and resources so as to pursue its objectives under the most competitively advantageous conditions, now and in the future.

At the entrepreneurial level, marketing is concerned with investigating and forecasting future market developments and customer requirements and how these may impact on the firm's assets—which are taken to include not only cash resources, plant and machinery, but also its products and services, trade-marks, brand franchises, corporate reputation, managerial and technological skills. It is concerned with reaching out beyond the present asset base, current operations and capabilities in order to identify and anticipate market opportunities that, in the first place, will enhance the value of the firm's existing assets and, in the second place, may call for asset renewal or additional assets, as well as for new and, perhaps, unrelated operations and capabilities.[3] The first obligation of management is to maximize the value of its existing assets, i.e., effectively to run the business it has. Its second obligation is to determine and provide the assets it needs to ensure its continued survival and growth.

At the operational level, marketing is concerned with doing everything that needs to be done to make it easier, more attractive and more beneficial for customers to do business with your organization rather than with a competitor's organization—by creating new first-time customers, by winning customers from competitors and by keeping both.

Thus, the adoption of the marketing concept has the potential to confer on firms—even large ones like IBM, GEC, ICI and Unilever—a flexibility of mind (to capitalize on tomorrow's market opportunities and to anticipate and pre-empt market threats) as well as a fleetness of foot (to beat today's competition on the ground).

ROLE OF MARKETING

The aim of a business—any business—is to be competitively effective. Competitive effectiveness is measured in terms of market response, and judged on the basis of commercial results, that is profitable sales. These results are external to the business enterprise in that they are only realizable outside the firm, in the market place.

From one point of view, therefore, it can be argued that the only thing that a business generates internally are costs. The market is the only place where profit can be made. Even where one firm sells its output, or supplies services to another firm within the same group, it is perfectly valid to regard the latter company as representing the market—or one market, at any rate—of the supplying company. Everything that a business unit does accumulates cost—whether buying in or selling out—right up to the point where cash receipts from actual sales flow back into the unit. Without an adequate cash flow, a firm cannot innovate and cannot finance future profit-generating activity. It is cash flow which determines whether or not the firm will continue to exist and, beyond that, the boundaries of its opportunity for success.

A business unit buys inputs from the environment—buildings, labour, machinery, raw materials, semi-processed goods and components—and sells outputs to the environment. Whenever a firm's own products—whether they be work-in-progress, or finished goods—stop moving, for any reason, on their journey towards the intermediate customer (who may be a processor, converter or distributor) and on towards the final user or consumer, they accumulate costs—of warehousing and storage, insurance, stock handling, stock obsolescence and deterioration, and working capital tied up in unsaleable or slow-moving inventory.

All of the firm's efforts are converted into commercial results, that is to say, profitable sales, by satisfied customers, which is why business may properly be described as a customer-servicing and customer-problem-solving process and not just a goods-producing process. In this context, competitive effectiveness means servicing the customer better than one's competitors. This means doing the better thing by the customer—identifying, anticipating and developing the better product and service packages, determining the better pricing, promotion and distribution policies in relation to the market's existing and emerging requirements. Neither technical leadership nor superior quality control is, of itself, enough. First and foremost, the business unit has to be organized to be competitively effective in terms of being in the right markets with the right products and services to sell at the time the customer wants them, at a price which the market can absorb and at a profit which makes it worth while to the supplier. Customers can be expensive or loss making as well as profitable. What matters in the end is profitable customer relationships.

A major concern of marketing is to determine what will constitute competitive effectiveness tomorrow, next year and five years from now. Your competitive effectiveness in the market place today is the result of strategic decisions taken sometime earlier, perhaps several years ago. Today's strategic decisions must be made with tomorrow's market requirements in mind.

Theory and practice

Various persons within the business unit have always been responsible for product planning and development, pricing, selling, promotion and distribution. But it has not always been the overall responsibility of one individual or group. It has not been uncommon in the past for product planning and development to be the responsibility of the production or engineering department, and for the promotion and distribution to be the responsibility of the sales department. There was not necessarily any coordination between the two beyond the understanding that it was the job of the sales department to dispose, as profitably as it could, of the goods churned out by the production department without having any or much of a say in what products ought to be produced. In this situation, a business unit was said to be 'production and sales oriented'.

'Selling', says Theodore Levitt in Chapter 15, 'focuses on the needs of the seller, marketing on the needs of the buyer. Selling is preoccupied with the seller's need to convert his product into cash; marketing with the idea of satisfying the needs of the customer by means of the product and the whole cluster of things associated with creating, delivering and finally consuming it.' The sales-oriented company sees the customer as 'somebody "out there" who, with proper cunning, can be separated from his loose change . . . and is not concerned with the values that the exchange is all about'. The marketing-oriented company on the other hand, takes a consolidating view of the whole business process and seeks to integrate all the elements—R & D, design, engineering, production, distribution and selling—in order to identify, anticipate, create and satisfy the customer's requirements profitably.

The marketing-oriented approach looks first at what the customer's problems are that he is trying to solve, then develops a product–service solution, puts together the most effective 'marketing mix', i.e., the most appropriate product/service/price/promotion/distribution combination, and gears up the production unit accordingly. Business units adopting this approach bring these elements together under a single management which may be represented at board level by a marketing director or commercial director. The title is unimportant; what matters is the function that lies behind the title, i.e., the coordination and integration of all the elements of the marketing mix.

This is the theory. In practice, there are wide variations in application, particularly as between industrial product manufacturers and consumer product manufacturers. In the case of the former, it is not at all uncommon to find a marketing services department which plans and organizes promotional services (advertising, public relations, technical literature, exhibitions, etc.) and provides economic intelligence and market research services to divisional general managers and corporate management. The management and control of the field selling and pricing functions, expecially with high technology products, may be under the divisional or product group manager who himself acts as the focal point for marketing coordination. The organizational solution to the problem of technical–commercial coordination has been attempted, with varying degrees of effectiveness, by (a) product manager systems focusing on the management of a specific product or group of products selling to a variety of market outlets; (b) market manager systems focusing on the management of a specific market or group of markets for the firm's entire range of products; (c) technical–commercial manager systems focusing on plant and product scheduling to meet sales requirements.

There is no difference *in principle* between industrial and consumer products' marketing. The difference is rather one of emphasis in the way in which the elements of the marketing mix are blended together to meet the particular needs of customers who may be a few specialized purchasers or a mass of consumers. The basic distinction lies in the purpose for which the goods are bought, i.e., goods bought for organizational purposes rather than for personal or family consumption. Certain goods can, of course, be bought for both purposes, e.g., typewriters, personal computers, motor cars. The combination of marketing activities can be very similar in certain situations and quite different in others. The more technical an industry, for instance, the more will the customer's needs be influenced by the results of the supplier's own research. In fact, the customer in such industries is often best served by being persuaded to modify his designs to use components or materials which will solve his problem more economically than those which he may have originally specified.

Specifier back-selling—the creation and promotion of trade-marks, brand names and the use of product and service differentiation for products (mainly components and raw materials) which have to be 'designed in'—with the aim of getting a particular product written into a tight specification, is a technique borrowed, with some degree of success, from consumer marketing.

Almost all selling involves face-to-face negotiation with prospective customers. What particularly distinguishes the selling of industrial products from that of consumer goods is the precise nature of these negotiations and the technical demands made on the salesmen. Industrial salesmen have to deal with expert buyers and, typically, more than one individual within the buying company will influence the purchasing decision (see Chapter 2). To sell capital equipment, the salesmen may face long hours of negotiations possibly spread over many months, sometimes years. Often it will not be a question of selling a standard product but of agreeing a specification which incorporates the buyer's and/or supplier's approach to a particular technical problem. The salesmen must be aware of the effect of design decisions on profitability. Planning will also be important, for a project may run into years and involve complex financial and contractual obligations. In such cases, the salesman must be a skilled development engineer and have the authority to negotiate terms on the spot.

What the industrial marketing executive needs to know

The marketing executive in an industrial firm needs to know something about the techniques of marketing research, since everything stems from an understanding of the customer, his requirements and his problems. The marketer's success will depend on understanding and anticipating these requirements and problems more accurately and coming up with better solutions than his competitors.

He must be knowledgeable about the appropriate distribution channels; about the habits, attitudes and requirements of agents, wholesalers, specifiers and contractors, who must be persuaded to handle and actively support the product before it can reach the customer.

He must understand the psychology and techniques of face-to-face selling—even if he is no great shakes at it himself. The firm's salesforce is the main instrument through which he must work in getting the product into key distributors or directly into the hands of the customer.

He must appreciate the part that advertising, sales promotion, exhibitions, technical seminars, specifier/installation/user literature can play in product presentation.

Although he need not be an expert in production, he must know enough about the potentialities and limitations of the manufacturing process to be aware of the effects of design and engineering decisions on the profitable utilization of plant and to persuade his research and development and production colleagues that modifications in the product required to solve customers' technical problems are necessary to build customer loyalty and to shut out the competition.

Marketing as a change agent

The basic challenge which all industrial managements face is the resistance to change within their own organizations. In order to cope successfully with the market conditions of tomorrow, domestically and internationally, it is necessary to make a habit of change today. You can go on reacting to one crisis after another and use the temporary expedients of cost cutting, axing the advertising or market research budgets, laying off workers or salesmen in response to adverse market conditions until the situation reverts to normality. The only trouble is rapid change is now the state of normality.

In order to operate in continuity, the firm's organizational structure and management's objectives, policies, strategies and plans must adapt to changes in the environment, domestic and international. Internally, most organizations tend to reflect built-in, accumulated historical experience or culture combined with straightforward, short-term extrapolations; in other words, an expectation that the future will not be too different from the recent past. The prevailing characteristic of organizations is, therefore, one of continuity.

The domestic and international environments, on the other hand, are characterized by discontinuity—political, social, economic and technological. The challenge is then very often one of breaking with the past (experience of which may offer little or no guide to the future) and of coping with novelty, innovation, disturbance of markets, disruption of operations and structural change.

The marketing concept can be an effective means whereby the organization can address this challenge and try to anticipate and plan for change and turn it to one's own advantage. Meeting change—and creating change—can be the dynamic that provides the forward motion of the firm and of everyone whose livelihood depends on it. Unless you make some attempt to plan for change, however loosely, you can only be reactive. In today's harsh competitive climate, the firm has to plan positively for innovation, product design and quality improvement.

However, this involves a profound and broadly based change in culture as well as in structure. The adoption of the marketing concept and its implementation through an effective marketing structure pose two entirely separate problems. The former is largely a problem of communication; the latter is a problem of organization. It is possible to have a marketing structure of sorts full of executives with the right-sounding titles, but without the will to implement the marketing concept. Equally, to adopt the marketing concept without a planned structure to make it operational is meaningless.

There is no short cut to winning acceptance of the marketing concept. Entrenched attitudes of mind are not easily or quickly changed. What is involved is a cultural transformation. No amount of reorganization or label changing will produce the right results. On the contrary, far from helping, cosmetic changes precipitately introduced can do more harm than good. The concept has to be sold. What is intended to be a fundamental change in outlook can be misconstrued as a change in individual responsibilities and status, a form of promotion by the back door for some, demotion for others. Product managers and technical managers will resist if they perceive the marketing concept as encroaching on their own areas of responsibility and status or changing their established ways of doing things. The salesman may feel seriously weakened if 'marketing' becomes the OK word and 'sales' an inferior one.

Far from these functions being devalued in a marketing-oriented organization, they should assume far greater effectiveness from being part of a totally integrated operation.

MAKING THE CONCEPT WORK

No two organizations are exactly the same and what may be best for one is not necessarily best for another. The extent to which an organization can orientate itself towards its markets and its customers will depend on the nature of its business and the particular characteristics of these markets and customers.

A company with a single base for development and production and a limited range of standardized products which fit into clearly defined market segments will have fewer problems than one which serves a diversity of markets with an extensive range of differentiated products.

One of the simplest and most favoured ways of coping with this complexity—but not necessarily the most effecient or economical—is to establish product divisions, each more or less self-contained, with its own salesforce, and serving only those customers it is technically competent to deal with. It is easy to see the apparent logic behind a product-based structure. All manufacturing businesses start with a particular product. The product is the brain-child of the man who starts the business. He is in love with his product. The people he brings into the business in its early stage of development are usually production people—engineers who develop and make products. A product is something tangible. Everybody can relate to the product which makes the money that pays the salaries and wages of everyone in the firm.

Firms wedded to this traditional structure sooner or later find that it is not necessarily the best way of serving the customer who finds himself having to deal with several representatives from the same supplier instead of one.

Achieving a better interface with the customer

An alternative approach, designed to achieve a better interface with the customer, is to structure the organization on a market- or customer-served basis comprising a number of market divisions each responsible for the entire range of the firm's products—laying out the company stall, so to speak, so as to be able to offer the customer a number of alternative solutions to his problem. While this may be good for the customer, it creates considerable internal difficulties for the supplier.

Whatever structure is chosen, and there are half-way houses between complete product orientation and market orientation, areas of conflict within the organization will persist. The production department is primarily interested in long runs of standardized products to meet high efficiency and low cost goals.

The sales or marketing department is primarily interested in product innovation and product modifications to meet specific and, increasingly, customized requirements and to give it a competitive selling edge. R & D may be more interested in technical perfection which may mean an over-engineered product at too high a price. The sales department is likely to be interested in a workable, marketable product that gives the customer good value for money.

A firm needs the expertise of its R & D personnel, designers, salesmen and production engineers; but it also needs to find people who can effectively span these industrial activities with ease, understanding and commitment. At the moment, such group activities very often behave like magnetic fields, occupying physically separated or, sometimes, adjacent spaces and volumes—or 'domains'—and, seemingly, magnetically opposed to their neighbours. Technical and cultural barriers or 'domain walls' separate the domains making it difficult to cross the boundaries between activities. Attaining the requisite degree of effective interaction and diffusion presents management with one of its most intractable problems. In the industrial firm a trained marketing person with a good technical background in the industry is perhaps best placed to move through and between the different domains, or weave from lane to lane, so to speak, in the interests of the organization's overall competitive effectiveness.

Major requirements for successful implementation

Successful managements will seek to achieve the best possible balance of trade-offs between these conflicting domains in the mutual interests of both the company and the customer and this requires that no single interest should dominate.

This is the paramount requirement for making the marketing concept work. The chief executive and his top management colleagues must be fully committed to the marketing concept and involved in its implementation. Too often, top management has professed belief in the marketing concept whereas, in practice, line marketing executives have been judged and rewarded on their short-term sales and profit results. While paying lip service to the concept, general management has sometimes, gullibly or deliberately, allowed or required its executives to employ means which carry no firm commitment to the customer's long-term interests and welfare. In other words, unless top management is fully behind the marketing concept—forget it.

The second requirement is the recognition that everyone in the firm, from the shop floor to the board room, is involved to some degree in creating added value for the customer or in minimizing the delivered cost of the product or service. A marketing-oriented firm encourages everyone to consider his or her own contribution to the enterprise in terms of its effect on the customer, from the managing director or works director to the telephone exchange operator or the person sitting at the reception desk in the front hall or office. It means getting rid of the idea that there are some people in the organization who serve the customer and others who do not or think it does not matter. In the end, we are all marketers to the extent that our efforts contribute to the achievement of effective results in the market place.

It also means designing, producing and testing for quality, reliability and ease of manufacture from the start; making sure that bought-in components meet the firm's own high standards; providing a high standard of after-sales service and a programme of product improvement based on continuous customer feedback.

The third requirement is good internal lines of communication and a planned programme of communication to explain and sell the marketing concept at *every* level within the organization. Everybody must be convinced that he or she can make a vital contribution to serving the customer; this is the firm's *raison d'être* and the only way it can continue to exist on a long-term basis and fulfil its obligations to all its employees, stockholders, suppliers, the local community and society at large.

The fourth requirement is that marketing men and women must shed their misplaced zeal in their own abilities to plan, coordinate and control the firm's entire future. Marketing management is not general management any more than is production management or financial management. The marketing function should be part of an integrated stream of research–

development–design–engineering–manufacturing–selling–financial activity in which no single discipline or specialist function has primacy over the others. The proper instrument for achieving the necessary planning, integration and control is not an all-powerful marketing department or marketing supremo, but a closely-knit top management executive group in which each of these major functions is represented and which, collectively, can take a consolidating view of the business. It is this group's task to build bridges between the different functions, to avoid or sort out the interdepartmental conflicts which will inevitably arise.

The essence of good marketing is team effort. It is precisely because marketing affects so many of the firm's resources and activities and requires the support of massive investments in production plant, materials and logistical services that the marketing group within the firm has a special obligation and responsibility to make the marketing concept work.

Nowhere, perhaps, is the need to establish direct linkages more important than at the R & D/marketing interface in order to shorten the pathway from laboratory to market place. The limited research that has been carried out to date indicates that the failure of many firms to exploit the results of R & D is a consequence of its divorce from marketing, particularly from market research into user needs. The failure would appear to be two-way. Marketing management has tended to steer clear of involvement in the research and development process, possibly because of the former's historical non-technical pedigree. R & D management has not understood the marketing function or its potential contribution to successful innovation, possibly because of its traditional non-commercial pedigree.

What is needed is more interchange of roles at the R & D/marketing interface, and a new approach to technical innovation management by attracting science and engineering graduates into the industrial management covering prototype work, production and marketing as opposed to pure research and development. R & D personnel must be exposed to the rigours of the market place; after all, a scientist or engineer, in the end, has to make a judgement as to what is going to work on the customer's premises. They must also be in a position where they are obliged to justify their ideas to all those whose support they need—production, marketing and finance. Once a development with market potential is identified, a project manager can be appointed with responsibility for producing a coordinated business development plan.

A fifth requirement, and a direct consequence of the last one, is not to draw up a shiny, new, grandiose **marketing plan** to replace the business planning that has gone on before. A marketing plan, as such, is an operational plan and a by-product of the **corporate business plan.** In so far as a marketing plan is concerned with implementing those aspects of the overall business plan which relate to the firm's activities in the market place on a year-by-year basis, marketing consideration should weigh heavily in the development of the business plan. As Theodore Levitt[4] has suggested, making the marketing plan *the* plan 'makes an assumption that you are doing something different from what ordinarily ought to be done'. Ordinarily, everyone will agree that some sort of business plan on an annual basis is necessary. Putting a marketing orientation into the corporate business plan has the particular virtue of not presuming that the marketing people are about to take over the running of the business and, to this extent, it reduces some of the resistance in the organization that you get. In other words, marketing provides a key input to the ongoing planning process and it is possible to introduce a marketing orientation by asking a number of pertinent questions. As Levitt puts it, if the plan says 'We shall do X volume of business next year' then the marketing people would ask 'Why?' The answer might be 'The market has been growing by 3 per cent per year, that's why we're going to get more'. Then it should be pointed out that this means the company is going to retain the same market share as last year. The next questions are 'Why are we saying that? Are we saying that our competitors have not got something new up their sleeve? That customers are not looking for anything different? That we shouldn't aim to offer something better?' In other words, the marketing orientation takes the form of questions that focus on the market place and the customers' requirements rather than the factory and the production department's requirements.

Following on from this, there is a great deal to be said for selecting an area where the new marketing orientation can demonstrate useful operating results. One such area is the closer integration of the selling and advertising function.

In many industrial firms, advertising is treated as an adjunct of the selling operation, where the function of the advertising department is merely to take a brief from the product or sales manager and produce an advertisement. Bringing in the advertising manager or agency at the earliest possible stage so that there is adequate time to translate product features into customer benefits not only has obvious advantages in terms of what the advertising has to say to prospective buyers but also helps people to think and talk in customer language. The closer integration of advertising and sales will also lead to the same kind of objective questioning described earlier—questions about the firm's knowledge of its customers and markets, about sales and advertising objectives and, most important, about the proper place and role of advertising in the overall marketing effort.

This is an effective way to begin to make the marketing concept operational. It makes people look outwards, highlights the role of advertising and other forms of marketing communication, exposes gaps in customer and market information, and draws attention to the potential usefulness of other elements of the marketing mix. Each of these elements is treated at length in the chapters that follow.

REFERENCES

1. Rodger, L. W. *Marketing Handbook*, 2nd edn. Ed. Michael Rines. Gower Publishing, 1981, p. 4.
2. Rodger, L. W. *The Chartered Mechanical Engineer* (Monthly Journal of the Institution of Mechanical Engineers), **23** (9), 1976.
3. Davidson, H. 'Putting assets first', *Marketing*, 17 November 1983. Recommended for an interesting discussion of asset based marketing.
4. Levitt, Theodore. 'Marketing: making the concept real', *Marketing*, May 1972, Haymarket Publishing.

TWO

ORGANIZATIONAL UNDERSTANDING— A BASIS FOR EFFECTIVE INDUSTRIAL MARKETING

Martyn R. Brown

Effective marketing strategies are based on an extensive knowledge of customer needs and wants, whether they be in industrial or consumer markets. Also of vital importance is a thorough ongoing understanding of the purchasing process the customer uses and the factors affecting that decision.

It might be said that the purchasing of industrial products is derived from the ultimate demand for consumer products or services. A component supplied to a manufacturer may, for example, be built into a product sold through high street retailers, into a ship sold to a major tanker fleet owner or into a product bought by hospitals, schools or prisons. In each case there is an ultimate consumer with needs to be met.

However, the same product will, in many situations, be sold to both consumer and industrial customers through the same distribution channel (e.g., cars, calculators), the products may be used by different types of people, in different situations for different activities. Nor can the degree of customization fully differentiate between industrial and consumer products and services. Certainly power stations, military aircraft and oil tankers are usually custom built, but then so too is a made-to-measure suit. Thus the ways in which industrial purchases are made and the purposes for which they are bought are key differences. More obvious and yet more important still is that industrial products are almost exclusively bought by organizations.

But concluding that industrial and consumer marketing are basically the same would be an over-simplistic conclusion. Basic principles may be the same but the focus of marketing orientation is significantly amended. In particular the emphasis in industrial marketing is very much towards direct selling to organizations and thus understanding how the purchasing organization works, thinks and makes decisions is of utmost importance.

Thus industrial products are sold to industrial, institutional or intermediate customers to be built into their own products, used within the organization or resold.

The 'industrial' category consists of customers who are buying products and services primarily for commercial production themselves and includes manufacturers, primary producers, agriculture, horticulture, forestry and fisheries. 'Institutional' buyers are generally involved in providing a service, not necessarily of a commercial kind, e.g., schools, hospitals, armed forces, local and national government, professions and hotels. 'Intermediate' buyers on the other hand are purchasing for resale (or facilitate resale) of other products or services in other markets, e.g., dealers, distributors, wholesalers, service trades.

BUYER BEHAVIOUR

Organizational and individual factors

In considering the differences between industrial and consumer markets it is often assumed that the organizational factors that influence purchasing choices somehow make more 'rational' and 'objective' decisions than consumer buyers who are seen as much more subjective and susceptible to a wider range of influences, even impulses. However, practical experience and considerable research tell us that many of the individual/subjective influences are also evident in organizational purchasing situations. The purchasing process is often extremely complex with individual influencers in the decision-making unit (DMU), but non-price-related factors such as supplier reputation, service and value are also extremely important.

Organizational factors The needs of the purchasing organization in terms of specifications, reliability, quality, delivery, price and service (e.g., to cut costs, increase output), etc., can be said to be 'objective' in that they are usually primarily defined by the nature of the organization, its process, objectives and operations. But they are also 'subjective' in that aggregated decisions were made by (probably) senior management in the historical development of the business. Concentration on objective needs has for many companies been the main preoccupation in the past, yet individuals and groups of individuals (whether formally or informally) actually make the decisions, not the 'organization' as such. They are the organization.

Individual factors Quite obviously, every individual who makes or influences a purchase decision to a greater or lesser extent is influenced by his or her unique and individual needs, preferences, desires and motivations. This is borne out by the numerous situations where supplier sales people are able to secure orders where on several objective criteria the product/service offering is uncompetitive; the value of the interpersonal relationship, for example, is always very important and often vital (see Fig. 2.1).

Considering organizational versus individual factors

When looking at Fig. 2.1, trying to position on the graph the dominant factors (whether organizational or individual), in the purchase decision for a specific industrial product/service is never easy. Taking high price, highly customized, low volume products such as capital industrial products (e.g., power stations or ships), experience has shown that the decision is affected by individual(s) influence much more than would, at first sight, be expected. The actual positioning of any one specific product/supplier purchase decision precisely on the graph is, of course, virtually impossible and unnecessary. Suffice it to say, that whereas the organizational factors are quite naturally very important so are the individual (people related) factors and quite often grossly underestimated by suppliers' marketing and sales personnel and plans. The purchasing decision process in the vast majority of cases is easily influenced by both organizational and individual, not to mention environmental factors.

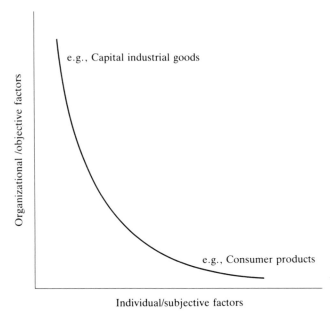

Figure 2.1   Objective and Subjective Influences on Purchase

PARTICIPATION IN THE BUYING DECISION

Decision-making units (DMU)

As already mentioned, the number of people within the organization who directly or indirectly influence buying decisions can be large. The people thus involved in this sphere of influence are known variously as the 'decision-making unit' (DMU) or the 'buying centre'. The actual size of this DMU will vary, be formal or informal, and its true size or existence may not even be obvious to its members. However, the number of variables means each company will be different.

Although a key marketing objective in industrial markets is to try to define the DMU, in practice this can be easier said than done. It is not purely the 'buyer' (who places the order), but a much wider group. In the purchase of fork lift trucks, for example, the influence of drivers can be considerable, and many of the most successful suppliers make considerable attempts to impress this group, because they indirectly (but strongly) influence the decision, either by the assertion of strong positive interest or in some situations by the virtual power of veto.

Some factors influencing organizational buying decisions

1. *Environmental*
   Economic/political situation and outlook
   Market sizes and trends
   Demand levels
   Technological changes
   Legislative implications
   Cost of capital
   Competition

2. *Organizational*
   Corporate goals and objectives
   Policies, procedures and systems
   Type of structure (centralized/decentralized)
   Financial (profits, sales, ROI, assets)
   Management style (autocratic/democratic/participative/irrational)
   Degree of centralized power
   Industry/organization type
   Performance/effectiveness trend
   Speed of decision making
   Degree of innovativeness
   Communication system (open/friendly/formal/defensive/bureaucratic)
   Corporate character (aggressive/conservative/creative/entrepreneurial/traditional)
   Mechanization/routinization
   Purchasing policy
   Purchase pattern

3. *Individual*
   Age
   Job position
   Education
   Intelligence
   Income level
   Personality
   Self-confidence
   Attitudes
   Motivations
   Perception of job responsiblities/obligations
   Attitude to risk (and perception of risk)
   Working experience (present position, time in organization, general experience)
   Informal organizational contacts
   Membership of outside organizations
   Span of control
   Achievement/power/affiliation personal orientation
   Life style
   Attitude to superiors/colleague/subordinates
   Career aspirations
   Decision-making style
   Criteria used in purchase/supplier selection

DMU roles

The following descriptions seek to clarify the generalized roles:

1. *Initiators*—perceive a need for a product/service; could be at any level but often in a senior position.
2. *Users*—members of the organization who will use the product/service. Can sometimes also be initiators. May play an important role in defining purchase specification, e.g., for machine

tools, an operative; for a fork lift truck, the driver; for an aircraft, pilot, crew, maintenance staff and passengers.

3. *Influencers*—influence decisions whether directly or indirectly; may often be technicians or engineers helping to define specifications and provide information for evaluating alternatives, e.g., for a new oil refinery, chemical engineers (formal) for furnishing a hotel, the manager's/owner's wife (informal).

4. *Buyers*—staff with formal authority for negotiating and placing orders with suppliers and possibly supplier selection as well. They may advise on specifying also. For very large, crucial or complex deals senior managers may also get involved in the negotiation stage, e.g., a buyer, purchasing officer or department or senior management.

5. *Deciders*—may have formal or informal power to select the final supplier. Buyers may also be deciders in many routine situations but senior management could be deciders in large, crucial, complex deals, e.g., new plant—managing director; machine tools—works manager or chief executive.

6. *Gatekeepers*—control the flow of information to other members of the DMU and may, for example, block supplier sales catalogues and even salesmen. Some technical personnel, receptionists and telephonists can also be in this role, e.g., buyer's secretary, buying assistant in drawing up list of potential suppliers.

Table 2.1

Buyer's relative influence	High	Low
Product complexity factors		
Product	Established	New
Product	Standardized	Differential
Technicalities	Simple	Complex
Purchase record	Purchased previously	First time
Application	Existing	New
Installation	Easy	Specialized
After-sales service	None	Technical
Commercial uncertainty factors		
Investment	Little	High
Order size	Small	Large
Commitment term	Short	Long
Consequential adjustment	None	Substantial
Potential effect on profitability	Small	Large
Forecasting the effect	Easy	Difficult

Table 2.1 shows that where product complexity is low the likely influence of the 'buyer' will be greater than in complex situations where the specialist, engineer or technologist will have greater influence.

Where the degree of commercial complexity is only low, again the 'buyer' will have relatively more influence than in a situation where the potential commercial risks of purchase make it actually (or potentially) a policy decision.

When both product complexity and commercial uncertainty are high the DMU is likely to be larger, and the buyer's influence less. The difficulty yet importance here of understanding DMU structure, roles and influence is of paramount importance.

Buyphases and the DMU

Identifying the stages of the purchasing process (i.e., buyphases) can be vital in understanding how the organization makes decisions, who is involved and when. This information can obviously be used in more effective marketing decisions and actions by the supplying company. Table 2.2 shows a simplistic relationship between buyphases and roles in the DMU.

Thus in the DMU or buying centre the purchase decision is not normally made by one person alone. Generally the more complex the decision is commercially and technically the less influential is the buyer's role.

Table 2.2 Buyphases and DMU roles

Buyphases	Users	Influencers	Buyers	Deciders	Gatekeepers
Indentifying need	×	×			
Establishing specifications	×	×	×	×	×
Determining alternatives	×	×	×		×
Evaluating alternatives	×	×	×		
Selecting suppliers	×	×	×	×	

Types of purchasing situations ('buyclasses')

Behaviour within the organization will change according to the type of purchasing situation. Some are almost automatic while others involve the possible consideration of alternative suppliers. These 'buyclasses' are as follows (see also Table 2.3).

Straight rebuy The simplest purchasing situation with re-ordering without any changes to specification by the 'buyer' or his department. The purchasing company can easily choose from its list of approved suppliers and will usually be heavily influenced by past experience of products, services and suppliers. In this situation it is obviously vital for the existing supplier to get a 'straight rebuy' with the minimum fuss and bother. There will be a greater chance of success by, for example proposing automatic re-order stock control systems, that make the task virtually or actually routine. Non-suppliers naturally enough will be attempting to create doubts in the buyer's mind, or make new or innovative offers or products/services available. The more the buying assumptions are reconsidered the better chance the competitor has. Generally, however, if performance is satisfactory the DMU is not involved in the process and the *status quo* is more often than not continued.

Modified rebuy This occurs when there is some change in the choice criteria, maybe in product specifications, prices, terms or in the supplying company itself. Usually the motivation for 'modified rebuy' is that the purchasing organization's needs have changed or it is looking for some improvement (of whatever kind). Some part of the DMU may be activated in this situation, and a greater number of people beyond the 'buyer' may become involved. Naturally suppliers get anxious and make attempts to hold the account while their competitors see it as an opportunity.

New task Situations when the organization is considering a product or service not previously purchased come under this heading. The greater the commercial risk, product complexity or cost, the greater likelihood there is of the whole DMU getting involved in the decision-making process.

Table 2.3 Buyclasses

Extended buyphases	New task	Modified rebuy	Straight rebuy
1. Identification, anticipation or recognition of need			
2. Establish characteristics/specifications of needed item			
3. Search for alternative suppliers			
4. Establish contact			
5. Set purchase and quantity criteria			
6. Evaluate supplier alternative offers			
7. Budget availability			
8. Evaluate specific alternatives			
9. Negotiate			
10. Decide/buy			
11. Use			
12. Performance feedback and post-purchase evaluation			

Thus, 'new task' situations offer the biggest opportunities for competitive suppliers, and the biggest threats for the existing supplier. The non-supplier thus has great opportunities to develop and exploit existing and new DMU contacts and provide maximum information and assistance.

The role of negotiation

Traditionally, selling has been the dominant process whereby the individuals in the salesforce, persuade individual buyers or contacts to purchase, and training has emphasized the persuasive aspects of communication.

But dynamic and turbulent market conditions with recession, increased overseas competition and the domination of fewer and fewer more powerful companies has put increasing pressure on margins and thus profits. Profits now have to be assertively negotiated, not necessarily just on price but increasingly by changing terms, conditions and specifications.

The companies doing the purchasing, whether it be products, services or ideas are having to face up to the tough complex realities of today and are becoming tougher and more demanding in their negotiations with suppliers but also more complex to understand, more professional and more aware of the financial implications of each and every purchasing decision.

One of the major implications for marketing and sales staff as a result of these changes is that traditional selling skills are no longer sufficient; skill in negotiating with larger more professional organizations is necessary plus a much better awareness of how the organization's purchasing decision-making process works, who gets involved in the decision, how they decide on supplier choice and why.

The relationship is thus changing from that of sales people 'persuasively selling' products and services based on their benefits and advantages to a greater emphasis on a concern for profit; not merely on the basis of once off profit per transaction but towards an increasingly integrated, longer term joint purchase/supplier problem-solving relationship, which is mutually profitable.

The purchasing organization then ideally perceives the supplier as a party which can be positively useful in helping to build profitability. This will often be beyond the level of merely thinking about discounts, but towards a mutually acceptable joint problem-solving exercise that will not just cut prices, but help build the purchaser's profitability. While one can argue that this should ideally be viewed as a potentially beneficial joint effort, in reality the initiation will and should be with the supplier.

Purchasing risk and perceived risk

All types of purchasing situations involve actual or perceived risk. New tasks (and to a degree modified rebuys) are different from straight rebuys in that the risk is perceived to be greater. These are not only organizational, commercial and financial risks, but also those related to individuals involved in the buying process.

Purchasing processes invariably affect many people who are naturally concerned about the outcomes for the organization and their own welfare and career development. No one wants a costly mistake either personally or for the organization.

All the problems listed below, plus many more, may cause purchasers to react, to whatever degree, in a risk-aversive manner:

New type of purchase
Large spend
Essential product/service
High complexity
Great importance of project to company
Limited experience of this type of decision
Unsatisfactory supplier experience
New possible supplier
Senior management involvement
Conservative purchasers
Indecisive personality factors
High risk venture
Unusual product type
High buyer accountability for purchase consequences
Extended purchase deliberation
Large company size
Decentralized decisions made by conventially centralized company
Lack of clear definitions of product specifications
Technical/product/supplier uncertainty
High resistance to change
Uncertainty with delivery dates or terms and conditions
Lack of objectivity by seller

Buyphase and buyclass relationship

It is thus very important, in terms of marketing/sales strategies and actions, to understand how the 'buyclasses' relate to stages in the purchasing process (the buyphases), and implications for the size of the DMU and relative influencers and influences. An illustrative example is given below for the buyphase/'new task' relationship.

1. **Identification, anticipation or recognition of need**—either for new product development, expansion of capacity, or on the basis of some analysis of operations. At this point a DMU will be activated depending on the type of need. In NPD situations senior management, R & D, line managers or technical specialists may initiate proceedings, although in expansion, mainly senior management, marketing and engineering will lead. In operational changes, generally only engineering and manufacturing will be involved. The actual DMU may well be similarly large for NPD and expansion situations, from senior management to technical specialists (marketing, engineering, manufacturing, purchasing). For operational changes line managers and technical specialists in engineering, manufacturing and purchasing will tend to be involved. Senior management will tend to be early influencers and consulted if large expenditures, resources or risks are involved. Technical specialists will dominate the early and evaluation stages, with buyers possibly acquiring information as well as being influential in final supplier choice.
2. **Establish characteristics/specifications of needed items**—much internal work and debate plus extensive information requests to suppliers, both formally and informally, to determine specifications. Forecasts may be used to determine new product quantities.
3. **Search for alternative suppliers**—intensive working sessions to identify and seek information from suitable suppliers (both capable and interested). Technical specialists interested in reducing number of prospective suppliers.
4. **Establish contact**—contact perceived appropriate suppliers, maybe with office and site visits. Requests for proposals.
5. **Set purchase and quantity criteria**—develop tighter list of criteria and fine-tune quantities.
6. **Evaluate product/supplier alternative offers**—after requesting, obtaining and analysing formal quotations, evaluate and work out realistic alternative suppliers.
7. **Budget availability**—rethink and rework of more precise budgets.
8. **Evaluate specific alternatives**—further shortlisting of those capable and willing to meet purchaser's requirements, analyse samples and tests, and refine specifications and other needs (e.g., for service). Technical personnel will be heavily involved. Senior management may introduce other non-technical requirements.
9. **Negotiate**—after the continuing reconsideration of the shortlist, there will be much negotiation on specifications, performance and quantities, some on deliveries, little on price.
10. **Decide/buy**—make final choice and negotiate on full range of requirements, price, terms and conditions.
11. **Use**—reacting almost as if it is expected that something will go wrong; expect instant response from supplier if it does.
12. **Performance feedback and post-purchase evaluation**—varies by organization but usually some form of review. New suppliers monitored very closely at first.

Reducing purchaser perceived risk and uncertainty

The implications of much of what has been said depend very much on whether the company is the existing supplier or not. Many of the opportunities (and risks) of better understanding purchasers have been discussed with the emphasis being on the need to understand their unique needs, requirements, problems and complexities.

The supplier (or potential supplier) should strive to get closer to the purchaser in whatever way possible. This may be more than just greater multi-level contact based on a better understanding of the DMU, buyphase and buyclass, but also on the realization that advertising, promotion and particularly PR can be used very effectively to reach people, not usually contacted. This may well be achieved by using different 'beneficial' messages aimed at different purchasing levels, probably in different media. But there are also examples of industrial promotional campaigns which are generically pitched at many levels. For example, a new offering may well be widely promoted actually deliberately emphasizing the risk inherent in not having that particular product, and aiming to generate a feeling of dissatisfaction with existing products/suppliers. The objective here may well be simple: to get someone to call the supplier for an initial product presentation.

Although it is obviously theoretically easier for the existing supplier to keep the business, the vast number of variables mean that suppliers are changed more often than is sometimes realized. Non-suppliers can often forget this, and make naive, half-hearted and unprofessional approaches, possibly just at the 'buyer' level. Gaining new large customers is often a lengthy, difficult and costly process which will lead many competitors effectively to give up when apparently blocked by an uninterested buyer. As already discussed, although the buyer may appear to have little decision authority it is unlikely that he is always willing to admit it. It must be concluded that many potential suppliers fail not just as a result of inadequate preparation, but also due to lack of multi-level contact over time. Purchasing organizations invariably, and often informally, gain an overall impression of non-suppliers who have tried to make inroads over a period of time. Often a supplier will almost take the position of unofficial 'first reserve' possibly without realizing it. If the situation changes, as it often does, for example for a 'new task' situation, a phone call may suddenly be received requesting a meeting. Yet if the potential supplier had completely terminated contact it might not even be seriously considered due to lack of perceived interest.

More than ever before, the need is for professionalism in all aspects of approaches with purchasers. Professionalism is quite obviously not a matter of claiming to be professional with general descriptions of company/product/personnel features, but through the demonstration of professionalism in the way the purchaser is treated. This can often be achieved by the analysis of the purchase situation and problems, and the presentation and discussion of an integrated and coherent approach with recommendations that take full account of the purchaser's situation, and provide the wide range of benefits that different parts of the organization and individuals will be seeking. It is thus a policy based on professional reassurance, removing uncertainty by understanding needs and problems, analysing them and presenting an integrated, coherent and multi-beneficial set of proposals.

Managing the relationship—a key to success

Much of this chapter has been devoted to emphasizing the need for a much closer understanding of what makes purchasing organizations, and the people involved in making purchasing decisions, tick. But many companies would claim that the biggest rewards come from converting this knowledge into some form of greater involvement with customers, almost on a strategic basis. This ideally means working jointly on some or all projects as a means of both organizations building growth and profitability. This involves not only the conventional exchange of products, services and money, but also of data, attitudes and corporate values. Both parties need to adapt to each other at many levels so that some sort of synergy can develop.

The trend for future success lies in the greater development of this type of longer-term joint relationship. Already some companies are realizing that by the selection of segments or individual customers where this type of relationship is possible, a basis is provided for new strategies which aim for greater returns.

MARKET SEGMENTATION

Many of the problems of understanding how and why customers choose suppliers have already been highlighted, but whether the differing needs and wants of the organization can be met fully is another matter.

Even if it were possible to serve all customers, their requirements would be very different, and they would require different products, services, back-up, etc. Some competitors would obviously be better placed, in whatever way, to seek and obtain the business. On the other hand, many companies are in the position to be able to meet the very specific needs of different customers.

However, it is usually possible, when analysing the market, to find natural sub-sets or groups with the same broad characteristics. In effect these 'segments' are separate markets which could conceivably be reached with distinctly different marketing approaches.

Market segmentation can bring many advantages in the development of marketing strategy and tactics. For example, the identification of profitable segments where they can concentrate, customize and build market share to achieve some sort of dominance can be more profitable than a significantly smaller share of a bigger market. By tailoring the marketing mix to specific groups of customers' needs it can often mean that the product/service offering is more closely matched and thus more attractive to the customer.

Deploying the supplying company's key strengths and resources appropriately in attractive segments with maximum advantage over competition can bring big rewards. Achieving maximum positive differentiation over competition in meeting customer needs can be a highly effective and profitable strategy.

Segmenting industrial markets

There are a great many ways in which industrial markets can be segmented and great debate about the most useful. However, it is remarkable how few industrial companies base their marketing strategies and plans on segmentation. Probably the most common and basic is by type of industry based on the differences between them, but this often needs refining to be more useful for target marketing efforts.

A useful exercise is to list all the possible segmentation variables, many of them at best partially derived from the factors listed on page 13 (Some factors influencing organizational buying decisions) particularly the following:

1. Customers' organizational factors (who are our customers?), e.g., geography, end-use of the product, customer type, customer size, 'buyclass' type (i.e., new task, modified rebuy or straight rebuy), the market served by the customer, purchasing profiles, supplier profiles, profit margin of customer, basis for competitive advantage, etc.
2. Purchasing factors (why do they buy?), e.g., purchasing policies, degree of 'buyer power', buyer's personality and self-confidence, buyer's tolerance and perception of risk/problems, buyer's relationship with others and workload, degree of conservatism, etc.

An approach which relates to both groups of factors above is that of 'benefit segmentation', based on the provision of a benefit or solution (by the supplier product/service offering) that is perceived to fulfil a need or requirement of the purchasing organization. Benefit segmentation is not an alternative approach so much as an additional aspect which often gives deeper insights.

The 'benefits' approach matches the conventional wisdom of selling techniques which reinforces the power of benefits rather than selling features, i.e., customers buy what the product can do for them (benefits) not just what it is (features). However, as already discussed, different members of the DMU will often have different perceptions of what the benefits are for the organization and themselves. For example, at the most simplistic level, the production manager may want a reliable functionally excellent product, the financial director wants the product to deliver the best return on investment, the user (possibly an operative) wants something that is easy to use and the buyer wants the lowest price.

The different needs, requirements and thus, benefits, sought from different DMU members mean that multi-level (or team) selling can often be effective, but may still fail to reach key personnel. Advertising and promotional approaches can be effectively used to reach, for example, more senior 'influencers' or 'deciders' which a conventional sales approach may miss. The medium used could often be quite different from that aimed at users, and stress quite different benefits.

Criteria for segmentation

If any segmentation analysis is to be useful there are certain criteria which must be considered.

1. It must be possible to measure, as far as possible, the segment's size and purchasing power to aid planning.
2. It is no good defining a segment which cannot then be easily reached (or accessed) by relevant promotional means, for example, to senior 'deciders' and 'influencers' if the cost is prohibitively high.
3. It must be large enough and profitable enough to warrant specific marketing efforts, but small enough to ensure that the approach is not too generalized. In other words any marketing investment must have a good chance of adequate return.
4. It must be different from other segments. That is, there must be a high degree of similarity on the segmentation criteria adopted, so that the selected customer segments are isolated within the total market to enable realistic and different marketing efforts to be planned.

In other words, the criteria for segmentation selection have to answer the following questions: Can it be reached? Is it identifiable? Is it commercially worth while? How is it different? Are additional marketing and other resources necessary to exploit it?

Reasons for segmenting

The benefits that can be gained by industrial marketing companies from the use of segmentation can be considerable yet may derive from both positive and negative reasons. Obviously some companies will view segmentation as a way of improving growth, sales or profitability from a strong base, while others in different situations may be forced, in tough times, to consider segmentation, almost as a means to survival.

There are different reasons and benefits that can accrue, for example to:

(a) position more effectively the company's offering versus powerful, large or numerous, similarly sized competitors by outflanking;

(b) position more effectively an existing product by concentrating on specific segments and attempting to dominate them;

(c) exploit parts of the market compatible with corporate strengths and resources;

(d) initiate strategies which demand a more 'customer satisfaction' orientated approach;

(e) identify gaps in the market which represent new (or amended) product opportunities;

(f) identify potential new users;

(g) maintain negotiating strength with major customers.

SUMMARY

It has been argued that in industrial marketing it is vital to understand the prospect organization: how it makes purchasing decisions, who is involved and when, the importance of individual as well as organizational factors, and the influence of different situations on outcomes. Also emphasized was the need for closer and more involved supplier/purchaser relationships as a key aspect of market segmentation and thus strategy. The need to understand organizational behaviour before segmentation was also stressed and various means of segmentation discussed.

THREE

NEW INDUSTRIAL PRODUCTS—THE MARKETING INPUT

Richard Skinner

The successful launch of a new product is the most rewarding experience industrial marketing has to offer. This is partly because it enables a marketing man to stand aside from the administration of an ongoing business, and feel afresh the challenge which has faced merchant adventurers since time began. The product at the moment of its launch is destined either to succeed or to fail. The man or woman responsible for introducing it stands up and is measured by results. That is for the record. But in addition a product launch can and should bring together the efforts of every member of the management team, and indeed of every member of the organization. A sense of common purpose is engendered which makes a company a good place to be.

These days the experience cannot be long delayed for anyone in marketing. As business becomes tougher and existing markets remain static, or even contract, the emphasis inevitably shifts to new products. The experience, however, is not always a happy one, because the development and launching of new products is becoming an increasingly risky business. Apart from a tighter and more competitive environment there are three main reasons for this:

1. The pace of technical advances which can shorten the life-cycle of any new venture, sometimes making it impossible to recover development costs without achieving a major market share.
2. The phenomenon of convergence, which can bring in competition from new sources. This is especially relevant for companies using microprocessor technology which can be adapted to many different applications.
3. The 'Gadarene effect', which will be discussed later. It is associated with the discovery of new markets, well publicized by journalists of the 'tomorrow's world' school, and results in a rush of competitors into what might otherwise have been a profitable field for two or three companies.

None of these factors should deter any manager from seeking new products but taken together they indicate a need for the application of a sound marketing input at each stage of the new product process.

The knowledge required is readily available,[1] but there are indications that, in the face of a greater urgency to expand the product range, its use is becoming at best intermittent. Some companies appear to be reverting to what used to be considered an engineering-oriented approach—'we can make it, so you can sell it'. This might now be considered in many cases as a software-oriented approach—'the product will do this, and this, so there *must* be a market for it'.

In either case the siren-song is speed, a natural desire to be ahead of competition and not to be delayed by time-consuming activities such as market research or field trials. The result is a high proportion of misguided effort and quite unnecessary failures. If speed is required, the answer must lie not in the abandonment of sound marketing techniques, but in finding ways of applying such techniques quickly, and without undue fuss.

This chapter will, therefore, look at the new product process at every stage, and identify where and how marketing can make a contribution. The marketing role cannot, of course, be taken in isolation. Other departments are inevitably involved from the outset, often occupying a central position in developing or manufacturing the product or in allocating resources. It will, therefore, be necessary to see how marketing, in addition to adding its own expertise, can relate to the other constituent parts of the management team.

THE NEED FOR NEW PRODUCTS

Each existing product is subject to a life-cycle which may be illustrated as in Fig. 3.1. Because sales will eventually decline, survival depends upon the eventual replacement of the product with something else at least as profitable. Since, even when no decline is in prospect, sales will level off, plans for expansion must involve either an extension of the uses of the product, or the addition of something new. All this is obvious without a graph to prove it, but *when* is the vital question. To plan product development effectively we need to know where we are in the life-cycle. In the example given in Fig. 3.1 it would be fairly obvious what was happening at A and at D but it might not be so clear at B, or at C, especially if price increases had taken place. Real sales graphs are full of ups and downs and the difference between a temporary set-back and a permanent decline may not initially be at all easy to distinguish.

The critical points which need to be defined in the life-cycle of any product are the approach of 'top-out' when sales cease to rise and the point at which a final collapse is imminent. The most

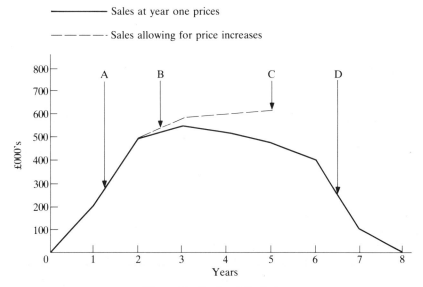

Figure 3.1 Product Life-Cycle

important factor is 'top-out', since once this point is passed a company is far more likely to be aware of the threat to continued prosperity, and to make contingency plans of one sort or another. In the meantime, however, it is likely to have suffered a set-back in profit, unless the situation was diagnosed well in advance and the necessary steps taken to bring on new products in good time.

How then can an approaching 'top-out' be recognized? Sales statistics offer no guide since they will only show a decline when the point in question has been passed. Furthermore, the vagaries of order input may well conceal a levelling of the trend line, until it is well established. This is particularly the case in companies where sales depend on the efforts of individual salesmen. No sales manager worth his salt will accept the excuse that the product has reached its peak, until he has exhausted all the devices of leadership in seeking continued expansion. His very professionalism may in that case postpone the recognition of a 'top-out' situation.

To predict signs of deterioration it is necessary to look outside the company and to study:

(a) the market potential;
(b) the competitive situation; and
(c) the development of alternative products.

Market potential will be discussed in greater detail later. Estimating it requires both imagination and analytical thought. At this stage it may be sufficient to say that the treatment it often receives in statements such as 'we are just scratching the surface', 'this country will follow the USA' or 'why worry when sales are expanding at 30 per cent per annum?' will simply not do. To take just one example, a market which is seen to be expanding at 30 per cent per annum is likely to be attractive to fresh competitors, which may in turn lead to over-capacity and a decline in sales for existing participants.

This puts emphasis on the second source of information, an examination of competitors' capacity to fulful market needs, and of any early signs of over-production. These can be reflected in price cutting, increased promotional expense or improved delivery. Of course such tactics need reflect no more than greed for a greater market share: they do not necessarily imply desperation. The best way to test this is by matching blow for blow in selected instances, without precipitating a full-scale price or promotional war. If over-capacity is diagnosed, a decision has to be made whether to ride the storm until some competitors drop out, or whether to reduce the scale of the company's own operation. The answer will depend on an analysis of comparative strengths, and of the future value of the market, but in any case the attractiveness of fresh fields in these circumstances is undeniable.

The third indicator requires a close liaison between marketing management and technical experts. If alternative products are under development that can do the same job more efficiently, sales of an existing product are likely to suffer just as soon as the new offerings are proven in the market place. Technical advice is often required because it is necessary to know not only what the rival product can do now, but also what it is likely to do in the future. Swiss watch manufacturers were understandably unimpressed by the appearance of quartz watches in their original cheap and gimmicky form. They lost a great deal of the market before themselves turning to quartz for quality watches.

No marketing department can be content simply to monitor sales of existing products. It should be perpetually scanning the horizon for signs of 'top-out' and be prepared to act accordingly. This is, however, the minimum it should do, and is essentially defensive. Most marketers will be thinking of new products not simply as a defence against the inevitable decline of products already in their range but as a means of expansion, of growth rather than merely of survival.

TYPES OF NEW PRODUCT

New products can be analysed into four main types:

Group 1—replacements for existing products;
Group 2—extensions to the existing range;
Group 3—additional products, outside the existing range, for sale in familiar markets;
Group 4—additional products for sale in new markets.

It is worth making these distinctions because the treatment each group requires may differ at some stage or other of the launching process.

The first category could range from quite radical innovations, for example the replacement of electro-mechanical devices with solid-state technology, to minor face-lifts such as a new colour range for cars. Group 2 is becoming increasingly important in the age of software when not only add-on gadgets but new systems applications can be found to extend and enrich the life-cycle of a basic product. Group 3 ventures enable a company to exploit its known marketing strengths, as for instance when a company established in the photo-copying field, launches a facsimile machine. Group 4 removes all existing points of reference. To the company launching it, at least, the product and its market are both factors previously unknown.

It will be seen that Group 1 products are primarily defensive developments, whereas Group 2 could be described as consolidatory, although to a competitor they may well appear to be aggressive. A similar description might fit Group 3, but Group 4 ventures are clearly aggressive and aimed at growth, unless by some horrible chance a company finds all its existing markets disappearing fast,[2] and has no choice but to adopt what is clearly a higher risk strategy than that implied in Groups 1 to 3.

All types of new product involve some degree of risk. How much risk needs to be undertaken will be determined by the situation of existing products and by the aspirations of the management team and the long-term goals that have been set for the company.

ESTABLISHING PARAMETERS

Whether a company's objectives are formalized or not, it is worth while forecasting future profit and looking at any gap that may be found to exist between what is predicted and what those in charge of the company would like to see. Such a forecast could include replacement products already planned, and any extension products foreseen. If a significant gap is found, additional products in Group 3 or 4 will need to be considered.

At this stage it would be as well to establish the parameters which any additional product should meet. These could cover the following aspects.

Market potential

The market for any additional product should have considerable unexploited potential. A fast growth rate in annual sales may look attractive, but if it means that potential will be saturated before any new entrant can recover the costs of launching a competitive product, there is no point in entry.

Sales volume

The product must yield sufficient volume, based on an achievable market share, to justify the effort involved in its development and marketing. What is or is not sufficient will vary from one company to another, but as one parameter, it might be agreed to consider only those additional products likely to produce a turnover of more than £x. The value of x will of course be different in a small, entrepreneurial organization where extra effort on the part of a few people can bring about a modest but profitable success, from that required in a larger company where lines of communication are longer and a more formal approach is obligatory.

It could also be considered desirable to establish different values for different types of product, coupled with differences in the timescale allowable to reach the required volume. For example:

Group 2 Extension products—£200 000 in first year.
Group 3 Additional (familiar markets)—£1 500 000 in second year.
Group 4 Additional (new markets)—£4 000 000 in second year.

Profitability

In a similar way profit targets can be developed. Most companies are implicitly looking for products that yield the gross margins to which they are accustomed. New ventures may have to be looked at afresh in this respect, but if lower margins are anticipated the volume required to fill the profit gap and the market share which this implies need careful examination.

Competitive advantages

Any new product will have to compete for its share of the market, and estimates of sales volume are related to the competitive advantages the product will offer at the time it is launched. If this is some time ahead caution is indicated. Competitors are after all likely to be looking to the future themselves, so that they too may be ready with improved products by the time ours is on the market. Furthermore, there is a tendency to overrate the competitive advantages of a product at the drawing-board stage. It is, therefore, all the more important to start with strong advantages, either in performance or in price, in order to emerge with something that will hold its own against others for long enough to produce the required return.

Fit

Some products, although otherwise quite acceptable, may not fit easily into the operation of a company as it has developed over a period of years. It is a matter of judgement to decide just how important this may be. Sometimes a radical change in marketing methods is in any case indicated. But if, for example, a direct sales organization is in being and is producing good results, it is wasting a known strength to ignore this and consider products which can be sold successfully only through dealers, and it would arguably be better to seek 'direct sell' products.

Technology may exert a strong influence on policies of this sort. As computers, for instance, have come down in size and cost, they have moved from being a product which could be sold only by experienced and well trained salesmen to something which can, at the lower end of the range, be distributed by dealers or even by means of direct mail. This has brought IBM, with some obvious reluctance, into a sector of the market which might previously have been ruled out on grounds of 'fit'. The product has been reduced in price to the point where direct selling can no longer be justified. So as a criterion 'fit' has to be applied with an eye to the future as well as to the present strengths of a company.

Once parameters have been established the discipline involved in their application needs to be considered. If they are treated as a series of filters very few ideas are likely to pass through every stage. Some compromise is inevitable; the value of stated parameters is not in establishing an automatic screening system, so much as in ensuring that all aspects of proposed new ventures are considered, and that those closest to the ideal are selected.

SOURCES OF NEW PRODUCT IDEAS

Ideas for new products can spring from a number of sources. Those eventually adopted are just as likely to have stemmed from some fortunate chance event, as from a systematic search. There are, however, methods which can be used to stimulate creative thinking. In considering these it is important to appreciate that marketing is only one source of ideas and in some respects one which is limited in its ability to produce radical suggestions. This is because of its close identification with the products the company is at present selling and the specific categories of customer involved. Other departments also have similar limitations, with the result that the emphasis falls most often on ideas for replacement or extension products. This is illustrated in Table 3.1, where it is suggested that even outside sources tend to offer only those products with which the company is already identified. In effect, only a brainstorming technique directed at new products and markets in Groups 3 and 4 is likely to throw up anything that could not be predicted without too much imagination.

Table 3.1 Sources of new product ideas

| Source | Groups proposed | | |
	Often	Sometimes	Seldom
Salesforce	1, 2	3	4
Service engineers	1, 2		3, 4
Production	1	2, 3, 4	
R & D	1, 2	3, 4	
Market research		1, 2, 3	4
Brainstorming session	3, 4	1, 2	
Offered from outside	1, 2	3	4

If ideas are required, a starting point could be the type of customer a company serves at present, with a view to finding other products or services that could be offered, even if these are quite new to the company. Alternatively, the skills already available in production, servicing or selling could form a basis for thinking of products for sale in markets at present unfamiliar. If a company sells to hotels, for example, what also could the hotelier be offered? Or if a factory exists which makes metal cabinets for housing its equipment, where else could its metal-working skills find an outlet?

Such ideas can be discussed informally until the decision is taken to measure them against the parameters for a desirable addition to the range, or they can be the subject of organized brainstorming sessions. If such sessions are planned, three rules are essential if anything worth while is to emerge:

1. The thinking is done by groups in which rank genuinely does not count.
2. No member of the group feels threatened by any likely result of the exercise.
3. No attempt is made to sift ideas against the parameters already established until the creative session has been completed.

The composition of the group is important, but even more so is a general understanding that everything is to be kept positive and that no points are scored by shooting down ideas at this stage. Screening comes later when the originators are less emotionally involved.

SOME ESSENTIAL QUESTIONS

Although marketing has no monopoly of ideas, and should welcome any positive contribution from any source, there are a number of questions which should be asked by the marketing manager before a project is accepted as viable. The most important of these concern the market in which a new product might be sold. Market research will be considered in greater detail in Chapter 4, but it may be as well at this point to outline the questions which need to be raised for any new product, without going into detail about how answers may be obtained. It is sufficient for the time being to say that answers can always be found, although the degree of accuracy with which they are invested will vary. Most major errors stem not from any inadequacy in research technique, but from a failure to ask the right questions in the first place.

What do we want to know about the market for our proposed new product? The starting point is what is loosely known as market potential. The term is used in a variety of ways, which often serve to confuse rather than to enlighten. Here **potential** is taken to mean the quantity of any given product that could be in customers' hands if everyone who could use it bought as much as he could use. This could be expressed in units or in value. In the case of capital goods it is a fixed figure at any given moment. With consumables it can be taken as the quantity that would be consumed over a given period (e.g., a potential usage of 500 000 transistors in a year).

Sometimes it is necessary to subdivide the concept of potential into **ultimate** potential and **immediate** potential. The ultimate potential contains the immediate, but the gap between the two often has great significance when constructing a marketing plan. For example the ultimate potential for motor-driven lawn mowers was always the number of households with lawns. But initially the immediate potential was considered to be only those households possessing a lawn large enough to justify the expense of a motor mower. A marketing plan based on all lawns would have been grossly over-optimistic. With time, however, the immediate potential grew to the point where virtually all lawn-owners were prospects for motor mowers. The lack of a motor was seen as reflecting on the status of the householder. Ultimate and immediate potential can now be said to coincide.

The judgement of what is the ultimate potential and where immediate potential stands relative to it can be aided by market research but remains to a large extent subjective. The ultimate potential for video recorders is clearly all households with a television set, or probably something even larger to allow for households with two or more sets. The immediate potential will be restricted by the amount of disposable income available, and that again has to be considered relative to the cost of recorders. It might also be influenced by the degree of interest in TV programmes.

Figure 3.2 shows ultimate potential represented by the area contained within circle A and immediate potential by the area contained within B.

Very few markets exist only in the mind's eye. Most have been exploited to some extent already, and it is important to know how much **penetration** has taken place, since this determines how much potential remains untapped and may also indicate how lively the market is. This is indicated in Fig. 3.2 by circle C. In the case of consumable items it could be taken as synonymous with annual sales so that circle C could be considered unnecessary. With durables it is essential to consider it separately and to look closely at those sectors of the potential market where penetration has taken place and those where it has not. Where the immediate potential is considerably

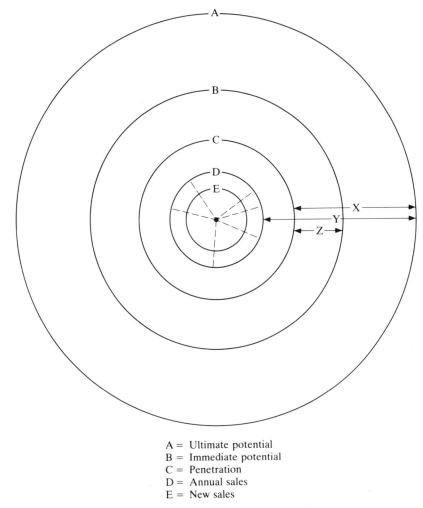

A = Ultimate potential
B = Immediate potential
C = Penetration
D = Annual sales
E = New sales

Figure 3.2 Quantitative Market Analysis

smaller than the ultimate it is usually the case that penetration is confined to certain groups of customers with well defined needs. The question then is when and how sales can be made to those other customers who form the wider potential yet to be exploited. This question may in turn be related to the price of the product, which again may reflect scale of production. Sometimes the next step forward depends on a decision to reduce cost by quantity production—provided the ultimate potential is there.

Annual sales are shown by circle D, and are taken to include all sales by all competitors. This figure can be estimated for past years and projected forward for future years as an annual sales expectancy. These rather clumsy turns are employed to avoid the ambiguity which arises from a vague use of expressions like 'market size' or 'annual market', which can cause confusion.

Circle E indicates the extent of new sales within the annual total. This is important since sales which replace products already in use have no effect on extending the overall penetration. The dotted lines serve to indicate the shares of annual sales taken by various competitors.

The need to ask all, not just some, of these questions cannot be over-emphasized. Sometimes annual sales figures can show an encouraging growth which masks an impending 'top-out' for the market as a whole, unperceived by any of the current participants. Annual sales of beverage vending machines some years ago were growing at 30 per cent per annum. Ultimate potential was publicized in the industry as one machine per 20 of the working population (the stated figure in the USA) against a penetration of one machine per 500 workers in the UK. The feeling was 'the sky's the limit' and new companies rushed to join the market. Within six months sales had topped out and one major competitor had admitted failure.

What had happened was that market research had concentrated on what seemed important questions at the time, such as leaf tea versus powdered tea, but no one had looked at the immediate potential which was in medium- or large-sized factory or office establishments. There were only a limited number of these and a high rate of saturation had already been reached. There was no way in which a growth rate of 30 per cent could be sustained. Of course, ample long-term potential remained, but the industry had first to recover from a shake-up and then proceed much more cautiously.

High growth rates should always inspire caution, unless the potential is indeed unlimited, because of the danger of the 'Gadarene effect'.[3] This can be observed when too many companies rush to join what is seen as a gold rush, but becomes a mad scramble to the brink of the precipice. It is particularly likely in times of change when firms are looking for new outlets for their existing technology, to replace those which have atrophied. In the case of vending machines, it was metal working companies which led the way. Later it was the turn of copying machines, following the lapse of the Xerox patents. Currently Gadarene markets may be identified in various sectors of the electronics market, with microcomputers well in the lead. Of course there is no reason why a new competitor with a much improved product cannot enter such a market and succeed, but he can expect a rough ride.

The position of competitors is another essential question, both in quantitative terms, when looking at competitors' shares, and qualitatively when considering competitors' selling methods and pricing structures. If a few powerful competitors share a market, and if, for some of them at least, the product in question is their main or only line, strong reactions to a newcomer can be anticipated. Current selling methods have also to be taken into account, since they may not match those of the new entrant, and an adaptation from, say, direct selling to selling through dealers, or vice versa may take a company on to unfamiliar ground, and increase the element of risk. Pricing also needs careful consideration since published prices may not be the end of the story, or even indicate where the main force of competition falls. Discount structures, sometimes of a fairly irrational nature, may already be established, or companies may compete in service or in add-on extras. It is important, and not always easy, to find out what is actually being paid for what product or service package.

The next question will naturally be about customers' buying practices and buying motives. Without a knowledge of these no effective promotion can be planned, and it is not even possible to assess the attractiveness of the proposed product. With the quantitative answers already gathered it should be possible to determine where the main potential lies, and not to be misled by one-off contacts with customers which may not be in any way typical. There is in any field of industry a handful of vociferous customers demanding something which is not yet available, and it is important to analyse how far this might represent a general trend. The customer is always right, of course, but only if he is prepared to buy in quantity.

In times of rapid change questions will need to be asked about product trends. Often the development department is working on something new which is well ahead of other products on the market, without considering that competitors may also be working on similar lines, so that any advantage could be short-lived. Worse still, changes may occur which outdate the product before costs of development have been recovered. At the least a knowledge of technical trends may enable an assessment to be made of the likely life of a new product, and consequently of the scale of operation needed to reap a profit in the time available. This coupled with the information already obtained about the market should make it possible to say whether a realistic share of the business would be sufficient to justify the proposed venture.

Finally, it is necessary to consider not only technical developments within a given industry but also market threats and opportunities arising from other sources. The phenomenon of convergence, which brings into collision industries which previously existed independently, is something which nowadays has to be taken seriously. Manufacturers of typewriters have found their markets invaded by companies marketing word-processors, which in turn are under attack from manufacturers of microcomputers with word-processing facilities. Legislation is also a factor which may bring restriction in the way of standards and regulations or may open up new markets, as has happened in the security field with new laws on fire protection and safety lighting. One man's restriction often becomes another's opportunity. Even an economic recession creates opportunities for accountants, debt-collection agencies and organizations engaged in youth employment schemes.

PROJECT ASSESSMENT

The process of arriving at a decision to go ahead with a given project is unlikely to be a tidy one. Some commitment has been necessary to answer all the questions which have been raised so far, and in most organizations there will be individuals with scant respect for the objective appraisal needed to weigh all the issues involved. So it is easy to find a team of people moving at different speeds and possibly with some doubts along a path determined more by force of personality or seniority than by logic. There is nothing inherently wrong in this. Without people keen to make changes and take risks, nothing would happen. But there is something to be said for a marketing executive, who will have the ultimate responsibility for selling the new product, producing a formal project assessment as soon as sufficient knowledge is available.

If a report is prepared it could cover:

(a) a definition of the product concerned;
(b) background information on the company's involvement and its objectives in considering the product;
(c) a market appreciation showing potential, penetration, annual sales and sales trends, competitors' shares and selling methods, market price levels, customer buying practices, etc.;
(d) a detailed description of the features and benefits of the new product, its competitive advantages, the cost at which it is expected to be produced and the price[4] at which it will be sold;
(e) a forecast of sales for whatever forward period is appropriate;
(f) a statement of the resources required in sales and support services, inventory, manufacturing plant (if appropriate), development costs, financial facilities, etc.;
(g) an assessment of profitability, including consideration of the expected life of the product, to ensure that sufficient time is available to cover the launching costs and yield a satisfactory return on investment;
(h) a clear statement of the risks involved;
(i) an action programme covering development and launching of the product.

It is often the case that the marketing executive is a prime mover in projects of this kind. If so, he will wish to sell his ideas to his colleagues and should involve them in contributing to the assessment report so that as far as possible it is drawn up with the agreement of all the departments that will be involved if a 'go' decision follows.

Most reports of this kind tend to avoid the question of risk, and to assume that forecasts are history written in advance. This is why item (h) has been introduced. A firm statement of what is at stake if things do not work out to plan should help to focus attention on the fact that a decision is required which involves a business judgement to which all departments will be committed. It may also put the project into perspective, and thus make it easier to secure agreement.

CONTROLLING DEVELOPMENT

Once development is under way it might be thought that marketing input is at an end until the product emerges and is ready to be tested. In fact it is during the development stage that the greatest peril lies. This is a phenomenon which can be called 'engineering attrition'. It ensures that what emerges at the end of the development process either does less than what was originally proposed, or costs more, or perhaps does less and costs more. It is largely an internal phenomenon, since when products are purchased from outside, both buyer and seller are subject to greater discipline, and penalties tend to fall on the supplier, rather than on the purchaser.

Herein lies one clue to controlling development and reducing engineering attrition to a minimum. The marketing department needs to produce a specification for the product. This is done quite naturally if purchasing from outside, but sometimes left vague if all work is internal. To allow sufficient flexibility the specification should be put more in terms of customer requirements, including cost as one of these, than of technicalities. In certain cases technicalities are essential since the product may, for example, have to meet national or international standards, but generally the product will be better if the development engineer is free to use his initiative and find alternative ways of achieving the desired results.

Often it is quite difficult for the marketing department to complete this apparently simple task. Lack of knowledge of future product trends which may affect the market is one reason for this. So consultation with engineers both inside and outside the organization is worth while. But a grasp of customers' future needs is the essential foundation for a product specification, and this responsibility lies firmly with marketing.

Assuming that the process has started on the right lines, the next problem is how to keep it running to plan. A launch committee involving all departments concerned in launching the product may help, and marketing can often take the lead in establishing this. It would be natural for a product manager to chair a committee of this kind. A common reading file might also be established to improve communication, but the important point is that departmental decisions taken outside the launch committee should be communicated to all concerned. A simple change in a component, made for good reasons, could have repercussions outside the knowledge of the engineer who approved the substitution. If unnoticed, engineering attrition will follow and it may later be difficult to regain the ground lost.

Perhaps the strongest check on engineering attrition should be the knowledge that any product developed is subject to customer acceptance. It should be a routine to test this acceptance before going into production and the marketing manager has to have the right of rejection. If this is understood a more commercial attitude will be engendered.

If in the worst possible case the product which emerges is unsaleable, or inferior to one which could be bought in from other sources, there is no sense in pointing to all the money spent in development as a conclusive argument for the necessity of going ahead. Development costs can only be repaid out of profit. If more profit can be obtained from selling products from another source, that is the quickest way to restore the situation and provide funds out of which further development may take place. Any other decision is based on motives which can only be regarded as outside strict business considerations.

FIELD TRIALS

Assuming that the perils of engineering attrition have been avoided and a product developed which meets market needs at a competitive cost, we still have to make sure that it works, not just in the laboratory, but on customers' premises. No specification and no series of tests is comprehensive enough to cover all the ways in which a real, live customer uses or misuses a product.

Field trials are, however, very unpopular with almost all of those whose efforts have gone in to producing what is believed to be a winner. The product has passed all its laboratory tests and is ready for production, the salesforce is eager to offer it to customers whose needs cannot be met in any other way, the man at the top wants to see a return on the money invested in the new project, and here is a marketing manager asking everyone to hold fire until field trials are complete. In the case of replacement products the situation may be even more critical since stocks of the existing product may have been run down in anticipation of the new version.

The feelings of frustration which can emerge at such times can only be controlled by an appreciation of the hazards involved in offering anything new, and of the damage to the company which results from launching a product which does not come up to expectation. Time and again quite respectable companies have lost money and reputation with product failures which could have been avoided by testing under conditions of actual, not simulated use. Industrial products are often complex, both in design and application. The best engineers cannot foresee all eventualities, so it is not really surprising if early cash dispensers did not work when sealed into a bank's outer wall, or if the advanced passenger train made passengers feel seasick. It would, however, have been better to have discovered these problems before, and not after, the product had been launched.

The choice of customers for a field trial is again a matter where marketing, as opposed to sales, influence should be exerted. Often prominent customers exist who have got wind of something new and would volunteer to be the first to try it. The salesman involved would love to offer the new product, but it has to be appreciated that providing such customers with the product, on whatever basis it is done, is not a field trial, but a launch in all but name. Ideally the customers chosen should be unconnected with large groups, fairly typical of the average user, and near enough geographically for an eye to be kept on the trial both by the development engineer responsible and by the marketing or product manager.

During a field trial, discipline is needed to prevent news spreading and the company coming under pressure to supply others. If this situation is handled firmly, and the trial is a success there will be benefits to be gained in launching with the certainty that the product does it job, and fulfils the needs of customers. The launch takes place in the knowledge that the product is already in use and that third party references are obtainable from the start. Once the salesforce has confidence in the company's procedures and in the products which result, field trials will be accepted and discipline will not present any outstanding problem.

THE LAUNCH

The actual moment when a product is officially launched often assumes an importance out of all proportion to its real value. As has been indicated, there are often pressures to launch before all is ready, training complete for both salesmen and service engineers, and stocks available. The natural impatience of senior managers anxious to see a return on investment may be compounded by the desire of a departmental head to be seen to be doing something progressive, eagerness to impress the public or shareholders, or a wish to beat competitors to the punch. Then there are trade exhibitions, real or imagined seasonal trends, the need to avoid holiday periods—all of which can lead to the establishment of unrealistic deadlines.

Another aspect of development which needs careful consideration, where industrial products are concerned, is the lead time required for components purchased from outside sources. It is becoming increasingly rare to find a product manufactured completely in-house. Electronic or mechnical devices are frequently incorporated which may have only one or two sources of supply. Delivery times fluctuate widely as new markets for such components are discovered or production is cut back in times of recession. All this makes it difficult to estimate exactly when the finished product will be available, or available in sufficient quantity for a successful launch. Promotional plans in industrial selling need to be made with the realities of industrial manufacturing well in mind.

Sometimes it is necessary to be ready in time for, say, an exhibition, but this would be true only if there were no other ways of contacting the buying public. A boat show might fall within this category, since potential boat owners are difficult to identify and not easily gathered together by other means. But for most industrial products there are many other routes to the customer, and an exhibition which raises enquiries which cannot be processed through to an order is more likely to create business for competitors than to do any real good.

It has always to be remembered, however difficult it may be at such times, that the public launch of a product is something entirely within a company's control. It will also pay to remember that the only valid point of a launch, or of any attendant publicity, is to obtain orders. Sometimes it is better to have salesmen recruited and trained, with practical experience behind them, before the main thrust of a promotional campaign takes place. The launch is only a beginning. It is the success which follows that counts.

FOLLOW-UP

It is hoped that by now the function of marketing in the choice and development of new products will be seen as something which starts at their very inception, the appreciation of the need for something new in one or other of the groups defined, and continues, in close liaison with other departments, through to ensuring that salesmen are fully trained and that customers will get the service they require. Some members of the team which organized the launch may well turn their attention elsewhere once the product is on the market. For the marketing manager the most anxious, and perhaps the most testing time is still ahead. He is about to be measured by results, and there will sometimes be those around him whose enthusiasm was less than perfect, waiting to damn with faint praise, if nothing worse.

False starts are quite common. The selling cycle may prove longer than anticipated and first results may appear poor, although perhaps there will be a rapid improvement when quotations mature. Alternatively, and especially with replacement products there may be a pent-up demand which leads to quick sales at a level not easy to sustain. These two situations are illustrated in Fig. 3.3. Here the long-term trend is the same in both cases, but in A sales move slowly at first while in B the reverse applies.

The dangers inherent in situations of this kind will be obvious. Nerves are not at their strongest immediately after a launch and the management team needs to show a steady confidence that targets will be achieved rather than react violently to initial results with

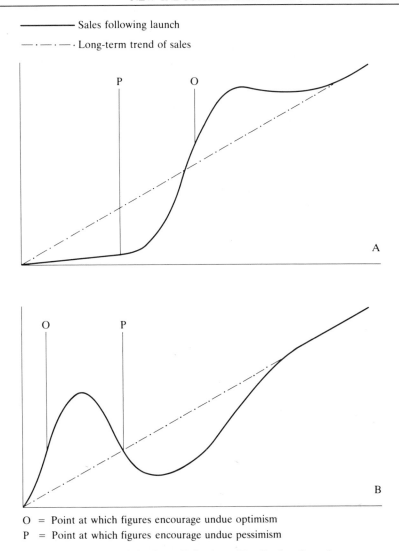

———— Sales following launch

—·—·—· Long-term trend of sales

O = Point at which figures encourage undue optimism
P = Point at which figures encourage undue pessimism

Figure 3.3 False Starts Following a New Product Launch

unfortunate consequences where the enthusiasm of the salesforce is concerned. A marketing man can be a steadying influence at these times but to keep his colleagues with him, he will need more than just ice-cold nerves. A very close look at the sales operation needs to be maintained. To help to provide an in-depth appreciation statistics on the following are useful:

Customers so far obtained—are larger orders to follow?
Prospective customers—are we yet in the most lucrative sectors of the market?
Outstanding quotations—how much business do these realistically represent?
Length of selling cycle—first contact to order.
Sales activity—ratios of calls:enquiries; enquiries:quotations; quotations:orders; calls:demonstrations; demonstrations:orders; and actual numbers of calls, etc., per individual.
Sales performance—of branches, teams, individuals.

Even when a steady trend is established and targets appear achievable the marketing manager cannot relax. Early enthusiasm may fade, and competitors may react to make orders more difficult to obtain. A second shot of indoctrination and training in the finer points may be called for.

Furthermore, where the salesforce carries more than one product it is necessary to guard against the 'chiasmus effect'. Since the salesforce tends to sell whichever product comes easiest to it a success with a new product may lead to falling off of effort on an older line. So while one graph points upwards another is moving in the other direction to produce the chiasmus (Figure 3.4).

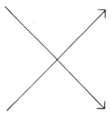

Figure 3.4

This effect is probably more prevalent than most marketing managers have chosen to notice. It is easily masked by talk of a declining market for the older product, but unless market research checks this out, suspect a very simple balancing of sales effort. Even where commission schemes are in force it is a mistake to assume that the salesforce will always exploit all the available opportunities. For most there is a point at which they will settle for a sufficiency and motivation to go beyond this has to be supplied from outside.

The chiasmus effect has a number of remedies. Often it is enough just to prove by market research that scope for continued expansion exists. Sometimes it may be necessary to increase sales coverage to ensure all opportunities are taken. If the market will sustain it, specialization in one line or another may be justified, but this is usually reserved for situations where sales are made in different markets, or at least to different people.

It is worth noting the chiasmus effect at the end of a discussion of marketing techniques for new products, since in time other new products will be launched, and they in turn may threaten the progress of the one which is now successfully off the ground. This cannot be allowed if full value is to be obtained from all the cost and effort that has gone into the launch.

What distinguishes marketing as a function from selling is the need to think analytically, to blend enthusiasm with a realistic appreciation of the situation, and to take steps to obtain all the information needed to plan a successful campaign. This is nowhere more true than in launching new products. A questioning attitude at every stage in the planning process will help in avoiding the pitfalls which cause product failures. Once a product is on the market, however, enthusiasm can take over again, since in the last resort it is this quality which achieves a satisfactory market share, and enables a company to meet the targets it has set itself.

REFERENCES

1. Skinner, R. N. *Launching New Products in Competitive Markets*, Associated Business Programmes, London 1972. This chapter makes use of material from that book.
2. See Theodore Levitt's comments in Chapter 15.
3. Gospel according to St Mark, Chapter 5, Verses 1–13.
4. For a discussion of pricing techniques, see Chapter 10.

FOUR

INDUSTRIAL MARKETING RESEARCH

Gordon T. Brand

During the interval of nearly 20 years since the first edition of *The Marketing of Industrial Products* there has been a significant extension in the provision of marketing training and education supported, in turn, by an increase in authoritative business journalism and literature emphasizing both the practical and theoretical aspects of marketing. Indeed, looking back, it might be said that industrial marketing practitioners, faced with the apparently immovable product orientation of their management colleagues, had to over-state their case in order to obtain the financial support needed for the implementation of marketing policies.

Marketing became associated with economic growth, not in the 'cause and effect' terms that good marketing would lead to economic growth, but almost in the sense that marketing (and thereby marketing research), could best be afforded when times were good. The danger of this belief is that marketing budgets might be cut or, at least contained, in times of economic recession. This, in fact, did happen in the immediate post-1973 period, but since that fundamental shock to the business system it is more widely accepted that marketing is not an 'extra' but a direct function of competition. Expenditure on marketing research, improved product development, rationalization, training and upgrading of the salesforce, support for distributors and more effective publicity are investments difficult to justify at board level if market share and profitability can be maintained without them. With nearly all companies facing forceful competition in home and overseas markets and from alternative technologies, marketing's contribution to survival as well as growth is more obvious. As far as marketing research is concerned, survival through market orientation without valid market information would seem to be far less possible than ever before.

Having survived the difficulties of the 1970s it can now be claimed that industrial marketing research has both literally and professionally become of age. The growing acceptance of market orientation has led to a growth in the demand for research services and increasing sophistication in technique will assist this advance even further. But the major support, however, still needed for the continued development of research into industrial markets is the greater understanding and acceptance by senior general management of its relevance and value.

GROWTH IN MARKET RESEARCH

The expectation of growth to date has been confirmed by figures regularly compiled by Simmons and quoted by Hooley and West.[1] Commissioned research in the United Kingdom increased in current values from £17 million in 1969 to £110 million by 1981. Quoted in index form at 1969 prices, a substantial real growth of two-thirds was obtained over the period as a whole in spite of a considerable decline in reaction to the post-1973 recession. Expenditure revived from 1975 to remain at a high but 'no growth' level since 1978.

The survey confirmed the concentration of this expenditure in the consumer goods industries with four out of five fast moving consumer goods companies claiming to conduct marketing research. The authors conclude from their survey results, however, that over half of the larger industrial marketing companies do not currently conduct any formal marketing research.

The research of the industrial companies is reported as being largely confined to the analysis of company records such as routine reports by the salesforce or secondary, published, data. Budgets are relatively small with only 6 per cent of the capital goods companies spending more than £25 000 a year on marketing research in 1982.

The reasons given by company respondents for not using marketing research were, firstly, that they had no need to assess their markets, or that they obtained the information required from first-hand experience. Secondly, that the high cost of marketing research, and doubts that the benefits to be gained would outweigh these costs, were other important factors preventing its wide use.

DIRECT SUPPLY AN ADVANTAGE

Taking the first objection, it is true that industrial marketers, in contrast to their colleagues in consumer goods marketing, are more likely to have the advantage of regular and close contact with the users of their products. Information on many areas of current tactical marketing interest can be provided by the sales representative covering a geographical territory or particular groups of industrial customers. The representative will be able to note changes in purchasing procedures and report any information collected on competitor product developments and prices quoted. As part of the sales technique customers will be questioned on trends in their markets and possible changes in administration or production processes that might affect requirements.

All this information, regularly and uniformly collected and analysed, forms an important part of the company's market intelligence. It represents an asset available to all companies investing in the cost of direct sales representation.

There are, however, important qualifications to the use of market information collected through the salesforce. It will be seen from Chapter 5, how comprehensive are the duties of the modern sales representative and how numerous the skills needed to conduct those duties with efficiency. In addition to product knowledge, he, or she, requires a full understanding of the customer's production methods and the technical aspects of product development and modification. In addition, there is a need to perfect selling skills and to be aware of the importance of different members of the decision-making unit in terms of their relative influence on the buying decision. Competition and attention to cash flows put greater emphasis on the need to appraise a customer company's annual accounts and to incorporate sophisticated financial packages into sales presentations.

If further demands are to be made on the representative's time and mental agility through requests for market information, those requests must necessarily be of a routine nature easily recorded on report forms prepared for this purpose.

RESEARCH BENEFITS

The doubts expressed, by some of the managers surveyed by Hooley and West, in the value of marketing research represent a more substantial objection and, consequently, a greater challenge to the professional researcher. A market research report, although physically represented on paper enclosed within well designed covers, can appear less tangible in terms of its contribution to company profits.

A most important factor, therefore, in the extension in the use of marketing research techniques by a broader spectrum of industrial companies is the need by both professional suppliers of survey services and those responsible for marketing in the companies concerned, to convince senior management of the profit contribution of research.

Four broad stages of development can be identified in the growth of the marketing research function within the firm. The first stage, almost unrecognizable as marketing research, is the analysis of sales statistics to determine, for example, the distribution of sales between the various users or sectors or between large and small customers. The second stage is present when relevant market information is collected from all forms of published material and representatives' reports. An analysis of information gained from both internal and external sources provides a great deal of market information but it will be found that gaps exist in this knowledge as the sources used for desk research are neither sufficiently detailed nor sufficiently representative to permit a correct presentation of the market situation. These gaps are filled by field surveys representing the third stage of development. The fourth stage is reached when the marketing research function or department is fully accepted as part of the management team, to be consulted on all new projects and initiating its own projects by commissioning research from specialist agencies.

The chances of reaching stage four depend very much on the ability of marketing research specialists to assess and prove, to the satisfaction of others, the intrinsic validity of information obtained through market surveys.

DIFFERENCES BETWEEN MARKETING INTELLIGENCE AND MARKETING RESEARCH

In preparing for this task it is as well to distinguish between the general description 'marketing intelligence' and the more specific 'marketing research'. Every piece of market information coming into the organization, from whatever source, can be embraced within the former, broader description, including official data from government and international organizations, the financial and trade press, trade associations, government and industry research associations, specialist libraries, company annual reports and commercial banks, buyers' guides, directories and all forms of bibliographical material.

Marketing research, more specifically, is information obtained from either secondary (desk research) sources or primary (field research) sources which is both unbiased in its method of collection, analysis and interpretation and subjected to checks and tests as to its validity. Market intelligence, once screened and validated, can be accepted as marketing research. A published report, for example, needs to be cleared as to the method by which its data were collected and for any strongly vested interest or bias in its originators. The source of a statistic used, for example, by a journalist to support a point he is making needs to be verified before the article or report can be accepted as market information for use in the company.

The multiplicity of market data, ranging from the relatively current and accurate sales statistics provided by internal sources to an official government updated output figure which can no longer be compared to previous returns or a rumour reported by a sales representative—all generate their own lack of confidence. Each source in its own right is a valuable contribution to the general flow of information available, but it becomes more directly useful and manageable once through the process of validation. It is the responsibility of the marketing specialists to see that the market information used by other managers in the company is sufficiently reliable to make a direct contribution to key decision-taking processes.

APPLICATIONS FOR MARKETING RESEARCH

Good marketing research data are not obtained cheaply. The collection of valid marketing data and their interpretation costs money which, in turn, requires the budgetary support and control of senior management. The support of senior managers is more likely to be forthcoming, not only when they can be assured of the reliability of research information, but also when they are aware of the full range of the company's operations to which research may be usefully applied. Many of these applications involve production, financial or technical decisions and are thereby outside the control and responsibility of the marketing staff and yet they relate directly to the company's commitment to survival through profitable market orientation.

The basic applications and the breadth of management functions involved in research findings are shown in Table 4.1.

Table 4.1

Basic applications	Management functions involved
Market size Structure and forecast	Senior general management (board) marketing; sales
Product/service features	Design and development; production and operating management; marketing
Pricing policy	Finance; marketing; senior and general management
Purchasing decision processes	Marketing; sales; advertising
Promotional policies Sales deployment Selling methods Advertising Sales promotion	Marketing; sales including area/regional sales management; advertising; finance; general management
Distribution Direct v. use of distributors Physical	Marketing; sales; transport; general management

CHANGING EMPHASIS ON MARKETS AND FORECASTING

In the pioneering 1960s and early 1970s some 60 to 70 per cent of all industrial marketing research appropriations were estimated to be allocated to studies of market size and important segments within the market.[2]

The need for information on market size is self-evident, both for a firm proposing to enter a new market and a company seeking a greater exploitation of an existing market. Knowledge of the total market size enables a realistic assessment to be made of the penetration which the company might hope to achieve. Further, the magnitude and intensity of all the other marketing activities can be linked to the total market figure to prevent over- or under-investment in market development. Regular accurate knowledge of market size for a company already in a market is vital for the calculation of market share.

The importance of market share as an indication of success or otherwise has declined in the last decade with the strong influence of management accountants and the measurement of success through rates of return on capital invested. Few would disagree with the appropriateness of the accountants' intervention but it is now also accepted that a substantial share of the home market is an essential base for the penetration of international markets. Market share data enable a manufacturer to assess untapped potential and provide important basic data in relation to competitors.

For those users of marketing research who have obtained market size data in past studies, now updated by routine assessments, the emphasis has moved away from total market size to the more detailed analysis of specific market segments.

Another important use for quantitative data is market forecasting. The simple techniques of extrapolation in tune with regular economic growth have not survived the turbulence of the international economy in recent years. Increasing competition, intensified by greater market fragmentation, similarly requires more sophisticated analyses of trends.

CHECKING VALIDITY

The range of professional industrial marketing research services available in the United Kingdom is very extensive and no marketing manager need be at a loss for advice on how to obtain detailed information relevant to a company's problems in home or overseas markets. The marketing research specialist is an expert in the techniques needed to collect and interpret information. With his cross-industry experience he can also assist the manager or client to formulate the problem in marketing research terms. Research proposals made more specific by the specialist in the formal research design need to be thoroughly scrutinized to ensure that the research survey offered will meet the needs of the sponsoring company. A useful question to check the relevance of the research approach is 'What would I do with the information if it were available now?' How would it be used to support a decision to enter a new market, for example, or substantially modify the product offered, change the emphasis of the sales effort or direct an advertising campaign? An additional self-imposed question before starting research is, 'To what extent will such measures have the support of senior management?'

Although validity *per se* must be the ultimate responsibility of the specialist researcher, the value of the research is dependent not only on its technical quality but also on the acceptance of that quality by the department or section concerned with the findings.

Research accuracy, therefore, has its basis in this very early 'terms of reference' stage with the researcher dependent on the client's openness as to why the information is needed and to what use it will be put. One of the most damning criticisms of a research survey and one most likely to weaken the confidence of senior managers in the techniques used, is that the information obtained was already known by managers in the sponsoring company. In such a case the researcher can only point to the agreed terms of reference and ask why the area in question was chosen in the first place. No researcher should attempt to win any arguments arising from this point. Having fallen victim to a poor research brief and a negligently approved terms of reference, the researcher has unwittingly supported those managers in the 50 per cent of companies who do not accept industrial marketing research as an aid to profitable operations.

CHECKING TECHNIQUES

The research design will include not only the topics and applications for the research but also the methods proposed to obtain the relevant information. A well prepared terms of reference and feasible research objectives will provide a proper basis for the research but the step to be taken to ensure validity of the ultimate findings is the evaluation of the research methods to be used.

Syndicated surveys

The increase in speculative research, whereby surveys of trends in a particular industry or market, financed by a specialist agency for resale to potential clients, has been a significant development in industrial marketing research during the past decade. The quantitative findings of these reports can provide useful 'ball park' figures to help judge the potential of a market. Similarly, the qualitative material can give a lead for more in-depth surveys.

The research methods of these surveys need to be well scrutinized before being released to key decision makers in the sponsoring or client company.

Sampling

This is particularly true if the survey is based on a sample of industrial respondents. Traditionally the concentration of industrial markets has given the industrial researcher an advantage over his consumer research colleague. The survey of a market with only 50 potential purchasers, for example, could be conducted as a census with all respondents covered. With the expansion, however, of interest from heavy capital equipment to surveys of 'industrial consumables', office equipment, microcomputers, private telephone systems for example, samples of such wide user populations have to be drawn.

Representative sampling has been achieved by thorough investigation of market structures, turnover, size and geographical location of establishments in the user industries. Data in this form will provide a frame from which the sample may be drawn. The decision must then be taken whether to draw a non-probability sample, such as the purposive quota sample, in which respondents are drawn in proportion to their representation in the market as a whole, or a probability sample. The numbers needed to fill the quota in the non-probability sample are indicated by the controls afforded by accurate knowledge of market structures. There are many advantages in this form of sampling which ensures that each segment of a market is represented. A major disadvantage, however, is that statistical analysis cannot be used to evaluate the data collected. Statistical evaluation to determine sufficiency of sample size and the degrees of error in the sample should be applied only to probability samples in which each and every respondent listed has an equal chance of being selected as any other respondent. This assumes that every potential respondent is known to the researcher.

Non-response

Another area to watch for in evaluating sample survey data is the degree of respondent non-response. If, for example, only 50 per cent of interviews, whether personal, by telephone or by postal questionnaire have been successful, a problem arises as to characteristics of the non-respondents. The 50 per cent achieved may be sufficiently representative or they may have specific market needs that differ from those not cooperating with the survey. Techniques have been developed to overcome this problem in postal surveys by sampling the non-respondents with a second copy of the questionnaire or by telephoning. One technique used to increase response to industrial surveys involves the prenotification of postal questionnaire respondents by telephone.[3]

A sample population of 75 purchasing managers was selected from a list of 460 members of a purchasing management association. A postal questionnaire was prepared containing 40 scaled response items dealing with the existence and usefulness of company policies in regard to various buying practices. Of the 75 respondents in the sample, 9 had left the company listed or had changed positions in the company. Of those remaining in the sample 34 were reached directly by telephone and 32 were left a message that the postal questionnaire was being sent. The overall result was quite dramatic in that 64 of the 66 potential respondents returned completed questionnaires.

Postal questionnaires v. telephone interviewing

The costs of boosting response rates of a postal questionnaire thus avoiding the danger of a bias through non-response, may reach a level equal to that of a full-scale telephone survey in its own right. Postal questionnaires still have essential features in comparison with the high cost of personal interviews when the survey requires respondent consideration of answers in depth or when a fact relating to past behaviour, consumption of raw materials, etc., has to be checked with records not to hand, but the unease of the professional researcher, and indeed his clients, with the difficulties of achieving high success rates with postal surveys has led in turn to the reinforcement and further development of the telephone interview technique.

The telephone interview has for long been an important industrial survey technique exploiting, as it does, the fact that all businesses are on the telephone and that key decision makers are rarely more than a few feet away from one.

As the use increases there is a need for the research sponsor or client to be satisfied that the supervision of interviewers employed in large-scale surveys and the procedures for editing and quantifying the data obtained are satisfactory. Regular telephone interviewing is an arduous task requiring stamina and a high degree of concentration to ensure the accurate delivery of the questions and recording of data.

COMPUTER ASSISTED TELEPHONE INTERVIEWING

Accuracy and thereby validity of telephone surveys can be improved by measures reducing errors in editing and interviewer fatigue by systems of computer assisted telephone interviewing (CATI) such as Quancept.[4] The traditional telephone method is for the interviewer to enter the respondent's responses on a conventional questionnaire. These answers are in turn punched on cards or directly on to tape for data processing. Data validation programs have to be used and prior coding involving code-lists of products and/or the preparation of code frames for open-ended coding.

The process may be speeded up by keying the completed questionnaires directly to a computer terminal using a data editor or by direct data entry (DDE) in which the computer, programmed as to the format of the questionnaire, can reject any incorrect responses as they are keyed in. This method removes the need for a separate EDIT programe. In the full computer assisted operation the interviewer is guided through the interview entirely by the computer. No paper is used. The computer terminal displays the questions one at a time together with the permitted responses. Special routing or 'skips' to other parts of the questionnaire are catered for by the program without any decision making by the interviewer. An even more advanced system caters for the use of open-ended questions.

TRENDS IN DEVELOPMENT AND RESEARCH

The potential for the expansion of industrial marketing research is assured by the need for market information in a competitive business climate. Greater use can be expected through the introduction of the techniques to companies not already using them and by an increased and more sophisticated use by companies and organizations with extensive experience. The level of expansion will depend, to a large extent, on how far research efficiency, particularly in field work, can be increased and thereby costs contained.

The prospects for cost control in industrial marketing research are good. Multi-client surveys by the larger specialist agencies go a long way to fill information needs without the loss of control or reduced relevance of the speculative survey. Many small 'two consultant' agencies are available to supply specific small-scale research services. The use of computers, both in techniques and in commercial data bases, will also help to reduce costs.

The professional standards of the industrial marketing research specialist can be expected to develop further with more education, training and the interchange of experience through practitioner bodies such as the Industrial Marketing Research Association.

REFERENCES

1. Hooley, G. J. and C. J. West. 'The untapped markets for marketing research', paper to appear in *Journal of Market Research Society, 1984.*
2. Wilson, A. *The Assessment of Industrial Markets*, Cassel/ABP, London 1973. Recommended for further reading as the definitive text on the subject.
3. Hasen, A., C. Tinney and W. Rudelius. Increased response to industrial surveys', *Industrial Marketing Management,* **12**, 1983, New York.
4. Katz, M. 'Computer assisted telephone interviewing', SGCSA conference, Nov. 1982, City University, London.

INDUSTRIAL SELLING

Hugh Walker

IMPORTANCE OF THE SELLING FUNCTION

Industrial selling, and the management of the selling function, is of supreme importance in the context of industrial marketing. A 'push' rather than a 'pull' strategy usually characterizes the marketing effort. Very seldom do industrial marketers rely on heavy advertising to pull the product through a distributive pipeline.

The part played by the salesforce is, therefore, a vital one, and the selling operation must be fully integrated into the total marketing strategy.

THE INDUSTRIAL BUYING DECISION

In the industrial buying decision lies the essential nature of industrial marketing. The buyer of consumer products may or may not be fickle, swayed by advertising, emotional in his decision making. But, certainly in consumer marketing, the purchase is an individual, at most a family, activity. In the industrial scene the activity is a very different one. The industrial purchase is an organizational choice (see Chapter 2). It is business selling to business. Many people, many different levels of buyers are involved.

Sometimes these people act as individuals, sometimes in groups, such as a committee of departmental heads, or the board of directors. The considerations in the mind of each will be very different. And price will be but one of these. Reliability, ease of use, compact size, reducing manufacturing costs, and many other expressions of value in use will be the concern of those in the industrial decision-making unit.[1] The roles that a person may play in a decision-making unit will differ importantly. They will include those of initiator, influencer, decider, buyer and user. All are important and the seller must be able to identify each one. The buyer, in the sense of purchasing manager, may be a powerful executive or may be a mere cipher, doing little more than rubber stamping decisions made elsewhere. Either way the sales executive will certainly need to see many others in the customer company as well as the buyer.

More and more companies are using value engineering[2] ('Is quality and reliability right for a particular product design and function?'), and value analysis ('Are costs reasonable for the product price?'). Many are practising the 'materials management' concept which looks beyond the buying function as such to include all functions involving the flow of goods from purchase of raw materials through to the distribution of finished goods.

The eight phases[3] of the buying decision process and the three distinct types of buying situation call for a careful and detailed selling strategy not only for the salesforce as a whole but also for each market segment—indeed for each customer or prospect.

BUYER–SELLER RELATIONSHIP[4]

All these considerations add up to a complex set of relationships between buyer and seller. It is the interdependence between buyer and seller that is the hallmark of industrial marketing and which places great responsibility on the industrial salesforce and those who manage their activities.

A CONCEPTUAL FRAMEWORK

A useful model for reviewing the decisions that have to be made about the role of personal selling within the marketing strategy is provided by Ryans.[5] As he points out there must be a good fit between the company marketing strategy and the actual behaviour of the salesforce (see Fig. 5.1). Often, however, this is not the case.

DESIRED ROLE OF PERSONAL SELLING

This is the key element in salesforce decision making. There are two aspects of role which need to be considered:

1. The emphasis on selling in relationship to the other elements in the marketing mix, and especially other elements in the promotional mix (such as advertising, public relations and sales promotion).
2. The particular set of objectives that each individual has to accomplish.

All too frequently the role of personal selling is ill-defined in the mix, and the sharp end of the marketing effort is blunted.

THE SIX QUESTIONS

To enable management to define the role of personal selling very specifically, these questions are useful.[6]

What are we selling? Not just a product answer, but a description of the benefit the customer is getting, the solutions to problems. Are we selling products or systems?

To whom are we selling? How is the market segmented? Is all the salesforce selling to all target markets: part to one and part to another? Who are typical members of the buying centre in the organization? What role do they play? What considerations are important for each member? Are groups of people involved?

Why are we selling? What is in our favour? What are comparative strengths and weaknesses in relation to market needs? What competition are we up against? What degrees of our success can be attributed to the superior selling skills of our salesmen?

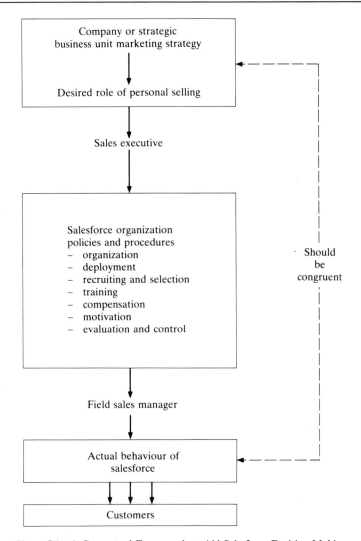

Figure 5.1 A Conceptual Framework to Aid Salesforce Decision Making

When are we selling? Time and opportunity. At what stage in the industrial purchasing decision do we get in the customer company? Do we discover latent needs? Or only serve needs that customers are aware of?

Where are we selling? Geographical? Where are customer groups located? Where does selling actually take place?

How are we selling? What methods does the salesforce use? What sales aids are available? Who, besides the salesforce, are involved in selling and customer service? What activities is the salesforce involved in?

These questions, carefully answered, will go a long way to produce a clear definition of the role of personal selling and the kind of sales executive needed.

SALES EXECUTIVE

One of the biggest dilemmas facing management focuses on the kind of sales executive needed. Should it be a technician who is taught to sell? Or a sales executive who can call on technical and specialist support? In some instances there is a clear case for an engineer, say, who can talk about engineering problems with the counterparts in the client company. In others, it is much more important that the sales executive is not a technician but someone who has a very good knowledge of the customer's business. An IBM sales executive, for example, selling to a building society needs a profound knowledge of the exact kind of management information system needed by head office and branches in that organization.

ORGANIZATION AND DEPLOYMENT

Clear thinking about the role of personal selling and the kind of salesforce needed must stem from decisions about the market segments to be served and the product offering to be made. In so many cases, what is sold is not a product as such but a complex system which includes a strong element of service.

An analysis[7] of the actual and potential customers in the given markets will indicate what those customers' service requirements are—and who should provide them. This analysis may show that in addition to purchasing and price negotiation, customers may need technical advice and support, samples and trials. Not only the salesforce would be involved in giving these but technical service managers, development managers, sales managers and sometimes the marketing and managing directors. Companies marketing to the building industry, for example, may well need to canvass architects, who are, after all, part of the potential customer's buying centre though not part of his company. Architects specify but do not buy. It is important that representatives who contact architects speak the same language. Often, therefore, architectural representatives are a special group within the salesforce chosen because they have some architectural training.

The traditional way of organizing the salesforce was on a regional basis. Latterly, the emphasis has shifted towards industry segment or product and technology. This can sometimes, in a multi-product company, lead to more than one person for the same company calling on a customer and could cause confusion if communication channels are not kept clear and discrete. The number of people needed depends, of course, on the job to be done. A useful formula for identifying how many staff are needed, and whether a particular person is fully loaded, uses the relationship between four factors:

$$\frac{\text{Number of actual and potential customers} \times \text{Call frequency}}{\text{Average daily rate} \times \text{Number of working days per year}}$$

This will involve categorizing customers according to their business volume and allocating call frequency appropriately. The organization of the salesforce will call for careful thought about the relationship between sales and service. Management will recognize the role the salesforce has in providing service and in summoning technical service from base. The value of the service engineer in a selling role has often been overlooked.

Because of the rising cost of personal selling, and the large number of calls needed to secure one sale, many companies now look carefully at alternatives to calling on customers in person.

The increasing use of telephone selling is a case in point. Either the salesman himself can devote some time to maintaining regular telephone contact with customers in addition to his personal calls, or telephone canvass can be carried out by a separate group permanently based at headquarters or regional office.

Industrial marketers have become more aware, too, of the potential for actual selling that service engineers may have. They often have lengthy contact inside the customer organization and are associated in the customer's mind with trouble shooting and problem solving.

The allocation of responsibilities must, however, be very clear-cut. The sales executive's responsibilities must be clearly defined and nothing must be allowed to erode his or her standing in the eyes of the customer. The sales executive's personal value to the company is unique.

Considerable work has been done in applying the methods of work study to the salesforce. Even if this is not carried out in depth, the questions used by the work study analyst are relevant: this involves looking at each of the sales executive's activities in turn, and asking questions to discover the purpose of the activity and whether it is being carried out by the best person, in the best place, at the best time and in the best way.

Often the salesforce is loaded with responsibilities which dilute its sales task. While part of the job is to provide informal market intelligence on a regular basis, the whole training and relationship with a customer works against the suitability to provide formal market research.

Territory organization and journey planning are activities to which too little attention is often paid. Sales executives sometimes claim that it is impossible to make plans and keep to them as they must be always on call for their customers. In fact, planning and organization are essential if good results are to be achieved.

The organization of a sales territory requires a thorough analysis and grading of actual and potential customers. These must be graded according to the call frequency they merit. Sales territories are typically much larger in industrial than in consumer marketing. Plotting the calls on a map will show concentration. The sales executive can then subdivide the territory into a number of smaller areas. Dividing territories into four or five areas ensures a regular call pattern in a cycle which can cater for the different requirements of the customers. There must be direction as to the appropriate blend of call on existing and potential customers.

Even if a customer signals a need for an additional call, appropriate territory organization and journey planning ensure that the sales executive will probably be in that customer's area in a matter of a few days and the additional call can probably be integrated into the journey plan without too much dislocation.

DIRECT OR INDIRECT

One of the most important questions to be addressed by the industrial marketer is whether to reach customers directly through the salesforce, or indirectly through a network of dealers. The decision will be to go direct, using own salesforce, if the unit sale is a large one, if there are a small number of potential users, if there are many organizational levels of buyers, or if it takes a long time period to consummate a sale.

On the other hand, if there are frequent orders and rapid delivery is needed, or if there are large numbers of small buyers, the reverse is the case. It will be well to appoint distributors or dealers.

In fact, of course, many organizations use a combination of their own sales staff, selling direct to large customers, and dealers who service the smaller customers. This may give rise to some problems. The distributors are themselves customers and become part of the salesforce's responsibility. But the distributor is an independent businessman and cannot be directed and controlled. He must be influenced and persuaded to put out the effort needed to sell the company's products. For example, the Caterpillar Tractor Company's[8] dealer network has long been one of its greatest strengths. All its dealerships are independently owned. The dealer can count on a steady income from service maintenance and used machine business. The dealers are considered as partners in the enterprise, not as agents or middlemen.

The distributive organization is perhaps the most permanent part of a company's marketing arrangement. Often, it is a matter of deeply rooted company policy to use—or not to use—dealers to reach the end-user. So it was with Dictaphone (UK). The decision to use dealers for its lower priced items proved to be a major factor in improving the company's profit position in the 1970s. The salesforce had been spending time and effort in contacting customers from whom only small orders were forthcoming. Once dealers were appointed, sales staff could concentrate on those with greater potential.

In some cases, the pattern of the industry will dictate what is to be done. The selling of feeding stuff or fertilizer to farmers will result in orders that are passed through the farmer's local agricultural merchant through whom the farmer does most of his business. The arrangement is a long-standing one which is tied in with credit and payment terms.

Sometimes, a company decides to go into a new market with an entirely new range of products. How should it handle the selling operation? A company that had a great deal of expertise in fan engineering and air movement design decided to become an original equipment manufacturer (OEM) in its own right. It decided to market mechanical extract systems to the building industry. A logical answer to its sales problem was the appointment of freelance sales agents who are paid on commission only.

RECRUITMENT AND SELECTION

The recruitment and selection of sales staff must hinge on the role of personal selling discussed above. There is no substitute for a very careful description of the job to be done and the profile of the person most fitted to do it.

In some cases, the situation will call for a technically trained person who then needs additional training to sell the company's products. In others, someone with special knowledge of an industry and existing customers may be the answer. In other cases, again, a company may wish to select on the basis of the right qualities and aptitudes and add the rest by training.

What are those qualities? Clearly, a person must be a skilled and persuasive communicator. Equally, there is a need to be a good problem solver with the ability to diagnose a customer's real needs and find solutions within the products and systems being sold. Perhaps less obvious but of great importance, he or she must be a good organizer. Over a period of perhaps many months, there will be a need to organize the complex and changing group of people in the customer's buying centre. Moreover, there will be the responsibility of organizing company resources, including technical service, research and development, quality control and senior management to meet with their counterparts in the customer organization and to reach decisions.

When personal qualities of sales staff are discussed, two call for special mention.[9] They are empathy and ego-drive. Empathy is the capacity for participation in another's feelings or ideas: the ability to know where the other person's shoe pinches. Ego-drive is inner directed effort towards a goal. 'When the going gets tough, the tough get going!' Neither empathy nor ego-drive will do on its own. Both qualities must be present in equal proportion.

TRAINING

Training is about knowledge, skill and attitude. Training and development of the salesforce must, therefore, be looked on as a continuous process. It does, however, divide into a number of parts.

Initial training will concentrate on company policies and procedures, company products and sales techniques. This will be the responsibility of the company's own training and line managers. Consultants may be used, though the depth of their knowledge of the company will be limited. Continuous training will be the responsibility of the field sales manager. It is vital to recognize this as a prime responsibility. In making calls with the sales staff, the manager must take the greatest care to keep a low profile and never to belittle the subordinate in the eyes of his customer by appearing to take over the sales interview.

Refresher training may take the form of attending external courses in sales techniques. This has the value of giving the salesforce the opportunity of meeting people from other companies and exposing them to the stimulus of fresh ideas.

It is important to remember that development also means self-development. The person has the responsibility for his own development. The market place is constantly changing and the salesforce must change with it and keep constantly up to date.

Selling, though it involves constant contact with other people, is a lonely job. The sales executive frequently comes face to face with negative, even hostile attitudes. It is most important, then, that he or she feels the support and backing of the company. Training must make a thorough professional, effective and efficient, 'doing the right things, and doing things right'.

COMPENSATION AND MOTIVATION

Motivation has a material and a non-material aspect. The compensation package in many industrial product companies relies less on a commission element than on the structure of their consumer counterparts. This is perhaps because the ultimate sale is often the result less of an individual than a team effort. In many cases, sales staff are remunerated on straight salary. Where bonuses are paid, they are often paid on a group basis. It is important that the efforts of those in the sales office and in the service back-up team do not go unrewarded.

The non-material motivators[10] are generally agreed to be the work itself (if interesting), achievement, recognition for achievement, responsibility and advancement. There is ample scope in the industrial products sale job for these rewards to be provided given proper management. Interestingly, salary, company policies and procedures, and interpersonal relationships with superiors are often found to be among those factors which dissatisfy people at work. It must be remembered, though, that even if all those negatives are put right no job satisfaction is obtained—only an absence of dissatisfaction. The conclusion seems to be that the sales executive needs challenge, plus the ability, which training and leadership bring, to rise to the occasion, to achieve results and to gain recognition, if only in the form of a timely word of praise.

EVALUATION AND CONTROL

The evaluation and control of the sales staff relate to mutually agreed objectives to which assent has been given, preferably between the person concerned and the manager.

The full name of MBO is management by objectives and self-control.[11] The conscientious sales person who is well trained, managed and led becomes expert in evaluating and controlling own performance. Clearly, though, what is needed is a management information system which, with a minimum of effort, gives the maximum amount of relevant information to the sales office and from there to all those in the company who need to know.

With the development of information technology, we are rapidly approaching the time when the sales executive will have a computer terminal at home or even in the brief case. There will then be a much faster response to customer needs than is possible now.

Hitherto, reporting for control in many industrial marketing companies has sometimes been sketchy to the point of non-existence, or the requirements have been cumbersome and pedantic. Sometimes, in the latter case, the demands have come from the marketing department with no explanation of the need for the information. This has been a contributory cause of the antagonism between sales and marketing that all too often characterizes internal communications. Since conflict within the company absorbs the effort that should go into achieving profitable sales, it must not be allowed to develop unchecked. This is part of the coordinating function of top management.

It is often thought that planning is a forward looking function while control looks backward at what has happened. This should not be so. Control, too, should look forward, should aim at preventing failure. Sales staff must keep a watchful eye on the future, never making promises the company cannot keep and giving their customers early warning if delivery dates, for example, look like being late.

THE FIELD SALES MANAGER

The role of the field sales manager is a crucial one. It is the link between headquarters and the salesforce in the field. The manager is the person through whom the staff report and it is he or she who must ensure they get all the back-up they need. This includes direction and guidance of their efforts, responsibility for their continuous training and some direct sales responsibility. It is important to avoid the two pitfalls:

(a) behaving as still primarily a sales person and so spending too little time and effort on administrative and management responsibilities;
(b) spending too large a proportion of time in the office rather than in the field.

The field sales manager and general sales manager (in smaller companies they are the same person) must not be selected simply because they are good at selling.[12] This is the surest way for a company to lose a good sales person and gain a bad manager. They must be picked for their abilities to manage. They must be trained in the duties that go with the new job. These duties are planning, organizing, staffing, directing, leading and controlling. They must have a thorough understanding of how the company works; they must have a good knowledge of the financial side of the business; and must be able to play a full part in the marketing decision making.

Successful industrial product companies are nearly always those who have carved out a strong marketing role for sales managers.[13] In practice this means:

- interpreting information on local market conditions and competitor moves;
- participating in discussions with other functional managers about various strategic options for building the business;
- helping to select the most promising options, and considering the commitments necessary for each alternative;
- agreeing on realistic volume and share of market targets under various options.

THE SELLING PROCESS

The actual process of selling involves a great deal of careful planning and preparation. In industrial selling, the salesforce is, more often than not, selling a system rather than a product, that is making an offering to the customer which goes far beyond the hardware of the product. The offering includes all the ingredients in the marketing mix, especially the service element. It includes the good name and reputation of the company marketing the product. Not least does it include the relationships that the salesforce has built up over a long period with its counterparts in the customer organization.

The salesman or women must know his or her customer's business intimately; he or she must make a thorough and careful study of the customer's customers and must know how the process of buying works, who are the members of the buying centre, their roles and their considerations. The sales person's concern must be to start the sales process at the earliest possible phase in the buying decision process. With existing customers regular calls will ensure that it is a straight rebuy. With new customers, the company must plan to be considered at the outset. If possible, it will be so organized that the specifications, when written, fit only the company's offering.

Conventional wisdom says that the sales person in a sales interview should focus on customer needs, customer benefits and product features—in that order.

Sony, for example, finds that its industrial products are so full of features that the strictest self-discipline is needed to avoid overloading the presentation with benefits that are of no relevance to the customer.

The SPIN[R14] model developed by Rackham and others is a development of the traditional approach. SPIN[R] stands for *s*ituation, *p*roblem, *i*mplication and *n*eed-payoff. They argue that the sales executive should focus on the sales situation, then on the nature of the customer's problem to arrive at the implied need, which can then be matched with the benefits of the product offering.

Situation questions are essentially background questions. They elicit information about the company's size, market and customers.

Problem questions probe for the customer's feelings of dissatisfaction with the present situation and try to discover the precise nature of the customer's problem.

Implication questions are intended to highlight the importance of a need implied by a customer. If uneven quality of parts supplied has been mentioned, for example, the question might be asked: 'How many customers do you estimate you lose through poor quality of parts?'

Need-payoff questions shift attention from the problem to the solution. They crystallize and make the need specific. As so often, in selling, the key word is if (e.g., 'How much would you save if . . .?')

All too often, an industrial salesforce is not trained to sell in this way. Instead of discussing the customer's business and his problems, the salesforce talks about its own products exclusively, frequently failing even to translate features into benefits by the simple means of 'this means that . . .'.

NEGOTIATION

The process of bargaining to reach a mutually acceptable agreement or objective[15] is required in a wide range of industrial selling situations.

Negotiation calls for the sales person to expect the buyer to have a wide range of requirements which have to be satisfied in whole or in part if a contract is to be concluded. He or she must, therefore, have a carefully thought out plan but be prepared to adapt it depending on the moves made by the buyer. A decision must be made in advance about what is the ideal and what is the acceptable outcome.

It is, of course, of the utmost importance that the sales executive and those who manage his or her efforts have a very clear understanding of the price, volume, costs relationship not only in their own company but in that of the customer. A sales person can sell effectively only if he or she can demonstrate, using the customer's own figures, the bottom line advantage of taking up his or her company's offer.

Selling to government—local or central—raises a number of special problems. The buying agency will usually ask several companies to tender for a contract. It must be the aim of the would-be supplier to get behind the purchasing department to those people who draw up the specification. It may be possible to influence them by technical argument to draw up a specification that only one or a few companies can meet. Again, good advice may be to look at those features which lie outside the specification and promote these.[16] The aim must always be to avoid competing solely on price.

SALES AIDS

It is well known that recall is much higher when we are both told and shown something than when we are told or shown only. It is folly to believe that a sales executive can achieve success by using the spoken word alone. Visual aids are needed. The best visual aid, of course, is the product itself. But it is the product in use that the prospect needs to see.

Often the product can be shown in use, either at one's own plant or on the premises of a satisfied customer. At exhibitions the product can often be demonstrated.

Films can be invaluable but they are costly to produce and cannot easily be revised once made.

The medium which has really proved itself in industrial selling is the video cassette recording (VCR). It is relatively inexpensive to produce professionally. It can be updated, and dubbed into different languages. It lends itself well to exhibition work and to demonstrations in an office.

G. and J. Hall of Sheffield, manufacturers of engineers' cutting tools, taps and dies, produce the Bradrad multi-diameter drill and deburrer. It weighs less than half a pound. Every time a trade exhibition was staged, machine tool equipment which weighed up to a ton had to be installed on the stand to demonstrate the product.

Then a 16 mm film was shot and later transferred to VCR. The programme shows the tool, explains how it works, demonstrates all its attributes and versatility without pauses and delays.

Still the most widely used visual aid is, of course, the brochure. When used in selling, it is important that the sales person uses it as an aid and does not allow the prospect to study it quietly instead of continuing the dialogue. The brochure produced as a mailing shot does not necessarily make a good sales aid. A sales executive often prefers to make up a personal sales organizer—a folder of visual material that will help in the presentation rather than become a barrier.

NEWER METHODS

Much of the industrial sales person's time is likely to be spent in exhibition work. Frequently, marketers take exhibition space because their competitors do—and for no other good reason.

A growing use is being made by industrial marketers, as a major part of their selling effort, of seminars in one form or other. These can take the form of a presentation by scientists or technologists of information on highly technical subjects connected with the products or systems that the company is selling. The presentation may be followed by demonstrations. Such seminars are obviously by invitation only and have the value that they combine education with selling. They enable the company to sell to a broader group of members of the buying centre within a company. Satisfied customers meet prospects. The reputation of the company within its field is greatly enhanced.

CONCLUSION

Many technical advances will change the product offering. The revolution in information technology will profoundly affect the way in which the salesforce operates and the methods by which orders are processed. It is hard to see any set of factors that will remove the necessity for the person-to-person encounter between sales staff and buyer. The skills of seeking out and sifting information, diagnosing problems, arriving at a systems solution that uses the company's products, and communicating it in a skilful and persuasive manner, will always be needed.

REFERENCES

1. Corey, E. R. 'Industrial buyer behaviour', *Industrial Marketing: Cases and Concepts*, 3rd edn, Prentice-Hall, Englewood Cliffs, New Jersey, 1983.
2. Ohmae, K. 'Analysis: the starting point', *The Mind of the Strategist*, McGraw-Hill, New York, 1982.
3. Robinson, P. J., C. W. Faris and Y. Wind. *Industrial Buying and Creative Marketing*, Allyn and Bacon, Boston, 1967.
4. Webster, F. E. Jr. 'Buyer–seller relationships', *Industrial Marketing Strategy*, John Wiley & Sons, New York, 1979.
5. Ryans, A. B. 'A conceptual framework to aid in sales-force decision-making', unpublished note used in 13th Strategic Marketing Course (College of Institute of Marketing) at Durham, England, Sept. 1983.
6. Willsmer, R. L. 'Where are we, now?' *The Basic Arts of Marketing*, Business Books, London, 1976.
7. Wilson, M. 'How to organise the sales force', *Managing a Sales Force*, 2nd edn, Gower, 1983.
8. 'Caterpillar: Sticking to basics to stay competitive', *Business Week*, 4 May 1981.
9. Mayer, D. and H. Greenberg. 'What makes a good salesman', *Harvard Business Review*, July/August 1964, Cambridge, Mass., USA.
10. Herzberg, F. 'The motivation–hygiene theory', *Work and the Nature of Man*, Staples Press, London, 1974.
11. Drucker, P. F. 'Management by objectives and self-control', *The Practice of Management*, Heinemann, London, 1955.
12. Strafford, J. 'Fred's our best salesman—Let's promote him', *Industrial Marketing Digest*, **5** (3), 1980.
13. Ames, B. C. 'Build marketing strength into industrial selling', *Harvard Business Review*, January/February 1972.
14. SPIN[R] is a registered trade mark of Huthwaite Research Group, Rotherwood, The Green, Penistone, Sheffield. The SPIN[R] model was developed by Rackham *et al*. Material on which this section is based was drawn from: Poppleton, S. E. 'The social skills of selling', in Argyle, M. (ed.), *Social Skills and Work*, Methuen, London, 1981.
15. Lidstone, J. 'Why negotiation?' *Negotiating Profitable Sales*, Gower, 1977.
16. Winkler, J. 'Competitor related pricing systems', *Pricing for Results*, Heinemann, 1983.

SIX

BUSINESS-TO-BUSINESS ADVERTISING

John L. Samuel

In some ways the advertising business shows signs similar to those of the cobbler's children. Perhaps that is good in its implication that we are absorbed wholly with our customers' communications and find too little time and incentive to worry about our own. But it may also be bad in that signs of lack of clear thought may not endear us to senior management with resultant uncertainty and even suspicion as to the worthiness of our contribution.

In the 'business-to-business' field particularly, this lack of clarity can be seen in the profusion of labels we give to jobs and operations—using words loosely, with little apparent concern for the clarity of their communication.

The word 'advertising' which heads this chapter, is in itself a piece of loose shorthand that covers the ground adequately for those of us in the business but is a palpable misnomer to those outside.

'Advertising' may be defined as that part of a company's communication which is not conducted face to face—'non-personal' as opposed to 'personal' selling. I prefer, in the business-to-business field, to ignore the mythical line above and below which advertising agencies choose to operate, depending on the economic climate and their resources. Again we may understand what is meant in broad terms, but it is a line that cannot easily be drawn in business market communication.

Instead we should see all communication effort, which in the end must be in support of company objectives, as splitting into two parallel but interdependent areas. Most clearly these can be called 'personal' and 'non-personal' communication.

Though somewhat simplified for purposes of clarity, this means the sales director will take care of those personal selling efforts conducted by sales and service people, while the communications executives will take care of those non-personal efforts that still address the market but do so without the benefit of visible response or counter argument at the time. Clearly, areas like exhibitions will straddle the two and use a mixture of both. So will the output from the growing AV field when used in support of sales presentations, for instance.

We will discuss in this chapter 'non-personal communication' and will acknowledge from the beginning, that that discussion will include many media—direct mail, exhibitions, audio visual, telemarketing, as well as press, television or radio advertising. You will have read the acknowledgment in Chapter 5 that some of these are woven inextricably into the selling fabric so the bridge between 'personal' and 'non-personal' efforts is perhaps stronger and more real than is sometimes imagined. Anything that breaks down the isolationist idea of 'advertising' as an activity operating on its own, must be good. The 'personal' and 'non-personal' concept I find helpful simply because it reflects reality, is clearly descriptive of areas of investment of money and time and, I believe, makes it easier for all to accept the interdependence one to the other.

INDUSTRIAL OR BUSINESS TO BUSINESS?

There is really not much in a name and, once more, fashion in our business dictates a constant move from one concept to the next. Over the years we seem to move in circles rather than in straight lines of development and, on that basis, 'trade and technical' will rear its head in one of the years ahead (and be as fashionable as it was in the 1950s) to describe this area of promotional activity. I have used as my chapter heading the term 'Business to Business' which more adequately describes the basic boundaries of our subject. Best of all would be 'non-consumer', but, even there, argument would resound as to whether specifiers and buyers in companies are not indeed consumers like anyone else. We do better to label the market place and not the buyers.

What we need to keep constantly in mind is that it is the differences in the market places that are important and not the overall activity. We are concerned as to how and why businesses buy and, therefore, with the different and changing format of communication programmes; with the differences which stem from the size of the decision-making unit at the customer end and in the more professional attitude to decision options.

Of course people in business still act as people and they have the same prejudices, hang-ups and opinions that everyone else has. But the real difference for the practising advertiser (and his agency) who sells business to business, lies in the complexity of the communication task from which he cannot escape. Individual advertising techniques stay relatively constant, needing only to be applied with skill, flair and enthusiasm, for we still seek to alter people's view and attitudes and to persuade them to our preferred line of action in the short and the long term.

First and most vital, we must take time to define our audience. This may be difficult and tedious, but without it, the relevance of what comes after may be unconvincing and ineffective.

THE AUDIENCE

The advertiser or agency who ignores the difficult definition of audience may produce some memorable work, but it is unlikely that it will seriously influence the market place. There has been, in these past years, a tendency to bypass this difficult stage as, for example, with corporate advertising which turns to the large-space, simple-brief, creative dominated advertising much beloved of agencies in the mass consumer field.

I have no doubt that the business advertiser and agency team must spend substantially more time on definition of market and audience than will their fast moving consumer goods (FMCG) colleagues. The reason is simple. The business team has very little easily available data such as guide its 'consumer' market opposite numbers.

The advertising person in most 'consumer goods' areas has a wealth of information available to assist in understanding the market in considerable detail. Facts and figures will be clear and unconfused in the main and the distribution chain and eventual consumer will be clearly analysed in terms which are consistent across the business and which are fully understood. Socio-economic groupings are meaningful, market share figures abound in most areas and 'shelf life' and buying patterns are familiar ground. The adoption, for instance, of a new client by an incoming agency (and vice versa) gives little problem in the understanding of the facts and figures while the pick-up of familiar talismans and guides means a quick start-up and immediate grappling with the planning and creative solutions.

Not so in the business market. Here, works managers don't define easily by socio-economic grouping. Their function may be identical (though that will vary from industry to industry) but they may be engineering graduates, operating for some years at senior levels of responsibility within the company or they may have been promoted from the shop floor with the same level of practical ability but with very different characteristics as people.

The ideal would be to have standard classification by job function but, alas, the few desultory attempts that have been made in the circulation and readership field have so far had little success.

That lack of clarity of individual characteristics can either be ignored or struggled with, but if we seriously believe ourselves to be contributors to the effective marketing of industrial products, there really is no option. Our concern must be the group of people within each company who can make or break a decision in our favour—who will accept or reject our proposition. Again that will seldom be one person except in the smallest companies, but rather will be three, four or five people making up the familiar decision-making unit.

Job specifications, therefore, are critical at this stage for the communications team. Undoubtedly, we must understand the attitude of each of the unit's members and acknowledge that, though there may be an individual with personal hang-ups and foibles, there is also the job specification held from the company, and decisions and recommendations will be made as much against that background as against any personal preferences. We must understand both sides.

This is the source I think of the much discussed difficulty of dealing with accountants and engineers. There is undoubtedly a tendency for men and women from professions and trades where precision is the order of the day (both in training and practice) to find it more difficult to embrace selling and communication and the inexactitudes it seems we expect them to accept.

So audience definition remains vital in the business market place and the acknowledgement is critical that several people of different disciplines are involved (and without their total acceptance we shall not win). The first time-consuming task is to think through the market in detailed terms knowing that little help will come from established practice or figures. The gaps in knowledge must be filled or at least acknowledged. New initiatives must be sought for the answering of basic questions that, initially, may seem so unanswerable that we are tempted to accept the inevitable and move back to easier ground. After all, if we are unclear to whom we are talking, we will be equally unclear on the separate nature of the message we have to deliver.

THE MESSAGE

Each person in the decision-making unit will find different reasons for acceptance or rejection of our proposition. The personnel director may welcome electric lift trucks in the factory for the environment will be less polluted, less noisy and the workforce and unions would approve. The production director may, however, believe them to be a hazard in that the material to be moved is too heavy/cumbersome/fragile to risk anything other than the imagined power of the IC model. The finance director may be resolute that there is no intention of replacing the current models anyway, being only two years into their life-cycle.

The senior radiologist in major hospitals may actively seek the latest generation of diagnostic imaging equipment simply to help stay in (and be seen to be in) the forefront of modern technology. Senior medical staff, however, may see its acquisition as a bid for a growing centre of excellence and an extension of their individual hospital's influence over others in the area. Surgeons, nursing staff and administrators may be more interested in the ability of the equipment to tie in with other electronic hospital records systems, in the future, in an attempt to make patient information more readily accessible when and where it is needed.

To each of our several members of the DMU, therefore, we need to be equally thoughtful about what we want to say. The proposition needs precisely formulating for each of them and that means a full understanding of their current attitudes and the part they play in the specification and ultimate decision. Apart from one or two books on that subject, there is not much recorded experience and the fuller use of research and investigative techniques must be a major contribution to clarity here.

It goes without saying that the creative team must have a need to consider the 'tone of voice' for each group though never should this be an excuse for becoming so technical as to be obscure; so introverted as to lose the market's interest all together. The danger of talking to yourself, after all the time spent on analysis, is real and must be avoided. The contribution of communication people is to get absorbed in market detail yet still retain dispassion in judging what is of interest to the market and this may be our major skill and asset. It is all too easy for manufacturers to over-assess the importance of their products but there is never excuse for publicity people confirming that view without proper thought.

But let us assume we have a series of messages to be passed to a series of people. How do we do it? What media can and should we consider? Convention needs upsetting here, also, for the custom of our trade runs deep, biasing us in favour of some media and against many others.

WHERE TO PLACE THE MESSAGE?

At the beginning, I suggested that we are always dealing with a broad spectrum of communication media. The list is long. Simply put, we have to find a non-personal way of talking to the people in our decision-making group which will penetrate to them. We can accept that 'advertising' messages, in the broadest sense, can be avoided; can be missed or misunderstood; can generate anti-reaction where none was intended, as can all 'advertising' anywhere.

It follows, therefore, that we should end up with a clear list of people to be influenced; an understanding of their current attitudes to our proposition; an understanding of their job function and, therefore, of their attitude and influence within the DMU; and a full awareness of the numbers and characteristics in their peer groups. That understanding will lead us to make a judgement as to what medium is most likely to be effective in persuading that group to our viewpoint.

The arguments abound in favour of this or that medium. Direct mail argues its case more and more avidly and articulately. Television has seductive arguments with a real basis for consideration.

Audio visual demonstrates its effectiveness without perhaps taking enough trouble to talk about how the resultant products can best be used.

In the end, at the planning stage, we must hang on to the characteristics of the market and weigh up the length, tone and type of messages against the sort of people to whom they are directed. If we really need demonstration, we must question whether our techniques can really help at all without the intervention of a salesman. If sampling is critical, then press advertising is unlikely to be of assistance except as a two-step operation to 'write for sample'. Direct mail on the other hand could take that sample straight into the hands of our market place provided we have a superb and accurate mailing list.

In an ideal world, the media pattern should emerge if we have done the right pre-planning and, at this stage at least, we should not be rejecting any candidate medium because it is perceived as unexciting, difficult to handle or unlikely to find acceptance with a prejudiced client (or agency).

In reality I accept that other factors will have to be taken into account by the time the final media programme is put into action, but at this stage we must ignore them and compromise with nothing other than the effective cover of the market place.

Almost always a multi-media programme results. If, at the early planning stage in the business-to-business field, you find yourself with a single-medium solution, I would strongly advise a reappraisal to see where you may have not fully considered the real situation. Of course, there are different campaigns for different sets of objectives, but I argue for a detailed and fair appraisal of each situation. If communication is to play a real part in the total selling of the company and its products and services we must be equally ready to acknowledge the reality in the market and tackle it in depth.

Nature of the audience and creative implications

Given an agreed and relevant message and an adequate media pattern, thought must be given (and skill applied) to the dramatization and transmission of the message—the creative process.

In business communication more than most, not only is the medium part of the message but so is the target audience itself. Creative teams must tread the knife edge between treating that audience simply as people, and over-acknowledging their technical prowess and status.

This is often seen as a difficult area and a graveyard for many talented writers and visualizers—or at least for their enthusiastic interest. For instance, architects, asked to judge advertising, will almost always opt for that which comes nearest to the information level of the data sheet or that which acts only as 'wallpaper' with little or no sales content. They will tell you they are uninfluenced by 'persuasive advertising' and, here, they may by typical of the creative team's problem.

Each of our many target audiences will have characteristics of its own, a high proportion of them being based on the job function and the custom, attitude and even tradition of that job, trade or profession. Don't ever allow those characteristics to inhibit a clear, simple message.

CORPORATE COMMUNICATIONS

You will find the word 'corporate' much used throughout this book with extensive reference to it in Chapter 7.

Far from there being a conflict, there should be agreement that corporate objectives for any company can exist in their own right, and should, as a regular routine, be assessed and monitored as elsewhere.

If and when it is apparent that action needs to be taken to project some corporate aspect of the company proper, i.e., some knowledge of the company as a whole which, if not properly understood, will inhibit its internal or external understanding and, thus, its commercial success, the need is for the same level of 'homework' as elsewhere with resultant, considered objectives.

These 'corporate' objectives will be arrived at in the same painstaking way as all others and I accept there will be differences in their build-up. But, equally, I would not accept that these objectives will be alternatives to those set by marketing/sales/product managers. Even if, in practice, the sound investment of limited budgets will demand a setting of a priority between different sets of objectives, the 'corporate' label cannot take priority simply because it deals with the broadest issue.

It must follow then that the definition of message and audience must be expressed simply but fully before the creative team comes to grapple with it. But it also follows that the team must, at worst, be sympathetic to what it finds in that brief and seriously try to achieve communication *within the parameters* given. It is said there is often a tendency for creative tails to try to wag the market dog—to find it convenient to rewrite the analysis of the market and to ignore the bias of customers to suit the creative preference. But the facts of sales life must apply and no such avoidance strategy is permissible.

None of this implies an acceptance of dull, unemotive, non-motivating words and pictures which simply reflect the *status quo* or past history. Instead, it should yield intelligent, hard selling publicity material which acknowledges people, their true motivation and the true nature of their 'sales resistance'.

There is *no* reason not to have the highest expectation of creative quality in the business area—clear writing, emphasis on benefits, memorable dramatization of a simple message which will be admired *and* remembered. But there is reason *not* to have elegant, irrelevant artwork (for instance) simply because we think quality of execution will intrigue our 'qualified' professional market *nor* to elect for complex and convoluted phraseology, thinking we match a market characteristic when we only impress the advertiser and seldom his customer.

Remember that we have defined a multi-media situation in most companies and that there are differing creative needs in each. Advertising, direct mail, literature—all have different jobs to do as part of the total campaign and each must have its own brand of relevant and skilled creativity to generate interest, get action or change attitudes.

Priority should be determined by market situations and the need for correction—long and short term. Companies cannot usually fund, at one time, all the ambitions of their individual departments. I have made comment later in this chapter under 'Organization' (page 70) as to how we can more effectively assess the priority between, and relevance in these internal demands and judge whether they are the same (and therefore alternatives) or whether all must seriously be achieved and to what extent they are interdependent.

It may be that pressure from the media will tend to make corporate advertising seem to be a special and separate skill when it is not. Of course, the media must continue strongly to project the benefits of their individual coverage but those of us operating in client and agency are expected to know how to build an effective programme from the mass of candidate media on offer. If we do not, we will merely increase the suspicion with which senior management views our capability and lengthen the time it takes us to influence the board room and show how British industry can more successfully sell.

MEDIA ASSESSMENT

Once we have defined our varying audiences (or 'publics' as the PR business would have us call them) we must be able to relate them to the promise of effective coverage made by any one of our candidate media.

Without exception, each medium has problems in making an adequate case for the same basic reasons as we have difficulty in defining markets, specifiers and buyers in the 'business' area.

Add to that a tendency for each medium to argue from its own strengths and, therefore, emphasize the communications task that suits it best, e.g., the *Financial Times* and television will concentrate on 'businessmen' in general and, therefore, emphasize 'corporate' coverage more than any other.

This range of effective coverage is one of the bonuses on offer and the planner will turn it to advantage in building a campaign format. If the media accentuate the positive, that must be good selling for them and that is their correct marketing stance—ours is the choice and the justification.

All media will produce supporting evidence of one sort or another—all of it must be in the form of a selling document and representatives cannot be expected to be dispassionate guides through the total media mix.

A word or two on each of the main candidate media may, therefore, be relevant, with some guidelines on assessment—before and after use. A special and extended word is needed on press media (or print media as the Americans call it) for that situation is particularly complex but, equally, shows most promise in assessment terms.

THE PRESS

At the end of 1983 we are able to see the total media expenditure for 1982. The Advertising Association's survey (produced annually) is exhaustive and covers press, television, cinema, radio and poster advertising.

The 1982 totals are further split by type of press—national newspapers, regional newspapers, magazines and periodicals, business journals and directories.

Comparative figures are useful and sometimes surprising. The 1982 figures show £928 million spent on television, £1296 million spent in the general press area, £124 million on poster advertising, £70 million on radio and £18 million in the cinema.

Taking the press expenditure alone, this breaks into these percentages—national newspapers take 30 per cent, regional newspapers take a surprising 25 per cent, magazines and periodicals take a further 15 per cent as do the business journals. Directories come in at a modest 3 per cent and the cost of production averages out at 12 per cent.

You can see, therefore, that the expenditure in business journals is a sizeable one and, for display advertising, reached a figure of £191 million in 1982. These figures all exclude financial and classified advertising.

The 1982 survey also attempted an estimate of media expenditure by product group but this related to 1981, acknowledging the difficulties of speedy collection and calculation of the figures. It is again interesting to note that there is an estimate of £302 million spent on household and leisure press advertising; £256 million on food and £204 million on drink and tobacco—all figures in the consumer advertising area. Compare that with £487 million in the retail field and £310 million in the industrial field (that includes classified advertising) and you get a different perspective again on the way the press is used and where advertisers make their investment.

It has been shown that industrial publicity press expenditure probably represents less than one-third of the industrial advertiser's total expenditure on publicity. But it is the largest single medium, and for this reason more thinking and planning time is needed here as is money to provide better information upon which to make decisions.

There are enough data available in the consumer area to let the media buyer reach proper decisions. The reverse is, alas, true for the industrial media planner with the result that he can be tempted to opt out or take a non-controversial approach.

The industrial sales or advertising manager is also often too close to the trees to see the real wood with the added danger that he may be familiar with old, established publications and fail to appreciate the growing value of new media.

Having accepted the need for a clear idea of what is being said and to whom, the problem then is where to place the advertising. This discipline will help enormously for the strengths of the business press journals vary extensively even within the same market or industry.

For instance, in a situation where reader replies are called for, the media planner needs to know just how necessary they are. If it is a real need, there should be a bias towards proven response-getting publications which may not figure among the most authoritative or respected journals in that field.

On the other hand a new product may require announcing via an industrial 'newspaper' which is unlikely to pull the same kind of active response as a monthly magazine.

Again it may have been considered that design engineers, production engineers and purchasing officers should be exposed to the benefits of a particular product (differently interpreted for each of course). Here it is vital for the planner to know the relative importance of reaching each particular job function and, in the brief, a system of weighting might be used to advantage to dramatize the importance of the various job functions.

The need for research—criteria for judgement

There have been attempts to produce better readership data in the business and industrial press but even joint client/agency working parties have found the snags too great and the impetus has gradually died. There was the Chemical Industry Survey as long ago as 1965 and the two-part Building Survey in 1969. Of course, there is the current Businessman's Survey and the agricultural market is well served, but, beyond that, there is virtually nothing apart from individual surveys from individual publications.

One successful, industry-wide venture was the **media data form** (MDF) and this has been the only live attempt to provide regular information on the vital statistics of industrial publications. It is a long way short of doing the job we really want but it is an excellent base.

Industrial media planners are, therefore, forced to judge on the basis of criteria other than the MDF alone. Some of these inputs may be factual but most are subjective. The criteria that should be looked at on each and every occasion are these: (i) Media data form. (ii) What do readers think of it? (The editorial policy, the quality of the articles and editorial comment.) (iii) Who reads it? (iv) What kind of publication is it? (Horizontal or vertical, frequency of publication, ratio of advertising to editorial, etc.) (v) Reader service facilities? (vi) Creative scope? (Colours available, quality of the paper, type of binding, etc.) (vii) How is it circulated? (Paid for, controlled circulation, etc.) (viii) Economy? (How do rates compare with other publications? Are there series discounts? Are deals possible, etc.?)

The future

Individual publishers continue to produce readership data over a fairly wide spectrum. The way the findings are reported needs to be approached with caution and the industrial media planner continues to find a lack of unbiased readership data which can be used to decide between one journal and another in most industrial fields.

That something needs to be done about this goes without question and some have felt compelled to try to bridge the gap in our knowledge by instigating private readership surveys in those areas where they have most interest. Such surveys cost a great deal of money and my agency, for instance, invests but can afford to do little more than the essential minimum.

We have carried out studies in the engineering, metal, electronic and electrical manufacturing industries including management and professional journals circulating horizontally across manufacturing industry as a whole. In each of these fields the object has been to find out the penetration of the industry by the media in terms of circulation (regular receipt); the interest with which a journal was read; and its usefulness to the readers in carrying out their normal day-to-day tasks. These parameters, in our surveys, are related in all cases to the job function of the respondent and the size of the establishment in which he works. It is on such a basis that the future lies and hopefully more money will be made available to enable this to happen. Reading and noting studies, exact analyses of the responses obtained from particular journals—these are vital additional pieces of information for the industrial media buyer.

The future will demand some hope of a European data form, perhaps. On the occasions when we have conducted this kind of operation, the responses received show radical differences from one country to another. Buying media internationally must be approached with considerable caution.

Possible further polarization into larger publishing groups, the current swing back from controlled circulation to subscription journals and the re-emergence of the narrow vertical journal, are all to be welcomed because they are likely to lead, in the future, to a general raising of standards. There is a need for more and more agencies to devote themselves to this industrial judgement, with professional appraisal and selection taking over from 'let-the-client-pick-his-favourites' attitude which sometimes seems to be the only basis for choice.

What we are all after is greater efficiency and cost effectiveness and the result of more united efforts could be better circulation and readership validation: syndicated media research with a higher level of information at the disposal of all concerned; and a move towards some degree of logic and the sort of scientific appraisal that is now commonplace in most other business activities.

TELEVISION AND RADIO

Coverage of 'industrial' markets is taken seriously by media owners in both these spheres and rightly so. All the advantages of television (colour, movement, possibility of demonstration, etc.) lend themselves very well to industrial selling. Stumbling blocks are cost and the strong mass-market connotations while the industrial advertiser has a healthy cynicism that agencies recommending television, may twist the objectives to suit their favourite medium rather than the other, and proper, way round.

There may be some substance in that but the facts alone make television a medium that must be considered, particularly when there is a regional connotation. One of the real advantages of the television network in the UK is the fact that it is highly regional, and agricultural manufacturers, for example, can advertise in farming areas at low cost and with real coverage justification. This would apply equally to radio and the combination of the two could be powerful. The support of merchants and distributors of all kinds is clearly critical and again this points to a regional effort. Would regional television or radio, however, be more effective than the regional press?

Many arguments have been put forward for television in the corporate field too and, also, its regional capability can play an effective part in employee relations in an area, particularly on a short-term basis. Reopening of factories after, say a strike or unexpected closures, has been effectively notified at short notice by using television or radio while production costs need not be as high as sometimes thought.

The feeling that industrial or business communication is the poor relation is nowhere stronger than in television and it should be combated at all levels. Those most at fault may well be the advertisers and agencies and not the media at all. More research is perhaps needed in radio where the arguments for communication with businessmen tend to be confined to in-car listening in the early morning and in the evening. To experiment and to test can be useful here if time and funds are on your side, but, at least, the medium should be considered and not arbitrarily rejected when it is recommended as part of a total, integrated programme.

DIRECT MAIL

In certain industrial or business environments, the mail still offers a very cost-effective medium for publicity. Each mailing may comprise nothing more than a truly personal letter from a senior executive to his opposite number in the market place, or it may be a letter covering the mailing of one or more pieces of literature, or a three-dimensional mailer containing a sample, invitation, business game, all purposefully designed to make a point and dramatize a benefit or selling point.

Company newsletters, annual reports, external magazines—all are basic examples of direct mail for they travel in an envelope with a stamp. The real element that makes the difference is not the creative cleverness of the whole thing but its fitness for purpose and the existence of a very well edited and updated mailing list. Do relate the cost of mailing fairly to the likely return or sales value. Being horrified at the 'cost per shot' is not very relevant if you are selling a £1 million scanner. Above all, perhaps, forget your bias and look afresh at D.M. Concentrate on that list—own it and keep it clean yourself. Not easy, but vital.

LITERATURE

The average 'consumer' advertiser may spend under 8 per cent of his budget on literature whereas the typical industrial or business advertiser spends nearly 30 per cent.

This considerably greater activity has nothing to do with the mass of instructional material. Technical publications (everything from a multi-volume overhaul manual to a simple sheet instruction leaflet) form a separate activity in their own right.

This near 30 per cent represents technical sales literature, brochures, catalogues, direct mail pieces, house journals, recruitment back-up material and the 101 wallets, booklets and other publications generated every day by business advertisers and their agencies.

Of course the reason for the volume and variety lies in the basics of business communication. There is often a requirement to convey a mass of relevant information presented in a form permitting study and reference over a period of time. Film and other audio visual techniques are helpful and gradually gaining in importance but still, today, there is no better method than printing words on paper.

Leaving aside judgement on the visual attraction of company literature, we should be able to plan publications to fall into a sensible pattern. Otherwise, inefficiency in the form of 'one-off' publications encroach upon budgets (especially today) which just aren't elastic enough.

As a guide, each advertiser is likely to need literature at three levels for external communication but can yet follow a logical market orientation. For example, let us assume a large organization, selling mostly high technology products and services, internationally.

First, at corporate level we can distinguish capability literature pointing up potential market benefits to be offered in any contract the company undertakes. Or a booklet directed at graduates emphasizing career prospects and potential job satisfaction. At the other end of the corporate spectrum will be the company handbook of products and addresses for all units and divisions.

Next, at divisional level, we again could have capability literature (for the division only this time) and other capability literature for certain narrower areas of the division's total market. A division based on just turbine technology for instance, might produce a divisional publication on R & D, production and installation across a broad front while, at the same time, requiring literature for appeal to the electricity generating market or for, say, marine applications.

Lastly, each unit (the ultimate profit centre) has its own manufacture, marketing and publicity. There is a probable need here for a unit capability book; system/equipment technical sales brochures; product information in the form of data sheets and catalogues. All of these should clearly match a market need and avoid, at all costs, 'me-to' imitation and any form of 'ego' involvement from whatever source.

The facts again favour market orientation. The market does not want to take the trouble to understand the manufacturer's organization or to admire his management structure. Introverted publications often delight the originator and bore the recipients. Tell the reader only those things of benefit to him and his dealings with your company—make them clear and easily understood. And audit your literature portfolio regularly to cut out waste!

EXHIBITIONS

There is a changing pattern at large today—perhaps a swing from the large exhibition to the smaller, more local and more concentrated one. The cycle is probably repetitive and reflects directly the market situation. Be that as it may, this is perhaps the most work-intensive form of communication, and yet the clearest example of the mix of 'personal' and 'non-personal' selling.

Here, the temptation to go for a costly design must be resisted. However you tackle exhibitions they are expensive and seem to be so perhaps more than any other medium. So it is critically important to integrate fully all selling efforts associated with this opportunity. Literature, PR, sales training and briefing—all are critical as is a clear idea of what you want to achieve.

All too often the task of designing and building a stand ('booth' if you're in the USA) is sufficiently exhausting it seems, to leave no reserve of money or enthusiasm for any selling or follow-up.

The handover of an exhibition on opening day by marketing services to the sales team is more than a ceremonial act. In fact the physical dramatization of such a handover can be illuminating. I have seen it done with effect at the sales briefing meeting the day before opening and it makes it all too clear why salesmen are there and what is expected.

On design and construction, you are well advised to design first and quote afterwards. All too often separate contractors, who apparently design for free, will give you exciting but non-comparable solutions. Instead of debating the relevance of the design and planning against the objectives set, you find yourself choosing between individual designers' taste and creative skills.

Better by far to get your design, and once agreed, put it out for tough tendering and detailed quotes; detail someone senior to be budget controller with authority to say 'No' thereafter. Repainting walls the night before, or finding room for a late, new exhibit is as astronomically expensive as thinking of the need for a new range of literature in six languages only three weeks before opening day!

Remember that sales people who will make use of the forum you create to sell are in a strange environment. Make up a helpful set of tips based on common mistakes or use one of the several films and audio visuals available which do it well.

Finally, count the cost and know who has visited for what purpose. Names and addresses must go to swell and correct the mailing list; leads must be fed to sales staff in the field for follow-up; quantified results must be acknowledged. *Post mortems* are valuable. If you are lucky, you will have the results of the visitors' audit which more and more exhibitions are offering.

AUDIO VISUAL

This is a burgeoning area where the technology is exploding and it is difficult not be fascinated by the hardware. Concentrate on 'what is wanted' once again and acknowledge real budgeting. The crossfade tape/slide presentation (or even one simple carousel) can still be very cost effective, more reliable for field work and an excellent and inexpensive work horse. If you must have a presentation with effects, three screens, six projectors and the rest, please do it somewhere where the facilities exist and where the crew to mount it is available and ready. And see you can afford it and justify it. Above all, do be clear how you will use your film/tape/slide. White elephants breed faster here than anywhere.

TELEMARKETING

The tendency for our business to rechristen if not reinvent techniques comes to us, today, in this guise. Telephone selling it was; telemarketing it is becoming. Is it personal or non-personal? Somewhere in between, but a growing area where non-face-to-face communication can help economically. We have all had calls from insurance brokers, double-glazing manufacturers, the local directory, and might be surprised to find the effort did produce results. With specialist services, it can be effective (if done well) in making appointments with senior people following a special mailing for instance.

It can be the rounder-up of an audience for a seminar in the last days. Like all media it can be used well and badly but it is there—and with conferencing facilities available in the UK and further afield and the growing use of Freephone and 800 operators, it is worth looking at hard.

So in a parallel field is telex—a cheaper more immediate medium it is difficult to find and cable and new frontiers of inter-office communication are all on the horizon.

OVERSEAS PUBLICITY

If the world is your market, communicating with potential customers is an ever-present problem. Manufacturers of consumer products with major commitments in a particular market will operate on the same basis as local advertisers. The operation will be carried out by nationals and the language barrier does not exist.

But, at the other end of the scale, a manufacturer of high-cost specialized equipment selling in small quantities in a larger number of countries is faced with a major translation problem among others.

Market research, however, must play an even larger role in overseas marketing and publicity. Very seldom can we assume that other markets' patterns of demand are the same as UK requirements. But defining the market and understanding communication customs and opportunities call for careful study. Again the easy option (of a pan European general campaign in international media) must be avoided. Ask, visit and talk with others if you cannot employ real experts. Call translations 'rewrites' and do just that. Allow time, allow for frustration and allow for extra cost. Remember the EEC is not an integrated whole—it is a series of nation states and each loves its publicity customs and styles as much as we do.

MANAGEMENT OF THE ADVERTISING FUNCTION

One of the problems of the business area is that titles and descriptions of our jobs abound with little consistency of meaning.

It is another reason we may be seen as a non-professional area of management. It is much less true in the 'consumer' goods area where the role of brand or product managers, account directors and managers is, in fact, more consistent and better understood. The test of swopping from one agency to another or one client to another would prove nothing like as traumatic as the same moves in a 'business to business' situation.

Companies can have advertising, publicity, communications, PR, public affairs, promotional managers in any assortment you may choose, or they can have none at all but simply a marketing manager or sales manager who adds responsibility for publicity to already overcrowded portfolio.

In practice, one must look at each and every company situation and understand how each chooses to organize to manage the communication function and not worry too much about titles.

This study will yield wide variation in standards of performance. It is my personal observation that, in the last 10 years, the standard of 'advertising management' in companies has risen markedly.

Business-to-business communication has in recent years become more acceptable and more competent people are taking well-paid roles in the management of publicity in these companies. Some agencies have developed a specialization, but generally agency standards were always quite high and have remained so.

In the slow battle to win senior management's acknowledgement of the value of communications investment, these changes within companies are much to be valued and welcomed. You may have noticed that my subheading to these paragraphs is intentionally not 'advertising management'. I worked with the Du Pont Company in Europe for many years and was enormously impressed with their programmes of training in the communications area. My title is not original—it belongs to the Du Pont Company and I freely acknowledge the source. The management of the advertising (or communication) function is a very much more respectable title in the company hierarchy for it puts management higher up the tree than the subject being managed. In the company board room, being skilled in management is more important than skill in advertising.

If you accept this longer, but more relevant title you will not need much thought to see the whole job in a different light. It takes the senior company executive away from the magic marker and sketch pad and into the management of large sums of company money and the direction and assessment of a highly complex area of activity.

In today's conditions, with the cutbacks in company communications staff, good management becomes more and more important. Only with first-class management can complex programmes of communications be thoroughly planned, integrated and monitored. That above all is what is missing from ineffective business-to-business communication programmes.

A WORD ON ORGANIZATION

On a slightly broader front, and reverting to the corporate discussion which is discussed more fully elsewhere, I am impressed by the willingness of many American companies to have, at vice president level, a communications executive. But I am even more impressed with the holding of weekly meetings on corporate affairs (probably under the chairman or president) which include contributions from all management levels—finance, R & D, production, marketing and communication. All have short- and long-term objectives to be solved and, in this overall company forum, corporate communications become a more easily discussed and credible subject which can be interrelated with all the others. The regularity and familiarity of these meetings means they are taken seriously and makes them practical, hard working contributors to solving company problems and defining strategy.

In my experience there are few, if any, British companies (or European ones for that matter) that have this regular discipline of discussion at which communications is represented at senior level with an equal voice. Inclusion of 'communications' as a matter of routine is infrequent—it therefore becomes 'special', artificial and is not taken seriously.

MEASURING RESULTS

I have tried to emphasize that in the business-to-business area, the differences (and therefore the problems) are found in the multi-media situation, the multi-specifier situation, the variation in message and medium and the integration of a complex whole. This is to be compared with the familiar consumer goods situation of large expenditure in a single medium with the overwhelming demand on advertising people being made to respond in the creative field.

Any assessment of results must, therefore, be more complex and more difficult. In my view it comes back to that initial planning which, if thoroughly done, will yield objectives that can be quantified and spelled out. It is against these that results can be measured but only if results are comparable, meaningful, regularly received and assessed.

Whether it is the receipt of bingo cards or replies to mailings or coupons, or whether it is researched shifts in attitude or beliefs, one task of the managers of the communications function is to take this whole subject seriously and to monitor and report it regularly. If 5 per cent of the communications budget is set aside to judge the value of the other 95 per cent, it is a very good first step.

My central forum with regular discussion overall would be an enormous help in this area. Communications people, like everyone else, can find themselves talking to themselves all too easily. Communications teams (client and agency combined) should find at least quarterly opportunities to talk to marketing and sales people for it is all too common for them to discover they are playing their game on a revolving football pitch. Goals set this quarter can be positioned the very next quarter at 90° (or sometimes 180°) to the originals. Not because these marketing men are contrary, but because they must respond to new situations as they meet them. If communication plans within the company thus become less relevant, the weakness lies in the lack of regularity of review.

Most communication is a comparatively blunt weapon (as opposed to the personal selling end of the business) and time is needed for our plans to be implemented and to take effect. Regular review and assessment need to be thorough, broad and meaningful and to have a higher priority even than the creative process itself.

FINAL THOUGHT

There will be little disagreement with the view that sales of industrial goods are critically important for Britain or, indeed, for most countries. That must call for the existence of a professional core of communicators willing to be interested in the different problems of business-to-business selling.

That industry should take this area of investment and the management of it more seriously must go without saying. Perhaps if I had to single out one area for development it would be in education for the better management of the communications function in business and industry. I would ask all chairmen and senior directors to demand it at board level and to take it as seriously as they do any other management area. By all means interfere in the detail but, for goodness sake, manage this area of investment and give the men and women in it the same respect and time you do in any other sphere.

SEVEN

PUBLIC RELATIONS

William Paterson

Public relations is the management function that evaluates public attitudes, identifies the policies and activities of an enterprise with the public interest and carries out a programme of action to earn public understanding and acceptance.

All enterprises, big and small, are therefore practising public relations in some way or other.

Full-time practitioners of this particular discipline have become necessary as a result of the growth and complexity of business and commerce. In the days when the proprietor-manager ran the company, he lived, worked and recruited his people from the immediate neighbourhood of the factory. As his firm prospered he became, often as not, a local benefactor and well known figure in the community. The factory was an integral part of that community. As technology advanced, so the economics of manufacture changed. Companies expanded dynamically or by acquisition and moved away from the local town. Proprietor-managers disappeared to be replaced by professional managers and the head office was established far from the original centre of activity.

These changes broke the close links that existed in the community and stretched communications so that more complex systems were necessary. Scattered production units and a distant head office made it difficult to keep in touch. Gone were the days when the boss knew all his employees by name and gone also were the days when he was able to talk to his competitors by lunching once a week in the town's business club.

Public relations in its present form was born out of necessity and propelled into prominence by the increasing intrusion of government in the affairs of industry and by a population that wanted to know more about the companies that exercise so much influence over the economic welfare of the country. The media were ready to assuage this new appetite for information; the age of mass communications had arrived. There is no mystery about the practice of public relations; its task is simple and vital—it matters little what the people who perform it are called.

Every enterprise must protect its reputation and promote its products and services in order to win and keep customers. Every enterprise must develop policies that expand trade and motivate the workforce. Every enterprise must be prepared to change as markets are reshaped. No enterprise can afford to ignore the competition from wherever it may come. Thus, communications to the external and the internal world are a very important part of a company's dynamic.

At an inaugural lecture at Henley Management College in September 1983 Professor Keith MacMillan re-examined the relationships between business self-interest, wealth creation and community well-being.

Regarding the need for business ideology he said:

When business's actions are contradicted or challenged, it becomes necessary for managers to reflect on the basic rationale for the firm's existence, what it stands for, its values, its very identity and the people and purposes it serves. When business is accused of some anti-social behaviour who exactly is being accused? Who is the business? Is it the shareholders? A large company may have many more shareholders than employees and today most shares may be held by institutions, faceless bureaucracies most of them, in their own right. Is it the employees? If so, is it all of them or just the managers; and all of these including foremen and staff functions or just the very top management? This is often a most difficult question to answer yet it may be of critical importance, for the identity of a business reflects its prevailing values, it's criteria for judgement and decision making; in other words what it regards as good or bad as far as its self-interest is concerned. It is only if the top management of the company has the imagination and vision to see the relevance and importance of this dimension of business policy that it has any prospect of widespread impact on internal decision making. Furthermore, it is only when internal decision making fully reflects this concern of leadership that the image of a business can be truly improved.

As has been argued by two best selling American writers recently, Peters and Waterman, 'the really excellent companies tend to have something more than illumined edifices; they tend to have a belief in themselves, in what they stand for, in their shared values, in feeling they are the best at what they do!' These tenets should provide the base upon which a sound public relations programme is built. A programme of work that is designed to contribute to the success of the organization.

And if this is to be done it must form an integral part of the business plan. The activities that stem from the plan are designed to protect the reputation of the organization, to promote it in areas of potential growth, and interpret and explain its policies and activities to selected groups of people. Finally, there is a monitoring role concerning events and trends that may affect the company's standing.

Within this range of activities the work falls into several specific areas needing careful planning and a sustained effort over a long period of time if success is to be achieved. There are four main groups of people whose well-being and interest are critical to the company: shareholders, employees, customers and the local community.

FINANCIAL COMMUNITY

The key sector for any public company is the financial community which is dominated naturally enough by the shareholders. The financial world needs information in order to assess the company's performance and provide data for the investing public. It is in the company's interest to provide such information in order to minimize speculation and encourage an appropriate market valuation for the shares. Perhaps the best starting point in a planned programme of communications is the annual report which is the single most important publication to be produced each year by the company.

Its primary aim is to inform shareholders about the financial position at a particular date at the end of the organization's financial year. But it is of interest to many other people among whom are employees, suppliers, customers, stockbrokers and bankers. The information requirements of the financial markets are rarely satisfied. Shareholders are expected to be given priority and although professional investors should not be accorded special treatment, their dominant position in the stock market with on average some 70 per cent of the equity stock has given them a powerful voice and a rapacious appetite for facts upon which to make their investment plans. There is therefore a need to build close links with the various sector analysts and provide information of a detailed nature providing that you keep within the constraints that govern the release of price-sensitive news. Naturally, such news must go first to the Stock

Exchange before it can be made public. Major investments or disinvestments are examples of this and substantial organizational changes would also qualify.

The financial journalists are an important community of special interest to all public companies but they will, in the main, make their enquiries at the company's reporting times and when there are major new developments during the year. The opportunities are there for a regular and planned programme of information, and the special interests of the different groups need to be recognized. For instance, the analytical writers want to be in a position to give up-to-date and accurate advice to their institutional clients about the investment prospects of the securities market. They cannot do this without keeping in touch with the major companies. All companies are better served by a steady market in their shares rather than one that moves dramatically in either direction. Stability is a valuable commodity.

Once each year the company and the board of directors face the shareholders at the annual general meeting. Although they are traditionally quiet occasions, these rather ritualistic set pieces can provide just the kind of platform sought by disgruntled shareholders. There have been some very lively meetings in recent years, frequently used by special interest groups who wish to challenge the company's performance and policies. As the press and a number of sector analysts normally attend, the AGM has become a useful occasion to publicize a point of view. It is, therefore, prudent to prepare a set of likely questions and answers for the board and to rehearse with board members any possible weak areas. The mock press conference is a very useful way to prepare for confrontations either at the AGM or at reporting times such as the half- and full-year figures. Naturally the company is expected at such moments to make a statement about the business. It is customary for the chief executive to give a brief account of the state of trade and to venture a comment on the future prospects for the business. This statement will be issued to the press and is one of the occasions when the company can tell the stock market what to expect over the coming six months. The share price tends to reflect the expected level of profits at that future period in the company's life.

Specific action

As the presentation of the company's performance is a vital part of the marketing effort it might be sensible to look more closely at results time—when the half-year and full-year figures are published. A little planning will help to make the best of the opportunity.

- Look back at the statement issued last year and the press comment that followed.
- Read the latest stockbrokers' reports as they will indicate what the City expects, and enable a judgement to be made on areas of concern.
- Read any public statements by the chairman or finance director—particularly the statement in the last annual report.
- Now draft the likely questions that may be raised by the press and analysts when the figures are issued.

The questions and answers brief is a useful document for all the key company people, and not only those who will be involved with the press. The answers will come as a result of discussions with the executive management and the finance director will provide a brief for managers in the company which explains the figures in some detail and gives the economic background to the company's results. It will be helpful when they talk to their own people.

The overseas companies and departments should not be forgotten. Telex the salient figures and any significant trade comments from the chairman that affect their business.

Look at the proofs of the advertisements and make sure the finance department has a chance to check them. It is not necessary to publish on the same day as the comments appear—a day or two later is fine and allows time to 'trade set' the advertisements. Errors are less likely by this system and the typography and layout is under control.

The package to various company managers is now complete and will comprise the press statement, the financial brief and the questions and answers.

The importance of good briefing down the line sometimes encourages companies to back up this written pack with a video cassette or tape slide programme. Detailed figures, graphs and bar charts work better on paper. The audio visual material should be designed to complement the brief with supporting data about new products and other activities that have played a vital role during the period under review.

The annual report will be issued after the preliminary figures at the year end and must be with the shareholders at least three weeks before the annual general meeting. It should be issued to senior managers and to the press. In some companies the report will also go to employees. There is a benefit in addressing it to their homes as it will give their families a chance to learn about the company.

The report is a valuable way of promoting the company in overseas markets and associate companies, agents and banking contacts should have copies to distribute. Its role as a marketing tool can be underestimated.

EMPLOYEES

There are many ways of getting the vital facts of the company's performance across to employees at all levels. In public companies the annual report is important, but it must be attractively produced to review the year's trade and investment programme in a readable manner. This is a better system than producing a special popular version of the accounts. It should contain a simplified section giving the principal figures which will be of value to investors, managers and employees alike. The local manager will find that this section provides valuable background data as an introduction to local presentations about the company's business in any particular area. Furthermore, the company is seen to give everyone the same information. This is an important point particularly with the trade unions.

Video programmes are able to capture the interest of everyone in the company more readily than other means. But they are not the place for figures and elaborate graphs. Excellent trade reports can be put together which give account of the business and how it is coping with the competition for markets.

A good company newspaper is also a powerful aid but it must be professionally done. Layout, typography and writing style are terribly important.

Communications are designed to change people's behaviour. All employees will respond to being kept informed, and the best will feel more motivated and committed to the company. Business education will feature strongly in any internally directed programme. The house newspaper is potentially valuable. That potential will not be realized if the paper is unprofessional and without style and impact. Its authority will be very limited unless the chairman and the board are behind it. They should be part of the policy committee that guides the paper's development. The editor should understand newspapers and he must agree the aims and objectives with the board. The policy committee needs to examine the issues to be tackled and the best way to deal with them in the paper. If it is to be of value it must tackle the economic problems facing the company and the steps being taken to win markets.

It is fairly certain that the majority of the workforce read the tabloids and not the heavies. Look at the former for style and presentation of facts. Exciting layout—dramatic use of pictures—'people angle' to the stories and no item more than a few hundred words. There are a number of good contract publishing houses that can give a professional service. With care in your selection, the house newspaper can make a significant contribution in the promulgation of views and news among the press, stockbrokers, agents and certain customers in addition to the employees. It is certainly of value on the industrial relations front. And it is in this area that public relations and personnel people will work closely together in a positive way to foster better understanding and commitment as well as handling the problems that arise.

Plant closure

Plant closure or retrenchment that causes redundancies can have a disruptive effect in the local community and among the employees at the company's other plants. Careful planning helps. A brief can be prepared with the local manager on the reasons for a closure and the other options that were considered. The possible effects locally and elsewhere in the company can be looked at with the public relations people. The following actions should be considered:

1. A statement of the situation for the employees.
2. A letter to customers and suppliers.
3. A letter to the appropriate union officials and the local MP. Other civic leaders may need to be included.
4. A statement for the press, and a brief for the local managers nominating and preparing those who may be called on to give press or radio interviews. Naturally the house newspaper will have an important role.

THE MEDIA

The government information services offer a wide range of useful activities designed to put British industry on the world map. Companies with major news stories, particularly overseas success, should always send information along to the Central Office of Information. They are able to get publicity for industry developments in many countries of the world where there are real trade opportunities. There are a number of rules about media relations. This may not be the place to catalogue do's and don'ts but no one should forget that information given to journalists must be accurate and capable of substantiation. Too often items of interest to one or two specialist magazines are sent also to national and regional papers, even radio and television as well. Indiscriminate action of this kind is very unprofessional and produces a predictable reaction from the press. There may be a few stories in the year that justify a wide broadcast, but these will be confined to major contracts, and technical developments having a profound effect on the company's profits. Or there may be significant changes in the boardroom. The most obvious exception to this general rule are a public company's normal reporting times when the quarterly, half and final year figures are issued via the Stock Exchange to all of the press including the relevant trade papers. Stories must be selected carefully and written to match the information needs of the readers. Specialist technical magazines will require facts and figures, diagrams and illustrations that other general interest papers will not want. Newspapers are more interested in jobs created and key personalities.

A regular flow of press releases is bad tactics and can have a deadening effect. It won't be long before stories are spiked before they are read. Adopt more personal methods such as talking to the key people and finding out how interested they are and the sort of information they want.

It is always useful and at the end of the day, of considerable benefit, to see the journalists who are interested in a particular business on a regular basis, with no special story in mind. There will be occasions when problems arise and when the last thing wanted is wide newspaper coverage for these. For instance, it does little for the company to broadcast a strike or a plant closure. However, a judgement must be made about its significance in the local community. For instance, the closure of the principal factory in a town or a large-scale strike will be of interest to the local papers and may attract attention of the nationals. But if the strike is small and unlikely to cause much disruption or if the plant is only a minor one in a large town, it will not be necessary to issue a statement but rather to prepare the necessary response for use if required. It is also important to brief all the managers concerned with a supporting paper which raises all the possible questions associated with this development. This question and answer system can anticipate the points that may arise from press enquiries and it gives local managers a chance to prepare for the questions that they will get from employees, customers and local traders. Naturally, a local MP must be informed as soon as possible and certainly before the news breaks.

The house newspaper provides a very useful channel to the external media. A paper that sets out to inform its readers about the business can be sent also to selected people in the press, both as background material and for use when the occasion arises. Once a house newspaper has become an established source of reliable information, it will provide an oblique method of issuing news to the press.

CUSTOMERS

There is a PR dimension to most activities and none more important than the way a company markets its products and services. Its good name can be damaged very quickly by ill considered acts, faulty goods, poor service or failure to innovate and meet changing tastes. PR people may have little chance to influence all of these activities but they should be fully aware of all the aspects of the marketing programme and be in a position to intercede at an early enough stage.

This is particularly important in today's climate when everyone must fight hard for market share. It is at times like this that some of the more extravagent sales schemes can come unstuck. These are times also when local communities are profoundly affected by the need to cut jobs and reduce costs. A company's reputation is a fragile thing but of inestimable importance to survival and growth. It is very significant too, in recruiting the best people to help in the development of the business.

Traditionally the PR department's territory is the media—national, regional and local. It may sometimes be concerned with one or two key magazines who need stories about research projects. It is often confronted with supporting features and news items on new products, personalities and investment stories.

Some simple techniques can be applied for planning a public relations programme to support sales. The following may be helpful.

- Be quite clear about the product—how it is made—who influences its purchase—where the principal markets lie—how it is sold to those markets.
- Talk to the company's customers who may tell of some of the problems they have experienced in dealing with the firm.
- Prepare a statement of policy which will establish the attitudes that management hopes will develop towards the company and its products.
- List all the public relations projects that could meet the expressed needs and put down the expected cost.
- Draw up a plan for evaluating results.

A lot is heard about building a company image and this activity is sometimes associated with something ephemeral and unimportant to the essentially practical people who run manufacturing companies.

Perhaps public relations people should take more care to demonstrate how a good reputation can build sales and increase profitability. Not long ago the predominant task of public relations was to sell the virtues of the enterprise itself and not its products. But with the emergence of the social sciences, which revealed a wide spectrum of variables affecting human behaviour and, more specifically, consumer motivation, the objectives of public relations have been associated with sales. When barriers to increased sales are the primary concern of management it may be found that acceptance of the direct message of advertising is blocked for a number of reasons. It may be ignorance, loss of confidence, fear or tradition—but if they are to be modified they may require the persistent diversified attack of public relations concurrently with other methods of sales appeal.

Trade exhibitions

Trade exhibitions are a valuable way of making contact with potential buyers and act as a forum to bring together people of influence. Their impact will depend on how well the preparations have been made. Apart from the displays and special literature, invitations must be sent to UK and overseas buyers, and arrangements made to entertain them during the exhibition. As the exhibition stand is in many ways a company's own shop window it should be prepared to provide back-up services to help trade visitors, especially those from abroad.

Markets must be identified and objectives defined in order to export successfully. Strategic planning is essential and the British Overseas Trade Board offers an Export Intelligence Service which gives information to companies about export opportunities. *Trade and Industry Journal*, a weekly publication, gives details of overseas markets, customs regulations and a full list of exhibitions and trade fairs is included from time to time. The London Bureau publishes the *Exhibition Bulletin* which lists most forthcoming exhibitions throughout the world, by trade and geographically. And the local chamber of commerce or trade association will provide advice. For most companies the choice lies between exhibiting independently in a trade fair specializing in a particular business sector or taking part in a British joint venture under the sponsorship of a trade association or a chamber of commerce.

The latter offers many advantages. There are, for instance, financial benefits in participating through the British Overseas Trade Board and extensive publicity through the COI, the trade association in many cases and the official government department overseas. And for events outside Western Europe companies can get 50 per cent of the air fare paid and half the freight costs of returning goods which remain unsold on the exhibition stand.

The Incorporated Society of British Advertisers (ISBA) has published some very useful guides about exhibiting. Press releases should be issued to local technical magazines about product news, either directly or through the organization's press office. At Hanover, for instance, as in most other places a press office is available on site for use by exhibitors.

WESTMINSTER AND THE EEC

Government involvement and public interest in business and commerce means that MPs and indeed MEPs can have an impact on the business environment. As relatively few MPs have business backgrounds, companies need to create a greater understanding of their problems and the tasks they face if we are to have more sensible legislation. Some of the greatest skills concerning industry/parliamentary relations lie with the public affairs consultants who specialize in political lobbying and the provision of day-by-day parliamentary information. Perhaps the key to the success of these firms is the quality of their intelligence gathering, and the access they have to the House of Commons library and computer. EEC regulations intrude more frequently as each year passes. The desire to harmonize seems uppermost in the minds of the bureaucrats at Brussels and many companies have been obliged to learn the hard way about what constitutes the most effective course of action. The local MEP can be very helpful and a personal contact here is invaluable. The Common Market Information Office in London will provide information of relevance to your business.

All companies should know their local MPs and the best point of contact is in the constituency and not at head office. The exception to this will be the special briefing that might need to be made from time to time to a selected group of members. The local MP should be informed about any development in the area affecting jobs and it is sensible, therefore, to establish a close working relationship. Factory visits will provide an opportunity for a walk through the departments and a chance to talk to employees. The MP is certainly likely to want to meet the shop stewards as well as the management.

Political lobbying, once thought to be a US phenomenon is booming in the UK now. Among recent more prominent actions was the well orchestrated attack on the Serpell report which effectively buried it before any damage could be done to British Rail. But the greatest amount of lobbying is done in the defence business, where very large contracts are at stake. A new missile contract valued at £250 million from the RAF was being pursued by both British Aerospace and GEC/Marconi. Some 3000 jobs would be created if the British won the contract from the Americans. The lobbying effort succeeded after the consultants were able to monitor Cabinet discussions through their own political contacts and by pooling information with the lobby correspondents. This enabled them to judge the right moment to brief who was then Chairman of GEC, a former Cabinet Minister. Another consultant was able to use his foreign office contacts to run the Unitary Tax Campaign which 60 British multi-nationals supported in an effort to stop individual US States from taxing them on their world-wide earnings.

LOCAL COMMUNITY

The ties that once existed between the factory and the local community mentioned earlier in this chapter, must be re-established. Industry has a responsibility for the social effects of its activities. As the future prosperity of the company will depend upon a stable society, it must play its part in helping the community to prosper. This may mean providing opportunities to young people for training or helping small businesses to survive. It will mean encouraging managers to help in local affairs and build closer links with the schools and colleges. The importance of good local public relations is obvious and so also is the need for pre-emptive action that seeks involvement, not for charitable reasons but motivated by closer identification of the company's own objectives with the interests of the community.

A company cannot survive in an impoverished community.

STAFFING THE FUNCTION

A public relations consultant is in a better position to take an objective view of the way a company should tackle public relations than the company itself. If an organization is determined to develop a planned and sustained public relations programme it can do no better than commission a report on the best way forward from an experienced consultancy. Thereafter many options exist. Perhaps one of the most efficient and cost-effective systems is in a combined approach.

It is always wise to employ as few people as possible on the staff and to make use of the very many supporting services available. But the staff man or woman should enjoy the complete confidence of the board of management. All major business decisions impact on a section of the public—perhaps on the employees only—and the way these decisions are promulgated will be critical. An input at the policy-making stage will ensure that the communications plan is thought out in advance. The leading firms provide an excellent service and are governed by a strict code of conduct. Fees are based on the time element which must include a calculation to cover general overheads and profit. In addition there will be a budget to cover photography, postage, stationery, entertainment and travel.

Perhaps the most important points to consider are:

- The quality and reputation of the staff, particularly those who will work on your business. You may see the top people at the initial meetings but get to know the people who will finally work with you.
- The reputation they have with other clients, journalists and key people with whom they may come in touch.
- The problems they have worked on and the experience gained which might be useful to you.

In recruiting a public relations manager it must be remembered that his or her contribution will depend upon knowledge of the inner workings of the company and the industry and acceptance of the PR manager at the highest level of management.

John Derriman gives a useful candidate checklist in his book *Public Relations in Business Management* (University of London Press).

1. Good education with a degree an advantage but not essential.
2. Imagination, curiosity and an interest in everything, with the ability to see both sides of the question.
3. A clear mind which can get abreast of a situation quickly, seeing the wood as well as the trees.
4. Ability at clear and persuasive self-expression for simplifying complicated material for the layman, for framing convincing recommendations for management, and for writing press material for publication (not necessarily literary standard).
5. A cool head and the ability to organize and to teach and instruct others tactfully.
6. A businesslike approach to administering public relations operations in a sound and economic way and an ability to see what is practical.
7. Initiative and persistence—he or she should be a 'self starter' who can find his or her own solutions to problems with a reasonable proportion of bright ideas and who keeps hold of a problem until it is solved.
8. Integrity and responsibility to the employer, the media and the public.
9. A personaltiy acceptable to management on the one hand (hence not too brash—well groomed and well spoken, free from arrogance but knowing his or her own mind) and to the general run of employees, journalists and the public on the other hand.
10. Some knowledge of the industry with which he or she will be concerned, though if the candidate is versatile this can usually be acquired after appointment.

EDUCATION AND TRAINING FOR PUBLIC RELATIONS

Communications, Advertising and Marketing Education Foundation (CAM) is the body responsible for vocational education and training. It is sponsored by the Institute of Practitioners in Advertising, the Institute of Public Relations, the Advertising Association and a number of other bodies in the communications field. Its examinations in the various disciplines are held at certificate and diploma level. Preparation for these practical tests of competence can be done privately, through a guided studies package or by attendance at specified colleges.

It may not be necessary today to hold a CAM qualification to get a job in public relations, advertising or marketing, but it is becoming an important consideration when all else is equal. And in a decade or so it may well be essential in certain jobs to hold a recognized professional qualification.

Further details of the CAM qualifications are given in Chapter 16.

EIGHT

DEVELOPING SUCCESSFUL PRODUCT–SERVICE STRATEGIES

Peter Beddowes

BACKGROUND

The 1960s and 1970s saw a growing emphasis on the role of service in the marketing of industrial products. In the 1980s, this brought about both problems and opportunities, and increasing attention has been paid to finding the right balance between the product and associated services in order to maximize customer satisfaction and profit.

In the 1960s (heady days viewed from a 1980s perspective) industrial marketing companies increasingly looked to the addition of customer services relevant to their product/market circumstances almost as a 'good thing' in their own right. These were the days when in a number of industrial companies the 'marketing concept' came almost as a 'bolt out of the blue'. The addition of customer information services, training, technical advice and after-sales services, for example, became accepted as a cost of entry for any reputable company in the market place. These activities and associated cost increases could be more than accounted for by market growth and very high profit margins achieved in that era. Also, of course, the better companies tended to gain a competitive edge so that the new services paid their way quite easily.

In the 1970s a different situation emerged. The severe recession of the mid-1970s and the emergent over-capacity in most industrial markets forced many companies to look at the provision of services as the major way of gaining a competitive edge. This was a time when new product development specifically and innovation generally were relegated to the 'back burner' as companies painfully moved to 'cash management' as the primary focus of attention. The attraction of services at this time was their relatively low cost of development and execution compared to new products or massive marketing campaigns. The provision of services thus became, for many companies, a defensive measure in the absence of other more creative marketing activities.

At the same time senior management, often aided by business strategy consultants, began to think more logically about the balance between product and service costs on the one hand and customer benefits and economic competitiveness on the other. Some companies appreciated that not all services had equal benefits to all customers and that new competitors whether from the Far East, or around the corner operating out of a garage or small workshop, might well have identified the needs of a particular segment of the market or type of customer more precisely than they had. This led to the conclusion that the role of services in the marketing mix depended on the strategic focus of the business. In some segments the provision of services would not only be an unaffordable luxury but also the 'kiss of economic death'. In others, services of the highest quality would need to be provided and product pricing and resource allocation decisions would have to take this into account. Cost and 'value analysis' of each service by market segment or customer group became a powerful decision-making tool for some companies.

The 1980s, therefore, see the product–service mix decision situation as reaching a level of maturity in an increasing number of companies. What is emerging is a clearer view about the role and relevance of different types of services for different marketing circumstances. For this reason decisions about the type and extent of services to offer have become a very senior marketing responsibility in many companies now, compared to a few years ago, when decisions might have been taken in a more *ad hoc* operational manner.

SERVICE STRATEGY

There are a range of factors to consider in selecting the service strategy for the company or 'business unit'.

Strategic positioning The segmented specialist, market niche, multi-segment strategy. Naturally the first step is to identify the needs of customers in the segment(s) being targeted and also to analyse the stance of competitors. Generally high volume/low margin segments offer less scope for the inclusion of services since the major concern of the customer is price and the supplier's focus of attention necessarily has to be efficiency, market share and scale economies.

Stage in market development The potential appeal of a particular set of services is often dependent on the state of knowledge customers have about the related product and its application. In the early stages of development customers are typically uncertain about various aspects of the product and this is the time of greatest scope for 'information-related' and 'confidence-building' services. These services help both to enhance your own company reputation and to increase the market quicker than would otherwise have been the case. In later stages when the market, or product, has reached a level of maturity, 'convenience-related' services are probably more appropriate. By now most customers are familiar with every aspect of the product or in some cases larger customers will have developed their own in-house specialist resources to deal with any problems. So at the maturity stage customers are most likely to regard buying and use of the product as a routine activity and will probably be attracted to ways of making it more convenient to handle.

Competitive situation Marketing history suggests that all too often companies copy the service activities of their major and most respected competitors. This, of course, runs counter to all marketing theory which is concerned with differentiation and positioning away from competitors. Nevertheless it is an understandable, if dangerous temptation and this pressure is heightened by customers who make it clear that they are comparing one company's level of services with another's. After all customers aren't usually aware that they have been classified into a segment either meriting or not meriting a particular service and neither are they always totally open about relating level of services provided and prices charged by you and your competitors. This is where independent research has such a valuable part to play. The marketing decision maker needs to have from research and informed opinion (for example sales executives, distributors, etc.) a clear view about the needs and expectations of customers in different segments of the market prior to developing creative services strategies which will both be relevant to customers and help in the task of giving the company a 'unique total offering' in the market.

SERVICES FOR TACTICAL MARKETING

As well as having a good understanding about the role of services in achieving long-run goals, services can be used to specific shorter-term tactical objectives too. In this sense the 4Ps of the market mix are inadequate and should really be retitled 4PS—price, place, promotion, product, service. Some examples of this type of use are:

- Provision of a particular service as the basis for a promotional campaign to build awareness.
- Quality reassurance campaigns to increase confidence in product quality.
- Addition of a 'free service' instead of reducing price to counter competition.
- Provision of a service agreement or a financial package which has the effect of tying customers to us for a longer period of time thus providing a defensive marketing tactic.
- Addition of a range of services in order to make straight price comparisons of one product with a competitor's more difficult.

Over the years the best companies have become clearer about the appropriateness of a particular service in terms of achieving a specific marketing objective. This more explicit understanding of objectives enables the success or failure of that service in achieving its marketing objective to be more easily measured through research and tracking mechanisms. Table 8.1 illustrates some major marketing objectives and examples of suitable services to achieve these.

The use of research techniques to measure the quality and perceived value of a service being

Table 8.1 Services—the main marketing objectives

Objective	Description	Examples
Resource support	Services that provide resource help to customers in order to increase sales	Financial support and payment schemes Technical help Training Loan of physical resources
Information	Services that help customers make better decisions so as to improve our relationship with them	Market information Purchasing search Joint research programmes Factory trials
Expertise	Services that improve customer skills in order to increase their business and ours	Training Consultancy Design Executive loan
Convenience	Services that make it easier for customers to buy and use	Bought in product to flesh out the range Purchasing services Integrated distribution and storage Materials management Sub-contracting Computerized re-ordering
Reassurance	Services to reduce risks for customers	Quality reassurance Delivery reassurance After-sales service Preventative maintenance Complaint handling

offered is a growing activity in the research world. More and more companies are commissioning regular research studies to compare their performance against competitors. In some cases large and professional customers are beginning to adopt the Marks and Spencer's approach of regularly auditing the performance of suppliers against a set of important service factors. Such audits will play a more important role in the 1980s in review discussions between suppliers and customers and is one practical technique to help improve the generally poor reputation British industrial companies have in this area.[1] Figure 8.1 illustrates problems for the 'Z Company' unless it has a viable long-term future as a low cost supplier, or unless major improvements to a wide range of services can be made very rapidly.

IMPLEMENTING SERVICE ACTIVITIES

Although the provision of services can play a very valuable role in industrial product marketing they do also create a number of specific challenges for the marketeer. These challenges fit broadly under five headings.

Communicating the benefits Products are physical entities which can be subjected to observation, examination and physical testing in order to measure quality and durability. Services are essentially of an intangible nature and, therefore, it is more difficult for the prospective customer to judge their quality and usefulness as well as to understand what is being offered. A useful approach that many companies adopt is to demonstrate the apparent quality of a particular

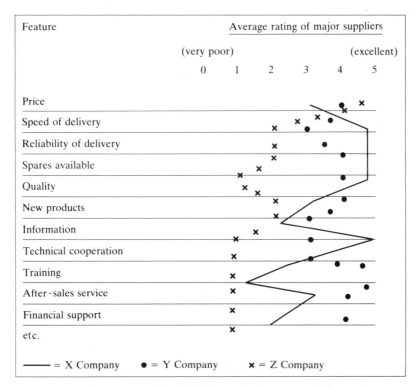

Figure 8.1 Research Suppliers' Rating of Competitors' Performance

service through the quality of the physical features that are needed to provide the service. Every opportunity has to be grasped to make use of these quasi or indirect bits of evidence to demonstrate in a tangible way the intangible benefits and quality of the service.

Organizing the service Marketing success requires close coordination of the various activities that impact on the customer. This becomes many times more difficult when services are added to the product offering. Services typically are people-intensive, therefore increasing significantly the number and diversity of people inter-facing with the customer. Often marketing staff do not have direct control over the activities of services staff thus making this situation even more complex in managerial terms. Careful consideration needs to be given to organizing for services looked at from a customer's perspective and special emphasis must be placed on training in customer appreciation and customer handling skills.

Product–service quality: cross-impact Companies that tend to drift into the provision of services rather than plan them tend often to fail to achieve the full potential benefit because of inconsistent quality standards. Sometimes there is a more *laissez-faire* attitude to the service quality than to product standards, particularly if it is provided free of charge. Unfortunately customers tend to judge the quality of the whole 'company offering' by the standard of the weakest element. In other words the provision of free training of a customer's operatives who are to use the machines being sold is only a marketing strength if the quality of the operative training at least matches the quality of the machines being bought.

Pricing This is probably the most difficult of all areas with regard to service. The choice is between absorbing the service cost into the product cost or on the other hand charging for it separately. There are other detailed variations on this theme. In previous years absorption pricing has been favoured but this raised the disadvantage of irritating those customers who have to pay for a service that they don't use or value. To some extent using a segmented approach overcomes this problem since services are targeted selectively to those customers in segments that require them.

Generally the trend is for a more open policy towards the costs incurred in the provision of services and, therefore, pricing for them separately provided this does not result in a very complicated set of price schedules.

Justifying the price Mainly because the supply of services depends on people intensity, they tend to appear very expensive from a customer's point of view. Normally, experienced and costly people are required too. Therefore, customers often tend to raise their own expectations about the quality of service to expect perhaps to an unreasonable level and it is necessary to handle the apparent let-down or disappointment they may possibly suffer. This problem is somewhat similar to the difficulty in communicating the benefits of a particular service. One method of approach is known as the 'Service Iceberg' which is an attempt to illustrate to customers the level of effort and resource (usually behind the scenes) that goes into provision of a high quality service (see Fig. 8.2).

SERVICES—THE FUTURE

The provision of services is one of the fastest developing areas of industrial marketing and the next few years will probably see significant developments.

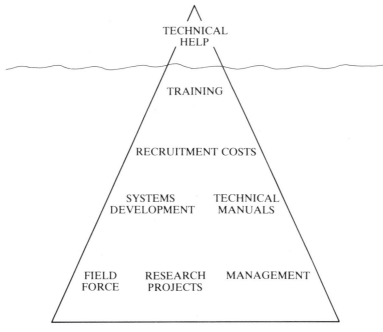

Figure 8.2   The Service Iceberg

In broad terms the stages in the development of services seem to be:

- Product alone.
- Product supported by a few services.
- Product and comprehensive range of services.
- Product and selective services targeted to appropriate segments.
- Balance of emphasis moving to the services with the product only being part of the package.
- Increased flexibility coming from the 'new technology' (for example flexible manufacturing systems and new communications methods) will create opportunities for even more targeted and tailored product/service offerings.

British industrial companies have generally lagged behind their continental counterparts in marketing effectiveness since 1945. We fell behind in product development partly because of an unwillingness to invest in major innovation campaigns. We have a unique opportunity to make up some of this lost ground on the service side of the marketing mix because the key to successful services in the 1980s will be harnessing creativity and computer-based systems; both areas where Britain has a relative strength. Successful services do not necessarily require major cash investments but a flexible and creative customer-oriented approach. They do, however, require first-class management of specialist people and it remains to be seen whether British marketing management is up this challenge.[1]

REFERENCE

1. Turnbull, P. W. and M. T. Cunningham. *International Marketing and Purchasing*. A survey among marketing and purchasing executives in five European countries. Macmillan Press, 1981.

DISTRIBUTION

John Leach

INTRODUCTION

For any company to function efficiently and profitably it must provide:

(a) the right product;
(b) well promoted;
(c) correctly priced;
(d) in the right place;
(e) at the right time.

Distribution is that aspect of the managerial process which relates to (d) and (e) above, i.e., the logistics function adds time and place utility to the intrinsic utility of the product itself.

In industrial markets it is increasingly found that the only way for the company to establish a competitive position in the market place is via the distribution (or logistics) function. Product differentiation is expensive and difficult, price competition can only be of short-term benefit (unless the company is truly the lowest cost producer), and benefits via advertising are difficult to sustain. Benefits of good distribution, however, are relatively inexpensive, relatively easy to sustain and the competition finds it difficult to compete with them. Several recent surveys into a variety of industrial markets indicate that reliability of delivery is often the key variable by which suppliers are judged, and selected. The NEDC, quoted in the CBI's 1983 publication *Working for Customers*, indicates that, for example, in the construction equipment industry sales are more responsive to reliability and service than to relative prices. The concept of service refers directly to availability of product and the ability to deliver it on the promised date.

For the logistics function to work efficiently, however, it is not just necessary to have the goods in the right place at the right time; it is also necessary that this is achieved in such a way that the costs and revenues of the operation are at the optimum level for the achievement of the company's profit objectives.

Logistics is a tremendously important area of the business, both in terms of its effect on the success, or otherwise, of the business and in terms of the resources and costs involved in the operation of the business function. Companies which consistently fail to have their products available where and when customers require them lose not only the potential profit on the sales which are lost due to non-availability but, in the long term, lose their credibility, and ultimately are not even considered as potential suppliers of the product; an example was reported in *The*

Times of 16 December 1980 in relation to the European launch of the Metro—'Sir Michael Edwardes, Chairman of BL, has given strict orders that adequate stock must be available to avoid the mistakes of past European launches. Supply shortages too often have prevented BL from benefiting from the favourable impact that new models make on European motoring journalists and dealers.'

Furthermore, the costs of the distribution function represent a significant proportion of an organization's operating budget. Any definition of the responsibilities of the distribution function will include the transport function, stock control (or inventory management as it is increasingly called), the warehousing function and material handling (plus decisions relating to the location of warehouses), packaging and communications between the customer and the company to ensure that the whole process can be coordinated effectively. Clearly these areas of the business absorb a large amount of resources and money: various estimates have been made relating to the costs of the logistics function and in some companies the cost is put as high as 50 per cent of the company's total costs!

Distribution must not be thought of as representing only a specific area of the business, however. For distribution to function satisfactorily it is dependent on the marketing and sales department to provide information with regard to forecast of sales—without this information it is impossible for an efficient distribution operation to occur. When this information is available it must be included with other information, of an economic and cash flow nature, to ensure that the right raw materials are bought and are available at the right place at the right time: i.e., if the company is to make finished products available to its customers in an efficient way then it must ensure an equally efficient supply of those items needed to produce these finished products. Furthermore, there must be coordination between marketing, sales, logistics and the **production** function to ensure that the latter department knows when the goods are required and in what quantities. The separate functional areas of the business are still responsible for the efficient operation of their departments, but within the constraints laid down by the overall plan of the company.

For example, a production department will invariably want to reduce unit costs of production with long production runs of one product, or one colour or design. This is because the overhead costs of setting up that production run are spread over a larger number of units and also because operatives become more adept over a long run and probably (a) produce more and (b) have fewer rejected products. Unfortunately, though, long production runs of one product will sometimes lead to non-availability of other products and the savings made by the long production run are offset (or more than offset) by the profits lost because of the non-availability of these other products.

Similarly the sales department, invariably anxious to make a sale, may promise delivery by, say, Monday. The company may have a scheduled delivery to that area on Wednesday but because of the promise a special delivery has to be made. This may disrupt the whole schedule of company deliveries and may well cost more than the profit from the sale. The sales department may well argue that it is a 'sprat to catch a mackerel', i.e., that by meeting this delivery date, other orders will be secured in the future, and if this is the case then the costs and potential benefits should be considered and evaluated. In many cases, however, (a) the customer might have accepted a Wednesday delivery and/or (b) the expected future sales do not materialize. Added to this is the potential danger that the disruption to the normal delivery schedule may result in established customers not receiving their orders on time.

A further example of the need for a coordinated approach could be found in the purchasing area. The buying officer might be persuaded to buy a larger quantity of raw material than usual because of a special quantity discount but this may impose cash flow problems on the company, or it may pose unacceptable strains on the warehousing function. Either of these factors could easily offset the savings made by the higher quantity discounts.

What the company must do is to take a 'total' approach to logistics, i.e., all of the areas of the business affecting, or affected by, logistics must consider the impact of their decisions, not only on their own department, but on the company as a whole.

For the company or any part of the company, to work efficiently it must have a clearly defined objective. In the logistics area of the business we normally use the concept of the 'level of customer service' (or service level as it is often called). This relates usually to the availability of the product and/or the time it takes for the company to deliver or make available the product to the customer. For some products the service level may have to be very high if sales are not to be lost (e.g., if the customer's preferred brand of paper clips is not immediately available then he will almost invariably buy an alternative brand), while for other products (e.g., machine tools, lorries, mainframe computers) the customer is happy to wait for a limited amount of time before taking delivery of his choice of product.

The main problem of logistics management is to set that level of customer service which results in the optimum set of trading results for the company. To achieve this it must be aware of

(a) the customer's likely reaction in the event of the product not being available (or not being available within the accepted time period); and
(b) the costs which are involved in making the product available at differing levels of customer service.

The company's aim should be to find that level of customer service which yields the optimum combination of revenue and costs.

To achieve the desired level of service, the company must take account of the important role played by distributors. The relationship between the manufacturer and the distributor, culminating in a sale to the consumer is known as the marketing channel and no study of logistics can be complete without taking account of the design and management of the channel, and of the way in which the channel works to achieve marketing objectives. If the channel is to work efficiently there must be a considerable amount of cooperation between the manufacturer and the other members of the channel and a considerable part of this chapter is about the way in which the behavioural elements of the channel can and do influence the achievement of logistical objectives.

For example, a manufacturer may implement a perfect logistics system such that exactly the correct amount of product is available when and where it is required, but the scheme will collapse if the channel intermediary fails to cooperate and does not fulfil his or her side of the implicit bargain, either by ordering at an inappropriate time, or by ordering uneconomical load sizes, or by not carrying out appropriate checks and running out of stock of product. To avoid these problems it is necessary to have a clear understanding of the complete channel.

SERVICE LEVELS

The distribution objective in a company must be measured in terms of a service level, which acts as a measure of the efficiency of the distribution function. For the company as a whole the concept of customer service will contain a variety of factors including delivery frequency and the lead time between placing an order and receiving the goods, back-up inventory, responsiveness to complaints or problems, equipment servicing and other forms of technical support. For the distribution function the concept is usually thought of in terms of the extent to which orders can be met from stock, and delivered to the customer, within a given time period. This approach to service level management makes explicit assumptions about the company's ability:

1. To forecast demand.
2. To ensure an adequate supply of raw materials.
3. To control production to ensure an appropriate supply of goods.
4. To store the goods.
5. To deliver the goods.
6. To understand the relationship between the costs of service and the effect of differing service levels on sales and revenue, and hence on profit.

One method of measuring the service level would be:

$$\text{Service level} = 1 - \frac{\text{number of stockouts in a given time period}}{\text{number of orders placed in that given time period}}$$

Number of stockouts means the number of times an order is not delivered to the customer, from stock, within an agreed length of time. The reason for the failure to meet the agreed delivery date may be because of:

(a) poor order processing;
(b) non-availability of the product;
(c) poor delivery of the product.

For example, if it is policy to deliver the goods to the customer within two days of receiving the order and if a customer places 20 orders during the course of the year and on three occasions the company is unable to deliver within the agreed two-day period, then our service level is:

$$\text{Service level} = 1 - \tfrac{3}{20}$$

$$= 0.85$$

or 85 per cent

If this service level is not satisfactory to the market then clearly the company has to examine the factors influencing the delivery time to ascertain where improvements can be made.

In the case of order processing, improvements can be made by the use of computers and/or faster methods of communications.

In the case of poor delivery of the product a change of transport mode, an increase in the number of lorries in the delivery fleet or a change of haulier may have the required effect.

In the case of non-availability of the product the problem is more fundamental and requires very careful examination. The cause of non-availability may be because of:

(a) a lack of raw materials or supplies to make the finished product; or
(b) a lack of finished products.

In both cases the cause of this problem will be because of usage or sales being higher than expected, i.e., unsatisfactory sales forecasting, and the time taken to replenish stock being more than expected.

In a perfect world there would be no variation in the time taken to replenish stock (known as the lead time) and usage or sales would be forecast with 100 per cent accuracy. In reality, of course, neither of these is likely to occur.

Under most circumstances either the lead time or the usage rate, or both, will vary and not be predictable with the required degree of precision. Under these circumstances we need **safety stock** or **buffer stock** over and above the stock based on usage rate during the lead time, unless we are to go out of stock, with the risks of failing to satisfy customer demand.

The amount of safety stock required is a function of the service level which the company wishes to offer to its customers, and this should be a function of the impact of different service levels on costs and revenues.

As the service level gets higher the costs, in percentage terms, rise disproportionately to the rise in service levels.

Thus the company must calculate the costs of the service level increase and evaluate those costs against the impact on sales. For example, a service level of 99.9 per cent means that a company fails to satisfy customers once in 1000 buying cycles. A 97.7 per cent service level would indicate a failure to satisfy customers once in 50 buying cycles while an 84 per cent service level would mean letting customers down once in 6 buying cycles. In many industries the increase from 84 per cent to 97.7 per cent, and from 97.7 per cent to 99.9 per cent would lead to very considerable cost increases. Clearly the question must be asked—what impact will these increases in service have on sales?

COSTS OF SERVICE

The main cost of service is that the company is to keep safety stocks which on many occasions will not be needed. Holding safety stock costs money in a variety of ways:

1. The cost of storage space.
2. The potential cost of obsolescence.
3. The cost of money which is tied up in stocks which could either be invested or be used to reduce the company's overdraft.

Offsetting these costs, however, are the costs of being out of stock.

It must be realized that it may not matter to the distributor whether he sells brand X or brand Y—he still makes his profit. Not only must the manufacturer have the product available, he must also make sure that his distributors have it available. (The relationship between manufacturers and distributors will be discussed later.)

HOW MUCH SHOULD BE SPENT ON SERVICE?

Clearly, as the level of customer service increases, the costs of providing that service also increase. On the positive side, however, a high service level will usually lead to high revenue because the level of lost sales is reduced.

The aim of distribution management should be to find that point where increases in service do not lead to appropriate increases in sales revenue, i.e., the cost of the next level of service is equal to, but not more than, the extra revenue which the higher service level generates.

Figures 9.1–9.3 show how this point of balance can be found in theory. Figure 9.1 shows how the cost of sales lost through poor service falls as the level of service increases. Figure 9.2 shows how the costs of offering service rise as the level of service increases. Figure 9.3 shows the *total* cost curve for service, and is constructed by adding together the costs in Figs 9.1 and 9.2 at the different levels of service.

Clearly the aim is to find the lowest point of the curve in Fig. 9.3. The diagram implies that this is easy but in reality it is very difficult to construct the diagrams with accuracy. It is not at all easy to obtain accurate cost information for different levels of service and it is extremely difficult to forecast sales at different service levels.

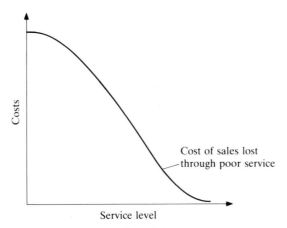

Figure 9.1

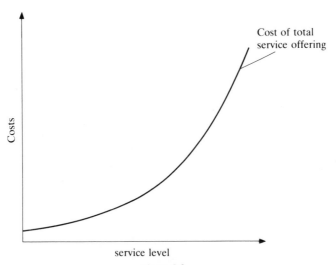

Figure 9.2

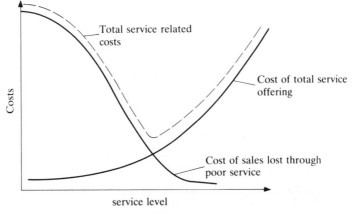

Figure 9.3

As a result of the difficulties of constructing absolutely accurate diagrams the attempt to find the optimum relationship is often neglected in favour of a compromise. The company may seek to achieve one of two things:

1. It may set a budget for logistics expenditure and then the logistics manager must achieve the highest service level possible within the constraints of the budget.
2. It may set the service level which it requires as a matter of company policy and then the logistics manager must achieve that service level at the minimum possible cost.

In market situations where service is of vital importance, method (2) will probably be necessary but if resources are limited then method (1) will be more likely to be used.

SERVICE POLICIES IN MULTI-PRODUCT MULTI-MARKET COMPANIES

Most companies manufacture more than one product and many companies sell their products into more than one market or type of market. In these cases it is necessary to set different service levels which are appropriate to the different products or markets under consideration.

For example, a company may be marketing products to the following customer types:

1. To consumers via retail stores.
2. To manufacturers via OEM arrangements.
3. To garages via factors.

Each of the above may have different responses to service levels and, therefore, the company should offer different service levels in the different markets. Furthermore, in some markets the company may offer a range of product types, from high quality, high price to medium quality, competitive price. It may well be the case that different service levels will be needed for each range. In the case of high quality products the customer may well be prepared to wait, and certainly the cost of holding this in stock will be very high, while for the cheaper ranges the customer will probably be indifferent among brands and, therefore, a higher service level is required.

What the manufacturer will choose to do is dependent on his costs and revenues and one approach would be to give priorities to products and to customer groups. The highest priority would be to a high service level product to a customer who requires high service. In this case we might seek to offer a 99.9 per cent service level availability and delivery within 48 hours. The lowest priority would be at the other extreme where the product availability is not important and the customer is prepared to wait. In this case we may offer, e.g., 84 per cent service level availability and two-week delivery.

In the case of a British component manufacturer a change of service level policy yielded spectacular results. The company was previously offering 10-day delivery on its complete range of 105 components. As a result of careful analysis it decided 20 components should have an improved service level, 25 should remain as they were and 60 become worse. Furthermore, it resolved that certain key accounts should have the highest service of all. As a result of these changes costs were increased by 6 per cent, sales increased by 24 per cent and overall profitability was increased by 9 per cent. In this market there is little brand loyalty and so delivery became very important. The key to the company's success was to find those products: (a) which accounted for largest sales; and (b) from which consumers were most likely to switch in the event of faster delivery being available from competitors (i.e., those lines where the consumer is indifferent between your offering and your competitor's offering).

A further complication, in the case of the multi-product company, is that the supplier may measure his service level on a per item basis while the customer evaluates the service of the supplier in terms of the complete order. Thus a manufacturer, offering a 95 per cent service level on each of six items may be perceived by the market as only offering a 70 per cent service level. This is because the customer gets the **complete** order when expected only on 70 per cent of occasions, i.e., 0.95 to the power of 6 (0.95^6). As most industrial marketing companies offer more than six items the dangers are obvious.

In many instances, however, speed of delivery is not as important as consistency of delivery.

CONSISTENCY OF LEAD TIME

If a company offers a consistent lead time then its customers are able to minimize their stockholding costs as the need for safety stock is reduced. Customers also like to plan and if they can rely on a consistent delivery time then their planning becomes straightforward and they will be more favourably disposed to the consistent supplier. This is particularly important in undifferentiated products or in markets where there is little brand loyalty.

An interesting instance of this was reported in *The Times Business News* on 13 March 1978. Alcan Metal Centres carried out a survey among its customers, checking the degree of desirability of six different product and service factors. Well ahead of everything else came reliability of delivery. It pushed product price into second place and left 'speed of delivery' nowhere. By concentrating on this fact Alcan reduced late deliveries from 19 per cent to 7 per cent and sales increased by 20 per cent.

DELIVERY FLEXIBILITY

If the manufacturer is flexible in his delivery policy this may be perceived as improved service by the customer. For example, convenient order quantities, delivery on convenient days, utilization of the product in a form compatible with the customer's handling system are all ways in which service is perceived by the customer.

SERVICE AND THE DISTRIBUTOR

For the distributor the concept of service levels may assume a different type of importance. For many products the consumer is indifferent between the different brands on offer and so if one of them is not in stock he or she will happily buy the alternative and the distributor loses nothing. The distributor's problems start, however, when products to which buyers are brand loyal are out of stock, or when a number of products are out of stock. In the first case the distributor will lose the profit from the sale of that product and may lose the patronage of the customer in the longer term if it happens consistently. In the second case it may be that the customer is not very bothered about any individual item but if a number of this type of product is out of stock then overall satisfaction with the supplier will decline and he may decide to give another distributor a try. The task for the manufacturer is to make the consumer brand loyal to his product and then the distributor cannot afford not to stock it or not to offer a high service level on it!

OPTIMUM SERVICE LEVELS

The main points to consider in the determination of service levels are as follows:

1. The profitability of the product.
2. The necessity of the product to the customer.

3. Whether it is a buyer's or seller's market.
4. The service policies of other companies in the market.
5. The extent to which the manufacturer has power in the channel.

Service is an important element of the company's total offering. Making the product available when and where the customer requires it may, in many cases, be as important as the intrinsic qualities of the product itself. The service level offered may be just as important, in affecting sales, as advertising or pricing. The manufacturing company must decide on the service level it aims to offer and this service level should be determined after a careful examination of:

(a) the costs incurred at different service levels; and
(b) the revenue generated at different service levels.

CHANNELS OF DISTRIBUTION

All that has been said so far about the work of the distribution manager relates to factors over which it is possible to exercise a considerable amount of control as they are internal to the firm. In a significant proportion of cases the industrial manufacturing company uses the service of distributors. When this is the case the distribution manager and the marketing manager have to take account of the fact in a number of ways:

1. They must use channels of distribution which enhance the prospects of the products achieving their objectives.
2. They must take account of the relationship between the manufacturing company and the distributor and between the distributor and the consumer, to ensure that the channel works as efficiently as possible. To this end it will normally be the case that conflict must be avoided and cooperation encouraged.
3. They must constantly monitor the buying behaviour of the market segments they are seeking to attract, such that any change in these habits is anticipated and the company is able to act rather than *react* and thus the company's products are constantly available via the distributors which their target markets choose to patronize.

We traditionally think of channels of distribution in the following ways:

Manufacturer–buyer
Direct channel, the most common industrial marketing channel.

Manufacturer–retailer–buyer
An indirect channel but fairly short—quite rare in industrial marketing.

Manufacturer–distributor 1–distributor 2–buyer
An indirect channel, but a long one. Useful in getting to distributors whose size does not justify a direct relationship, and also useful if resources are limited and a large salesforce is impossible.
Channels of distribution should be considered under the following headings:

1. Channel strategy and design.
2. Factors affecting channel decisions.
3. Channel cooperation and conflict.

Channel strategy and design

When deciding on the strategy to be followed in the design of a channel of distribution it is necessary to take account of the interaction of this strategy with other strategies of the company because they should all be associated with one another and, as such, will act as constraints on each other. For example, the channel design should affect and be affected by the advertising used. This applies not only to the copy used but also to the media used. The target market at which the product is aimed will patronize certain types of distribution channel and read certain professional journals. Clearly these factors must be coordinated. Similarly, a company which can afford only a small salesforce and/or small accounts receivable will probably have to use a channel which includes distributors as it will not have the manpower to call upon sufficient buyers. Also a company with a narrow product range would find it difficult to compete in some markets because it would have the same salesforce overheads as the major operators but only a few products over which to spread the overheads. As such, it would be unlikely to be as profitable as its larger competitors. The choice and design of the channel type and of the specific channel must be seen as part of the overall plan of the company. To do this the company must have clear objectives relating to channel policy.

Channel objectives These objectives will usually include the following:

1. To make the product readily available to the market at which it is aimed.
2. To obtain the active cooperation of distributors to enhance the prospects of a sale or sales being made.
3. To receive fast accurate feedback of relevant information, e.g., sales trends, inventory levels.
4. To achieve cooperation regarding factors such as order sizes, delivery times, material handling, promotional efforts, point-of-sale, etc.
5. To minimize the costs of the system.

Having determined the objectives of the channel it will be necessary to consider a series of factors which affect the decisions to be made regarding the design of the channel.

Factors affecting channel decisions

Market characteristics The main point is that we must use those channels and types of outlet which our potential customers use. Other important factors include the size and distribution of the market potential. Large, widely dispersed markets will usually use longer channels while markets containing only a few buyers in a limited geographic area will be associated with short channels.

Product characteristics Often characteristics of the product will impose constraints on the channels available. For example:

1. High priced items are easier to sell direct because high gross margins will cover the costs of distribution and sales.
2. Complex products will usually require direct selling because many middlemen will not have trained staff capable of fully explaining the product to customers.

Channel characteristics The manufacturer should follow a two-stage process:

1. Does the intermediary under consideration serve the buyer in the way required?
2. If the buyer is served in the way required then the decision whether or not to use the intermediary will depend on his or her efficiency compared with others. (Efficiency will include factors such as the average size of orders placed, sales ability and enthusiasm, etc.).

Competitive characteristics The company must take account of the activities of its competitors. It must then ask whether it should be trying to sell the product alongside those of its competitors.

Company resources The factors mentioned earlier are all important, but in the final analysis it will be the marketing capabilities and the financial strength of the company which are most important in the determination of the channel strategy. Companies which are financially strong can afford a salesforce, field warehouses and large accounts receivable and are, therefore, able to use short channels (i.e., manufacturer–customer). Weaker companies, on the other hand, will have to use intermediaries who perform basic functions on a commission basis, and these companies, therefore, lose much of the control of their marketing effort and, of course, of their logistics effort. For example, however good the manufacturer's service level policy is, it will suffer if the wholesaler or retailer is not equally efficient in terms of re-ordering in sufficient time. Once the manufacturer loses control then the chances of the intermediary being efficient diminish and the service level to the consumer declines.

To develop the most effective strategy it is necessary to start with the consumer. Having determined what service he requires and what type of outlet he wishes to use, we are then in a position to decide on a strategy. What in effect we are doing is applying the marketing concept (giving the customer what he wants) to the time and place utilities, as well as to the product utilities. Having determined the ideal channel it is then necessary to create an operation which achieves the goals of the strategy with the maximum amount of cooperation and the minimum amount of conflict. Having determined the type of channel we wish to use we must then decide how many intermediaries we wish to use at each state of the operation.

Setting a distribution policy Our distribution policy will affect and be affected by our other strategies and by the type or types of customer we attract and the type of product we distribute. The three basic policies are as follows:

Intensive distribution If our aim is to achieve maximum availability then we need to use the services of the maximum number of distributors.

Selective distribution This policy is applicable when we are aiming at a particular market segment or segments. Here we do not try to get into all distributors which might handle the product but only those which are particularly attractive to our targets.

Exclusive distribution Distribution is limited to a single outlet in a given geographic area. This may be applicable where the distributor is required to invest in facilities to promote the corporate policy of the manufacturer.

Having assigned a channel system we must next select the members of the system. The selection criteria will usually include:

1. Financial stability.
2. Territorial coverage.
3. Product lines carried.
4. The distributor/retailer's sales strength.
5. The distributor/retailer's logistics capabilities, e.g., his warehousing, delivery, stock levels, etc.
6. Other criteria—including managerial capabilities and enthusiasm.

Once the system is in operation it must be continually appraised and controlled. The major criteria used in the appraisal of channel systems are sales data and cost data:

Sales data We should be seeking information on sales for each type of outlet in a sales territory.

Cost data Ideally one should have figures to determine profitability by line by outlet. To get this information one needs precise details on time spent per account, and on logistics costs. Often this is impossible but it is useful to know which accounts are most 'difficult'.

As said earlier, for the system to be efficient there must be cooperation and a minimum amount of conflict.

Channel cooperation and conflict

Conflict within the channel of distribution will invariably lead to a sub-optimization of the system.

Unfortunately the problem is that what optimizes one person's sub-system may well lead to sub-optimization of another's. Thus there is always a potential for conflict as the individual members of the channel attempt to achieve sub-system optimization. Clearly, efficient operation of the channel requires cooperation between and among the members of the channel; each party within the channel must know what to expect from his or her opposite number.

SUMMARY

Distribution has long been recognized as an element of the marketing mix. In industrial marketing it has a key role to play in the effective marketing of products which are often difficult to differentiate, already competitive in price and both difficult and expensive to promote. An efficient distribution system is a powerful marketing tool, as it is so difficult for competitors to match.

TEN

PRICING IN INDUSTRIAL MARKETING

Ray Willsmer

Industrial marketing has many points of similarity with other types of marketing. Certainly, it is the case that most pricing techniques described in any standard text are applicable in most industrial markets, if not in all of them. Nevertheless, there are important differences.

Perhaps the most important difference comes about because of the very nature of the industrial transaction. The demand for industrial products is derived. The degree of freedom of action that an industrial marketer may have over pricing policy will depend to a considerable extent on the amount of freedom that the customer has to vary price.

To complicate matters even more, different segments of the same basic market will find different benefits from the same product and, thus, value it differently according to the amount of benefit derived and the importance of that benefit in their own production or selling mix.

Competition is usually more important in price fixing in industrial markets. The option open to the consumer marketer to create a set of psychological benefits to complement those presented by the product itself exists only very seldom when businesses sell to other businesses. Where product specification and performance are the ultimate criteria, the prices tendered by competitors assume far greater significance.

Add to these problems the additional one of businesses that seek safety and continuity of supplies by insisting on multi-sourcing and, therefore, will buy from several candidates offering the right specification. This also tends to create price pressure from those not on the sourcing list.

These problems undoubtedly exist and in many industries are extremely difficult to surmount. Nevertheless, it is more often than not possible to overcome them, at least partially. It has been shown over and over again that when a business buys a product or service to improve the efficacy of its own business operations, it looks for more than simply a product (or service) at a price. To take a simple example, a promised product at a lower price has no precedence over a delivered one at a higher price when orders are waiting to be filled.

The ingredients of the industrial pricing decision are:

1. The product and its benefits.
2. The degree of augmentation (or extra benefits added).
3. The cost of providing the product or service.
4. The customer.
5. Competition.

PRODUCT BENEFITS

Ideally, products will be created in response to an analysis of the benefits sought. In practice, many technological developments make possible new benefits that the users have not perceived. On the other hand, customers often derive benefits that are totally unexpected to their suppliers.

Profit is possible according to the degree of risk undertaken by the supplier and the extent of differentiation from competition. Although the economist may define profit as the reward for taking risk, any industrial supplier knows there are customers who have never heard of that philosophy. Profit is far more often the reward for being different in ways that the customer perceives as benefits.

A product that cannot be differentiated in performance or in any added non-product benefits can only be effectively separated by price. Price competition, even to the extent of chaotic pricing, is the lot of the totally undifferentiated producer or supplier. At the other extreme, the supplier of a unique product or service can charge a premium price *provided* the uniqueness represents real user benefits.

In between, there is a whole host of possible positions. These represent various combinations of product and non-product differences and similar gradations of price/quality relationships. At the low price end, it is likely that small amounts of product difference will not in themselves be significant enough to escape from price competition and need to be supplemented by similar amounts of non-product additions. However, the more significant the degree of product differentiation, the less it will be necessary also to provide extra non-product benefits. To do so would be gilding the lily, possibly to an unnecessary extent.

The gradations of price/quality relationship run through the fairly obvious stages of little higher quality, little higher price to significantly higher quality at a very much higher price to the in-between stages of significantly higher benefit levels for only a small increase in price.

DEGREE OF AUGMENTATION

Mention has already been made of the fact that satisfactions other than product quality and price are required by most customers. It is a fact of life that customers differentiate suppliers by their own criteria. Ideally, suppliers will decide on their own augmentation patterns in order not only to control their marketing activity but also, more importantly, to reflect those activities in the prices they receive for their goods or services.

There are four areas of such augmentation. The first, most obvious, one is the area of product-associated benefits such as ancillary products and benefits, add-ons, product extensions, compatibility with other products and services, etc. Almost as obvious is the area of financial benefit. Here one may include terms, discounts, the length of credit allowed, special financing arrangements that make it possible for customers to buy or buy now rather than much later. Also 'sale or return'.

The areas where augmentation most commonly produces real selling advantage that can be reflected in prices are in pre-sales and post-sales policies. This is not to denigrate the product and financial possibilities. It is simply that for many industrial companies 'extras' of that kind are necessary ways of doing business and are provided by all the competing companies.

It is also in these two directions that the industrial marketer finds it possible to apply psychological and attitudinal factors.

At the pre-sales end of the spectrum, perhaps the furthest back a customer or potential customer may look is towards the supplier's experience and relevant reputation in the industry; the work that has been done for companies with similar requirements; the place of the supplier in the industry. When IBM launched its highly successful small business and personal computer, the company was able to fall back on its reputation as a supplier of business machines in general and mainframe computers in particular.

How far back along the pre-sales line a company starts will vary widely from business to business. Many will offer consultancy services designed to help the potential customer arrive at the best decision for his business. Problem solving is an area of very common involvement for most industrial companies, whether at sales person's level, sales engineer or high technological standard. It is worth remembering that in many industrial transactions, several years can elapse between enquiry and contract.

Training is another means of augmentation that may happen well before an order is placed or firmed-up. For many, it will be used as an inducement to order. In the early days of computers, the leading suppliers ran programmer training schools in the hope that those trained on their computers would influence the purchase of their machinery. Often, training takes place after the placing of an order but before the delivery, so that the product can be employed usefully from the day it arrives.

Perhaps the most vital piece of post-sales augmentation is in the delivery area. Good delivery will be one of the factors leading to the company's reputation among potential customers. If pre-sales training has not taken place, this could be the time to introduce training schemes. Plant is often sold with the promise that the supplier will commission the machinery and train the new operatives, not leaving the site until the machine is up and working under its new operators. Reliability in delivery promises is also of importance.

A ready supply of spares and servicing probably come next in the order of precedence (although they will have come much earlier where no commissioning or prior training is necessary). Thereafter, the factors taken into consideration by the customer or considered as valuable augmentation by the supplier tend towards the attitudinal. They are factors like the degree to which the supplier is likely to be in the forefront of technical advancement, his financial state and possibly independence and, obviously, any potential threat of the supplier integrating vertically into the customer's business.

COST OF PROVIDING THE PRODUCT OR SERVICE

Analysis of industrial pricing methods inevitably reveals a very high proportion using no other basis than a mark-up on the cost of providing the product or services concerned.

Obviously, costs must be taken into account. So too must the company's aims in terms of its target returns on assets employed. There are, nevertheless, two significant dangers with cost-based methods. The first is the possibility that the provider is undervaluing the offering and that a higher price could be obtained. The second is that it is not always possible to assess accurately the true costs of selling and servicing at the time the price is set. The result is either rapid price increases (which the buyer must interpret as paying for the services) or a subsequent loss of profit rate.

Perhaps the greatest problem with cost-based price fixing is the attitude of mind it engenders. There are many manifestations of this state. It leads companies to judge their competitors by their own standards. One continually hears forecasts of impending doom for companies selling at the prices they are, on the grounds that 'our costs prove they cannot possibly be making a profit'. Even companies practising 'reverse engineering' (stripping down a competitive product and rebuilding it costing the operation as they go along) are not immune to this mistake: it is their costing they are using, not the competitor's.

Above all, it leads to an obsession with costs. This, in turn, leads to other potentially dangerous practices such as 'keeping the factory working'. Often the only way to secure enough orders to keep the workforce employed is to bid for business at marginal profit rates or even prices that only contribute towards total costs. The prices used to secure business in bad times may seriously compromise the ability to raise prices later. At the very least, the starting point is lower. A company that has set prices based on what the customer is prepared to pay may have a bigger safety net to fall back on.

However, the greatest danger with cost-based pricing is that it is indicative of a production-oriented approach to the market. Emphasis on costs leads naturally to an emphasis on features in products or services. Customer-based pricing, on the other hand, enforces consideration of relevant benefits: relevant and significant enough to justify prices that satisfy the provider's targets.

Nevertheless, cost must be covered. What is required is a complete analysis of all likely costs that will be incurred in providing the best mix of customer benefits and satisfactions. That means consideration of the augmented approach, the extent of that augmentation and the way the cost of benefits provided is to be recovered.

In industrial markets, where specifications may be similar if not exactly the same, the role of additional benefits is heavily underlined. There are several ways those benefits may enter into price.

1. They may be fully costed into the product and thus included in the final price charged. They become disguised 'free' benefits in that they appear to be extra to the buyer but have been fully recovered by the provider.
2. Costs may be partly recovered in the sense that although an extra charge is made, the operation is subsidized to some degree.
3. They could be conditional, i.e., a pre-sales survey is charged for at an economic (possibly a full profit) rate but the charge is cancelled if an order is placed within a qualifying period.

Which method is adopted should depend upon the degree of augmentation decided upon by the supplier and the degree to which the supplier wishes to make the extras manifest to customers. The ability to achieve the latter aim will obviously depend upon the competitive situation. The supplier will wish either to provide the extra benefit at the same price as the competition or at a price differential which the customers will perceive as offering good value for money because of the degree of augmentation provided in the product or service.

It is worth observing that the third alternative, used in appropriate circumstances for appropriate benefits, offers significant advantages. It means that services provided which do not result in orders are fully remunerated. Customers frequently interpret that circumstance as affording a higher degree of independence in the recommendations made. Income and profit do not depend entirely upon the customer placing an order. Perhaps this is one of the major reasons why services that are paid for seem to be more highly valued than those that are not. A company operating in the field of industrial safety carried out hundreds of free surveys every year with an average conversion rate of 1 per cent. The problem was that the services provided were required by legislation in only a small sector of British industry. However, there were strong fears that the legislation would be widened. There were also pressures from trade unions for companies to provide these safety factors. In effect, companies were using the free surveys as a means of estimating the likely cost of compliance so that they could calculate the effects on their own costs and prices.

The recommendation to charge for the surveys was received with great fear by the survey division. They claimed that no one would want the service if it was charged for. To the proposition that it wasn't worth providing if the conversion rate was around 1 per cent, they countered that valuable goodwill was being established that would yield higher returns if legislation duly arrived. The change was made. Full profit prices were charged with the proviso that the charge would be taken off the price of any order placed within six months of the survey taking place. In the first year, the number of surveys dropped by 58 per cent but the conversion rate within the six-month qualifying period rose to 24 per cent. However, all those who did not subsequently place an order paid an economic rate for the service. The hoped-for legislation has still not been passed. The survey division, whose demise was widely prophesized when the change was made, is carrying out roughly the same number of surveys annually that it did before. The conversion rate is now around two-thirds of all companies surveyed. The expertise of the company in making recommendations based on its surveys is widely praised in industry.

The method may not work in all circumstances. It is nevertheless well worth considering. When the alternative to charging is not providing the service, the true value to the customer may well appear for the first time.

And that is the problem with all cost-based pricing systems: they may disguise the value of benefits to the customer and establish price levels—which are, in turn, reflected in customers' prices for their products—that become very difficult to raise.

THE CUSTOMER

The customer is central to all that has gone before. It is important to consider the types of benefit the customer may seek either through the product or service purchased or additional to that item.

Endemic to the industrial purchase is the role it plays in the customer's operation. This can vary from a central one (e.g., a prime ingredient or component), through operational ones (such as machinery, a crane, typewriters) to ancillary operations (the need for paint to decorate and protect the factory, paper to process invoices, etc.).

The role is vital for it affects the customer's ability to recover costs in his own prices. Central items can be completely recovered. So, too, can most operational items although their closeness to the central or core items will determine this. It is items in the last category that can cause problems for they are graded from essential overhead items to very optional ones. They are seldom variable with output and they directly affect the margin obtainable in the sense that anything that does not affect output becomes a cost that competes for the margin available for profit.

The main benefit sought by customers for core products is product (or service) performance in ways that allow the user to profit. Thus anything that affects productivity is important. Operational products are frequently fixed capital items and their cost has to be spread across numerous operations. Profitable productivity is the key here and that may well include the assurance of adequate servicing and ready availability of spares. With the ancillary items, the user will need to feel that company efficiency is improved by their use. In new markets, pioneers must be aware of the role of the product or service they are selling in order both to augment it effectively and price it accordingly. In developed markets, standards will have been set for performance factors in each role: newcomers must, therefore, seek either effectively to differentiate their products, provide increased benefit in the areas sought or compete on price.

Customer-based pricing policies are described by the emotive term of 'price discrimination'. Although they include some which quite rightly raise our ire, the term also covers many quite standard practices. Prices may differ:

(a) by customer;
(b) by time;

(c) by place;
(d) by version;
(e) by volume;
(f) by country.

Discrimination by customer

Discrimination by customer is not always at the behest of the supplier. It often arises from customer pressure and, not surprisingly, the supplier wants to keep the news from his other customers. Almost as often, the situation arises because the supplier *imagines* that pressure will be brought to bear unless an attractive price is offered. This form of discrimination is often at the heart of the 'keep the factory working' school. Large orders absorb overhead and fixed operating costs which make it possible to obtain higher profits from subsequent orders . . . if there are any!

The ability to establish different price levels for different customers depends upon:

1. The fact that they may have different degrees of price responsiveness. Identical products sell at very different prices in the automotive and aircraft industries, for example.
2. The intensity of the demand differs. As we noted early in this chapter, a higher price will be paid for a product needed and delivered now than for one promised in a week's time.
3. Customers have different levels of knowledge of ruling prices. Advantage is taken of this situation far more often than may be supposed. In industrial markets, and especially where users are placed well apart from each other, differential costs may be used to explain differences even where they do not account for the whole of the difference (e.g., transport costs). Many suppliers feel constrained from mounting seminars or exhibiting because of the fear that their customers may find out what others are paying for identical products: an area of clear danger.
4. Discrimination may reflect different levels of product knowledge, a situation quite common in the computer market.
5. Different timing of demand may permit time-based discrimination, e.g., night shifts allow the company to take advantage of off-peak power rates.
6. Fundamental to many types of discrimination is the belief that price differentiates quality or service.
7. The role of the customer. It is usual to give different terms to distributors and factors but that is only to be expected if they are to profit from their sales. It is far from uncommon to give different prices to OEMs than are given to other customers.

Discrimination by time

We have already noted that many public utilities have different prices for different times: off-peak electricity; off-peak travel; summer rates for coal and fuel, and so on. Time-based discrimination normally arises because demand fluctuates but costs do not (or not to the same degree). In effect, time-based discrimination involves contribution pricing (pricing to recover at least some of fixed and overhead costs) or even marginal costing as a basis for setting price.

If time-based discrimination is contemplated, careful thought must be given to the ease with which customers may be able to change their buying patterns. From the buyer's viewpoint, this involves a calculation of the benefit of the lower prices against the increased costs of stockholding.

Discrimination by place

This can occur when different prices reflect different positions or different geographical locations. Airline seats are examples of differential pricing by position. Ex-works, c.i.f. or f.o.b. discriminate against the buyer furthest from the supply point. Prices may be identical but the final cost to the buyer differs. It is this final cost that will be compared with what competitors have to offer.

Multi-zone delivered pricing is widely practised, usually by drawing boundaries based either upon actual distance or ease of delivery (e.g., taking account of motorways, etc.). Basing point pricing is another favoured method, although it is banned in many countries. Price may be common but delivery charges are based upon selected basing points. These may not necessarily be supply points. This could penalize those customers close to a supply point but not so near a basing point.

Many products do actually carry a degree of unconscious discrimination in that they are offered at the same price irrespective of distance from the manufacturing point. Thus, those close to the factory are, in fact, subsidizing those further away.

Discrimination by version

Many product lines consist of versions based upon a common base product. The prices of the derivatives do not always reflect either directly attributable costs or marginal costs. Two approaches are used. The first is to price the base product relatively low so that buyers are tempted to trade up. Full profit rates are earned on the extras in the derivative versions. (This is widely practised in the automotive industry.) The second method is virtually the reverse. It assumes that the base product will be the most widely purchased and full profit contributions are based on the sale of that version.

Once full recovery of fixed costs has been earned and target contributions from sales have also been achieved, it is possible to accept a lower rate on sales of lesser versions based on the fact that they now have to bear lower costs. Obviously, a swing in demand in favour of one of the lower priced versions could have damaging results.

This type of discrimination is frequently used as a discouragement. Thus, where a product breaks down into distinctly separate units, the complete item is sold at a price lower than the combined prices of the individual units. This can be a very useful tactic where components are available from competitors and it is necessary to reduce the temptation to make up a total package by buying from different suppliers.

Discrimination by volume

Long before large customers tried to exercise their buying power by asking for lower prices, manufacturers offered lower prices (or a lower total, final price) to those able to buy in bulk. Fulfilling large orders gives long production runs and economical utilization of resources. Consequently, costs are covered more rapidly and profits earned sooner than by filling large numbers of small orders.

Invariably, price discrimination based on volume reflects the fact that costs form plateaux and moving from one level to another justifies different final prices. These plateaux may arise in the production process itself or after the product has been made—in delivery, for example. Orders that permit the use of differential transport rates allow some of that benefit to be passed on to the customer.

It is worthy of note at this point that what is termed 'differential pricing' here is what the customer would regard as the final cost he has to bear; thus 'price', in this context, includes deals and discounts.

Discrimination by country

This is an area which has received a great deal of attention in recent years as more and more cases of differential pricing in different countries come to the public attention. The EEC is firmly committed to eradicating such distinctions throughout the Community.

By and large, two factors account for differential pricing in international trade. On the one hand, marketing outside the country where the product was produced adds costs not borne by the domestic sales. These costs account for most, if not all, of the differential. They assume, nevertheless, that either there is no effective local production which can compete on lower prices based on lower costs or, alternatively, that the product can bear a premium over such domestic competition. On the other hand, a great deal of differential pricing across national boundaries simply reflects the fact that products are valued differently in different countries and the prices charged reflect the willingness and ability to pay.

Conditions necessary for discrimination

The ability to charge different prices for identical products depends upon the existence of market segments willing to pay those differences. Thus, the very first requirement is that the market must be capable of a marked degree of such segmentation to make the policy worth while. The demand intensity between those segments must differ sufficiently to encourage the payment of the higher prices. It is probable, but not inevitable, that those segments exist because the different parts of the market have different price elasticities of demand; obtaining a higher price depends upon a relatively inelastic demand curve in those segments.

Obviously, it is a prime requirement of a discriminatory policy that there is little possibility of being significantly undersold in the markets where the higher prices are charged. If there is product switching to lower priced competition that does not discriminate in its prices and follows a basically non-segmented approach, then price differentiation will fail.

However, the fundamental requirement is that the discriminating company can feel confident that a net gain will result from its pricing policy compared to one of single pricing.

COMPETITION

Throughout all that has gone before, the stumbling block has been competition. A unique product or service has opportunities for setting prices and for discrimination between segments that are not available to a non-differentiated one. At one end of the scale is the completely non-differentiated product for which there is no meaningful service or other non-product differences that will produce benefit to buyers; competition will then be based exclusively upon price. At the other end of the spectrum, the unique product has no need of additional benefits to sell and will justify a premium price.

Three main types of pricing policy stem from the need to consider competitive prices.

Going-rate pricing

Often called 'pleasant pricing', the policy is simply one of not disturbing the market or causing reaction; thus, one simply follows the market leader which has established the 'going rate'. There are two great dangers. Firstly, it assumes that your cost levels are the same as, or lower than, the market leader or else you must accept a lower profit rate. Secondly, you have no idea what the price-leader's target returns are. The price-leader may be able to take a longer view of the market than you; possibly the company is looking only to short-term returns.

Plateau pricing

Essentially, this is agreed prices. In most developed countries, price agreements, in all their various forms, are illegal—except when proposed and promoted by governments. Many industrial products are subject to regulation of the final net price by government subsidy. Often the basis of 'unfair competition' in international trade is found to have its root in such agreements.

Competitive tendering

Competitive pricing reaches its zenith in competitive tendering. This is a complex area in which there have been many significant developments in recent years which it would pay those involved in such business areas to study. One's policy on bidding will vary with the intensity of the desire to gain the business. At times, most businesses will consider tendering at prices that do not yield full profit rates in order to establish a foothold in a business sector or even to register a success that makes them appear more serious contenders for future business on offer. At other times, the same businesses will tender at outrageously high levels, in effect declaring that they do not want the business but they are willing to take it if it affords them abnormally high levels of return on the project.

Theoretical assistance is to be found in Bayesian analysis and in games theory.

However, the biggest problem that any business faces is knowing how to react to price competition. We have already noted that the ability to resist buyer pressure on prices tends to be lower in business-to-business situations. It is also more difficult to resist the pressures created by competitors reducing prices.

Analysis using the format of Table 10.1 has been found extremely useful in reacting to such problems as well as in setting prices. In the first column it is important that the buying factors used reflect the benefits sought by buyers and not the features promoted by manufacturers and suppliers. To each factor determined, a weight is assigned. When used for the first time, it is often found easier to use simple numbers. The ideal is to ensure that the sum total of all the weights equals 1.0.

Thereafter, the columns show the scores on each factor for your product and competition. Again, to start, it may be found easier to score each factor out of, say, 50. The ideal, however, is to adopt a system in which a total score of 100 is shared *for each factor* among all the products listed (your own and competition).

The end result is that it is possible to produce scores for weighted factors which produce a total weighted points score for each product. Your own product's score is then shown as a proportion of each competitor. Thus, in Table 10.1 your product score is first compared with competitor A, then B and so on.

If the analysis reveals that your scores against competition all produce figures in excess of 1.0 then, other things being equal, you should be able to outsell competition if prices are the same. If prices are not the same, the greater the amount above 1.0, the greater your ability to resist competing on price. If, on the other hand, you fall below the magic 1.0 score, price reductions may be your only salvation.

Table 10.1 Price/benefit analysis

Factors	Weight	Our product		Competitor A		Competitor B	
		Score*	Score × weight	Score*	Score × weight	Score*	Score × weight
Product features	0.25	40	10.00	40	10.00	20	5.00
Product quality	0.30	45	13.50	30	9.00	25	7.50
Reliability	0.10	33	3.30	33	3.30	33	3.30
Availability (channels)	0.05	45	2.25	25	1.25	30	1.50
Availability (supply)	0.10	40	4.00	20	2.00	40	4.00
Pre-sales service	0.05	35	1.75	45	2.25	20	1.00
Post-sales service	0.10	40	4.00	50	5.00	10	1.00
Training support	0.05	50	2.50	40	2.00	10	0.50
Totals	1.00		41.30		34.80		23.80

$$Ratios: \quad \text{Our product to A} = \frac{41.3}{34.8} = 1.19$$

$$\text{Our product to B} = \frac{41.3}{23.8} = 1.74$$

$$\text{A to B} = \frac{34.8}{23.8} = 1.46$$

* Scores add up to 100, i.e., score for a product is a percentage of all the scores for that factor.

Several other important points emerge from this sort of analysis. If all the scoring accurately reflects customers' views of the relative strengths of competitors, the way each competitor's score is built up will reveal its product marketing strategy. In a similar manner, a table can be constructed featuring pricing factors instead of buying ones. The inclusion of net price, discounts, over-riders, special prices, deals, etc., will reveal the overall pricing strategy of competing products.

The value of the analysis in setting prices should be clear. It facilitates judgements about the level of differential that a product might bear against competitive ones.

SETTING PRICES

On the assumption that one is not going to set prices simply by marking-up cost levels, two methods of pricing new products exist.

The first possibility is to set prices low enough to encourage rapid trial and penetration of the product: hence the name of 'penetration pricing'. The alternative is to set prices high and milk profits from the market until competition appears: then prices may be reduced, supported by the profits built up during the period of *solus* operation. To give it its full name, this method is known as 'skimming the cream' although 'skimming', 'creaming' and even 'milking' are used interchangeably at times.

These alternatives are shown diagrammatically in Fig. 10.1. Starting at A involves 'skimming'. Beginning at D involves a 'penetration' pricing policy. If A in market 1 represents maximum profits and D in market 4 the minimum acceptable level, then a 'skimming' price could be successively reduced until it reaches that lowest level. In the diagram, this is achieved by selling

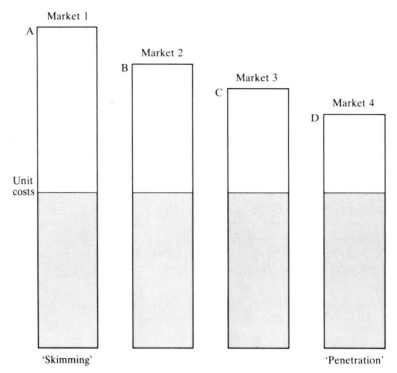

Figure 10.1 Introductory Pricing Policies

at different prices in different markets. It could just as well be different stages of selling in the same market. However, while it may well be contemplated that a 'skimming' policy will lead eventually to lower prices to deter or repulse competition, a 'penetration' policy seldom allows the possibility of subsequent price increases.

If a penetration policy is to succeed, there are four basic requirements:

1. The product and its back-up must be good. Penetration pricing offers a rapid way for customers to learn the faults in a product or its delivery.
2. It will not succeed if capacity cannot meet demand. Almost by definition, penetration pricing will be used in cases where it is relatively simple for competitors to copy the product or service. Any gaps in delivery will simply encourage that competition.
3. The company must have existing distribution channels or adequate arrangements for delivery to direct customers.
4. It should be a product or a service that customers can adapt to rapidly, accept readily and use soon after introduction. Any delay invites competition.

It has been assumed, thus far, that a penetration policy will be used for a new product in a new market. It is, in fact, just as feasible to use it for a new product in an existing market. However, competitors already in the market may match or beat those prices either because they defend their business by accepting reduced profit rates or even marginal rates or, alternatively, because they have previously been 'skimming' the market and have profit 'fat' to fall back on. The policy is, therefore, more successful for new products in new markets. It will work best in existing markets when the newcomer can achieve cost advantages (possibly based upon new production techniques) that existing companies in the market cannot match.

The problem with 'skimming' is deciding when, if at all, to lower prices. In theory, the policy will be adopted up to the point where competition is about to enter the market: then prices will be reduced both to defend the existing position and to discourage new entrants. In fact, it is difficult to be emphatic about what will happen. On the one hand, competition may elect to accept the higher prices, and higher profits established by the first entrant. It may decide to compromise and set prices only slightly lower than the ruling price. Alternatively, it may go for an outright fight for business and price very low. The skimming company may not decide to lower price at all, believing that the franchise it has established with customers justifies holding prices up. If it has had a lengthy period of *solus* operation. It may well find it unnecessary to respond on lower prices.

'Skimming' works best where the company has a protected position. This could be legal protection, as happens in the UK ethical pharmaceutical business, government protection, as happens in many countries, or the protection afforded by lengthy lead times to enter the business.

RESPONDING TO PRICE CHANGES

This is perhaps the most difficult area in any business. If you reduce price and competition responds, share may remain the same but profits are reduced. Raise prices and competition stays down and share may be lost with consequent loss of profit. A price reduction that does not gain business leads to loss of profit: a price rise that neither loses business nor gains new orders increases profits. There is a great deal to be said for price increases and little to be said for decreases. It is interesting that price-leaders are invariably those who lead prices upwards; those who lead prices downwards are those with low shares or over-capacity, hence the increase in price cutting during periods of recession—surplus capacity abounds.

Price cutting creates greater problems in undifferentiated markets, as we have seen. If it is simply the product that is undifferentiated, it may be possible not to have to respond to lower prices. This assumes that there are non-product benefits that enable a premium to be justified, albeit a small one. Often, a product that is undifferentiated sells through different channels, and this may be enough to justify a price difference. Even where there are neither product nor non-product differentiating factors, it may be decided *not* to follow a price reduction by competition. It might happen under these circumstances:

1. If the loss of profit from dropping price is thought likely to exceed the loss of share to lower priced competition.
2. If the prices quoted are below your operating costs.
3. If the decision has been taken to milk the product by sacrificing volume but holding on to profit rate.

The non-differentiated product has obvious disadvantages. The problems argue strongly in favour of policies of deliberate product differentiation and customer segmentation as a means of escaping the worst ravages of price warfare. It opens up possibilities of non-price competition.

NON-PRICE COMPETITION

Inferior and undifferentiated products have to sell on price. Quality and differentiated products (and quality is a prime differentiator) do not. Price competition always appeals to the price conscious. There is a great deal of evidence to indicate that the price conscious are always price motivated. Those who buy at your low price will also buy at the next lowest price that comes along. Loyalty is not a factor in the behaviour of the price-conscious buyer.

Very few markets exist that do not have price-conscious and non-price-sensitive sectors. Where price is not the prime factor, service, delivery, reliability and quality tend to be the prime prerequisites. Disaster befalls those who compete in the quality end of the market with products that do not match up to the quality needs and equally to those who compete in the price-sensitive sectors at prices that are above competition. If you compete on price, you need to go all the way on price. Similarly, if you compete on quality, you must be prepared to maintain those standards at all times.

It may seem strange to conclude a chapter on pricing with a section on non-price. However, non-price considerations can be crucial in industrial marketing, just as psychological ones can be in fast-moving consumer markets. If it is intended to give the company the best possible chance of avoiding the pitfalls of price competition, ways to achieve this objective are:

1. Product differentiation to produce required benefits for customers.
2. Careful segmentation so that those benefits are promoted to those who appreciate them most and are willing to pay for them.
3. Development of valid non-product aspects, such as better delivery, pre- and post-sales service, etc.
4. A policy of deliberate product augmentation.
5. Developing that augmentation by attention to all the marketing mix factors.
6. Attention to company and product image as developed through product attributes, quality and the degree of augmentation decided upon.

If all those things are given the attention they deserve, prices should be set with reference to the competitive advantages that the product benefits present to customers. Whether or not this approach will permit a 'skimming' policy for product introductions will depend on the novelty factors involved in the product or service and/or the length of lead one might reasonably expect in the market.

The reward for adopting this approach is access to less volatile markets and greater long-term security.

FURTHER READING

Gabor, Andre. *Pricing-Principles and Practices*, Heinemann Educational, London 1977.
Winkler, John. *Bargaining for Results*, Heinemann on behalf of the Institute of Marketing, 1981.

ELEVEN

INTERNATIONAL MARKETING

Alfred Alles

The fact that British industrial performance, for many years compared unfavourably with other industrial nations has been analysed, reported on and critically dissected in numerous essays, surveys and studies.

Engineering industries in the UK, as in other countries, face rapid changes in patterns of production methods, product design and product demands and they are wide open to foreign competition both in the UK and in other markets. These are by no means new problems but in difficult times they are aggravated by financial stringencies, in turn worsened by inadequate performance.

On the principle of 'working from strength of experience' this chapter is aimed mainly, although by no means exclusively, at the vast array of industrial products that have a substantial content of advanced, frequently complex, technological features. These products depend on technological performance and state of art position for their marketability, and on attributes of excellence, or at least of good quality and service, for their non-price competitiveness. To achieve success in the market they also need, and deserve, the application of high standards of technical and commercial competence coupled with an attitude of pride in quality and achievement, seemingly lacking or lost of late.

A hard and detached look at the dilemmas of the situation leaves a strong impression that while there are no doubt many viable products and attractive potential markets which justify a full programme of marketing operations (so thoroughly dealt with in the relevant chapters of this book) there is also an urgent need for a modest **launching platform** for marketing initiatives that can exploit existing resources more effectively and can be implemented by means of low-cost, low-risk techniques. It is suggested that the concept of a **Strategic Opportunities Search (SOS)** for industrial products meets this need.

The shortcomings of technical education in Britain have been discussed, and numerous solutions and prescriptions have been advanced to remedy them ever since, prompted by what was seen at the International Exhibition in Paris in 1867, a Commons Select Committee was set up to inquire into these shortcomings. More recently not only the technical qualifications of engineers and their presence in the management of engineering industries, but also their social status in the community was investigated. Of necessity the practices in the UK were compared with those of competitors abroad and in the context of international marketing of industrial products it seemed appropriate to devote a section of this chapter to the relationship between **engineers and international marketing efforts**.

International exhibitions are yet another example of early British pioneering endeavours that were neglected, underexploited and left to others to develop. It is an open question to what extent the absence of truly international industrial exhibitions in Britain during the post-war years deprived British engineers of the impact and stimulus of competitive designs and technical developments and to what extent the prolific growth of the main European exhibitions contributed to the more successful export performances of many European industrial products. A section of this chapter deals with the capabilities of international **exhibitions as universal marketing tools**.

For the sake of brevity the term 'products' is used to mean: products, accessories, auxiliaries, components and materials; complete systems, turn-key projects, services, competences, expertises. The term 'markets' is used to mean: markets, market sectors or segments, special or unique demands, technical or commercial cooperation, joint ventures, know-how and manufacturing licensing arrangements. The term 'engineer' means professional engineers or graduates of engineering.

INDUSTRIAL MARKETS

Before the advent of marketing as a management philosophy the conceptual separation of the home market from export markets was accepted in the same way as home sales and export sales were regarded as self-contained functions often remote, if not divorced, from other mostly product-oriented activities. This separation emphasized the differences between markets as if each domestic national market was one homogeneous unit which must be compared with another, foreign, homogeneous national unit. Analysts who took great pains to examine, dissect and classify the various sectors of the domestic market retreated into generalizations and summary treatments of foreign markets. It was only when marketing was accepted as a concept and selling as one of its many functions that exporting was also recognized as being only one of many international marketing functions.

When the markets for industrial products were explored and more closely examined it became apparent that, perhaps with some exceptions, the similarities of industrial markets at home and abroad were much more significant from a marketing point of view, than the differences which they obviously displayed by being located in different national and geographical environments.

It seems, therefore, logical and reasonable to include the UK in the totality of international markets and international marketing strategies, the more so as the UK is a prime example of a cosmopolitan market for industrial products ranging from the simplest components to the most sophisticated high technology communication and exploration equipment. The UK is also host to agents, subsidiaries and multi-national corporations engaged not only in imports but also in extensive international marketing operations.

So-called 'indirect exports', i.e., products supplied to UK exporters for incorporation into exported and re-exported products, must comply with the precepts and specifications of foreign markets as much as if they were 'direct exports'.

Industrial products imported into the UK are on the one hand direct competitors of UK products, while on the other they open for other UK products opportunities for incorporation in the imported equipment. This applies particularly to such products as power units, auxiliary equipment and accessories, where the UK producer offers the importer advantages of compliance with UK standards, regulations, stock availability and widespread service.

Imports of some industrial products reach quite a high proportion of the UK market. A manufacturer and distributor of fasteners commenting recently on an upturn in demand stated that: '. . . the low manufacturing capacity for stainless steel fasteners in Britain means that a good 90 per cent of these products have to be imported, from approved European sources, to meet existing demand'. As the fastener industry is often regarded as an indicator of trends of most manufacturing industries the lessons are here for all to learn: how to benefit, what to guard against, how to be cautious and how to be bold.

The recognition of the **UK as an international market** requires no more than a change in marketing attitudes. It simply means that for a UK company this particular international market offers special privileges and advantages. There are, of course, companies which export anything up to 70 per cent of their output, even if not to a single foreign market. The acceptance of the UK as an international market can influence product design and marketing strategies which, even if initially aimed only at the home market, can take early notice of the implication of international competitiveness.

Marketing influences and environments

As industrial products can range from screws and rivets to turn-key installations of whole industries, the technological and marketing environments of potential markets have to be examined with the technical nature of the products as principal guide. There are, however, other influences and environments of a target market which can have an impact on its receptiveness for a specific product and on the marketing effort required of a particular company.

Geographic spheres of influence Usually based on national boundaries, these are important marketing merit factors which cannot be determined in a generally valid way but must be assessed in relation to a company's marketing objectives and capabilities. Whatever the definition and character of a market, all marketing activities have a space element. They have definable territories or geographic areas of past, current and planned future activities. It is from this point of view that the geographic influence factor is important. The definitions of spheres of influence are of necessity fairly open. Thus local may mean a sizeable town, an industrial or urban conglomeration or a market town and its agricultural hinterland. A national sphere of influence needs no comment, but an international sphere of influence can range from two small neighbouring countries to many large ones. A sphere of influence which due to special circumstances extends over the whole of the North American continent could be classed as continental, such a sphere extending to both Americas as intercontinental. From the point of view of Company 'A' conventional geographic areas may be of no more than formal conceptual value and the company would have to construct its own categories strictly related to its marketing strategy. From the point of view of Company 'B' one or more, or a combination of several geographic categories, could provide the required basis for marketing operations.

Economic environment factors Such factors have the most direct influence on the marketing environment, and generally they are also best documented and widely communicated. Information about changes in internal credit conditions, investment policies, politico-economic conditions, industrial groupings and similar factors is less readily available and in markets inclined to reticence in publishing such information, deeper probing is required. Impending changes in import quotas, tariffs, custom duties are obvious factors requiring timely observations. The prevailing trading pattern in market sectors which are of particular interest, the ratio of private to public trading, the importance of government trading agencies should be reviewed. Existing or projected agricultural or industrial development schemes, investment subsidies or aid grants, tax concessions, international loans should be related to marketing objectives.

Marketing infrastructure factors These can influence the merit of a target market. Container terminals, free ports, free trade zones or free transit zones are important marketing environment elements, particularly for market entering and market penetration objectives. Associations of import agents, consumer protection societies, government or official test and approval agencies must be considered as influencing the overall market environment. Sophisticated publicity media, numerous and frequent exhibitions, can strain modest resources of a new entrant to the market, or provide opportunities for expansion to an established one.

Scientific environment factors The presence or proximity of universities, technical colleges, scientific institutes, research laboratories can influence the merit of target markets located within their radius of influence or access. The buying expertise of customers can be augmented by calling on the services of members of faculties or specialists. Testing and experimental facilities of institutes can be used for assessment purposes, both by the buyer and by the seller. The claims made for advanced designs or progressive concepts are subject to scrutiny by people with up-to-date knowledge, even if often only theoretical, of the latest achievements. Sophisticated scientific environment will be favourable for progressive equipment or for products based on sound design and operational principles, and unfavourable to products with overt or hidden characteristics of design or operational obsolescence.

Political environment factors These can affect the decision to enter an apparently attractive market and can influence the scope and mode of the marketing operation. An unfriendly political climate could indicate that it would be wiser to use a modest approach, an exceptionally friendly one could encourage a more sumptuous effort than would normally be considered. In an unstable situation a diplomatic absence may prove less embarrassing at a later date than entry during a time of impending change. Products of direct or indirect defence character are particularly affected by this factor. Discrimination by the public sector against suppliers on the basis of their national origin and prejudices of the private sector can adversely affect the merit of the market. A friendly political environment, the establishing or renewing of political associations can affect it favourably.

Legal environment factors Legislation can affect the choice of products and under certain circumstances of marketing techniques and price policies which have to be adopted, e.g., monopolies and antitrust legislation, standards requirements, price regulation, distributors and agents' legal protection, exclusive market arrangements, franchises, unfair competition legislation, advertising restraints.

Aesthetic environment factors This aspect implies the assessment of esoteric values of aesthetics generally and of appearances and taste particularly and is full of pitfalls, yet the aesthetic environment of a market deserves serious consideration. To disregard that aspect of the marketing effort is as inadvisable as to disregard the now acknowledged emotional, status and prestige motivations of industrial buyers and decision makers. The aesthetic environment of the product, of the sales literature, of publicity and PR will be different in Scandinavian countries and in Switzerland, in Hong Kong and in Brazil, in Mexico and in India. Ultimately the question of what is bad, acceptable or excellent will be decided by the beholder, i.e., by the customer.

INDUSTRIAL PRODUCTS

The major classes of industrial goods, their subdivisions, their relation to industrial buyers and to the buying process are dealt with in Chapter 2. A traditional, popular but facile classification recognizes only two classes—consumer goods and industrial goods. The division is unambiguous for such goods as turbines and cosmetics but it loses validity for goods on the borderline of the division or those straddling it or changing from one sector to another depending on application. However at the so-called consumer durables end of the range the dividing lines between consumer and industrial goods become somewhat blurred and some products make their way from one category to another. The high technical content and service requirements of some consumer durables bring them much nearer to the family of industrial products. On the other hand many industrial products like fasteners, hand tools and consumable tools are distributed and sold like consumer goods. The crossing and re-crossing of the imaginary consumer–industrial frontier by such products as do-it-yourself equipment or packaging, further clouds the issue.

A very significant marketing characteristic of industrial products is the fact that the majority of them are used in connection with some other industrial products, so that all producers and sellers of industrial products are at the same time buyers of other such products. In this transposition process some industrial products pass through several phases of incorporation and a considerable time span can elapse between the date the product is first manufactured and the date it reaches the ultimate user.

Many industrial products move through several industrial markets or across horizontal or vertical layers of the same industry. In their travel some lose their identity on the way from the first product to the ultimate user. In some cases this is a requirement of the buyer, in others it is the unavoidable result of incorporation or assembly.

Very often the final user of a complete industrial product becomes aware of the conflicts and dilemmas arising from the incorporation factor only when forced to compare the publicity promises made for the complete product with disclaimers of responsibility for its components made in small print in the warranty.

An 'itinerant' industrial product travels not only across consumer–industrial boundaries but also across national frontiers, occasionally returning to its country of origin incorporated into an imported foreign product.

This internationality of industrial products and thus of their markets is best illustrated by the following: An illustrated weekly magazine, under the heading 'The car that's made in Britain . . . and a few other places' displayed a technically explicit multi-coloured drawing of a popular mass-produced car with 19 components and accessories indicated by the national flags of the 11 countries from which they originated. The car was being assembled in the UK, in West Germany, and factories in Canada and the US were producing versions for the North American market. Several components and products (wire harness, cylinder head, tyres, battery, glass) came from three or four different countries. These 'multi-national' products probably in turn contained materials or components from still other countries.

A review of products imported into the UK can yield valuable information on several counts. Directly and indirectly competitive products will disclose their technical and marketing strengths and weaknesses, the extent of their coverage of third markets, the chances of the UK product to compete successfully in the foreign product's home market and in third markets. Imported equipment containing products of the kind produced by the UK company can indicate opportunities for incorporation into the foreign equipment on the strength of the UK product's inherent advantages or of the UK company's superior service and/or replacement facilities in the UK and perhaps in some third countries.

Auxiliaries, accessories and so-called 'idiosyncratic components' (e.g., electrical fittings and accessories made to BS specifications or regulations) have the greatest chances for incorporation opportunities. Similarly, products like electric motors, power units, engines, familiar to the UK user, can offer to the foreign manufacturer considerable advantages, providing of course that the UK company can justify requirements of performance, quality and reliability of supply and service.

Exhibitions in the UK provide a good opportunity to obtain and supplement information about both competitive products and potential outlets. Exhibitions abroad, particularly in the foreign competitor's and potential customer's home market, can give early warning of their plans for the UK and other markets.

STRATEGIC OPPORTUNITIES SEARCH (SOS)

The decision to initiate, expand or modify international marketing operations is a management policy decision circumscribed by the tenets of the marketing concept as interpreted by an individual company. Normally market research is enlisted in the search for new, attractive and viable markets and marketing research provides the information required to form an effective marketing strategy.

In the present international economic climate many industrial markets are rather erratic, if not unpredictable, in their reaction to contemporary technical developments and in their impact on the social and industrial fabric of a market. Medium-term trends, let alone long-term ones, are more difficult to forecast and speculation often takes too prominent a part in the prediction of trends. Market research abroad, when conducted from a UK base, absorbs considerable personnel, time and financial resources and is fairly expensive when commissioned abroad.

Britain's particular predicament of corporate frugality creates an atmosphere in which budgets for such abstruse activities as market research are cut to the bone—for all that instinctive feelings mitigate against such cuts. It appears that the pressing issue is not a question of how to conduct orthodox market acquisition or penetration studies, but how to devise a cost-effective, low-risk search for exceptional marketing opportunities for products, competences, expertises, from within the current range of activities, how to identify products with singular merits, how to find market niches for special products—in short how to find rare whirlpools in stagnant waters rather than embark on an exploration of the great seas.

The attempt to devise a generally valid method for an opportunities search for sophisticated industrial products led to the concept of a Strategic Opportunities Search (SOS). In broad outline such a study is a persevering investigation process with a lengthy, perhaps even perpetually sustained, timescale which is based on technical and marketing audits of a company's current products. The scope of the search depends on the structure of the company, its range of products and its present, direct or indirect involvement in international markets. The intensity of the search waxes and wanes under the influence of a company's marketing policy; it is affected by technological developments; it reacts to changes in markets and responds to stimuli of exceptional or unusual demands.

On a more modest scale an SOS study can be designed to produce a short- to medium-term basis for identifying attractive marketing initiatives for a limited number of selected products and target markets. Thanks to its structure even a modest scale SOS study will reveal existing shortcomings and thus provide an impulse for product modifications, incremental improvements, market-led innovations and will define valuable bench marks and research targets for more extensive surveys. The implementation of an SOS study is not only a matter of following a course of actions but also, most importantly, a matter of engendering flexibility of thought and the application of pragmatic imagination.

Structure of the SOS study

A well-worn truism, familiar in the consumer market place, but equally valid in industrial markets, postulates that the most favourable condition for a marketing initiative to succeed exists when there is a coincidence of a market demand pull and a marketing push exerted on the same product.

This proposition when applied to an SOS study opens two search routes for its implementation: the company product route and the market demand route. The first route leads from a selected product to its target market, the second from an identified market demand to its target product.

The sequential programme of the two actions is shown in Fig. 11.1 and the two areas in which these actions operate and interact is shown in Fig. 11.2. In practice there is, of course, an overlapping of the two search routes and of their actions and thus most probably a cross-breeding of opportunities for marketing initiatives. Neither the programme of actions nor their concepts and attributes can make any claim to completeness, but they are meant as examples and

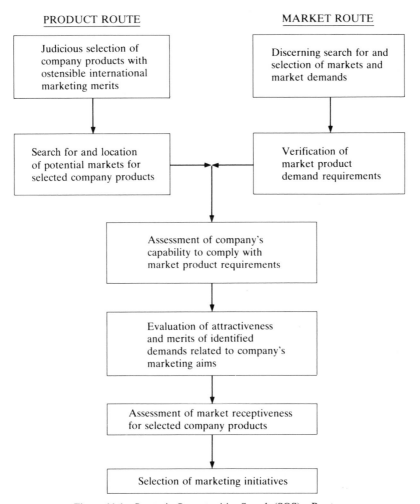

Figure 11.1   Strategic Opportunities Search (SOS)—Routes

PRODUCT ROUTE

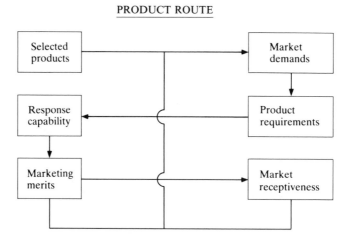

MARKET ROUTE

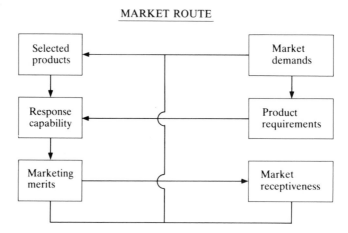

Figure 11.2 Strategic Opportunities Search (SOS)—Action Areas

guidelines for the required scrutinies and evaluations. In a real life situation directives, concepts and attributes are adapted to the special characters of the products and markets involved.

The term 'company product' is used for the sake of brevity and embraces a company's products, systems, services, competences and expertises and is used to distinguish it from the 'product' as needed or demanded by the market.

The technical audit

The structure of the industrial buying and decision-making body is dealt with in Chapter 2. 'Complete products', i.e., products nearest to the ultimate user depend for their marketability mainly on the primary criteria of performance, state of art position, and supporting marketing attributes. 'Inclusion products' depend on the primary criteria but also on the functions and characteristics of the 'receiving' or 'associated' product, and this combination of influences determines the 'incorporation potential' of the offered 'inclusion product'.

In times of economic stringency and tight markets it is particularly important to identify positive product attributes which can offer to some, to many or to all relevant buying influences and decision makers, tangible and realistic benefits and advantages.

In their circumscribed market outlets industrial components, accessories and auxiliary equipment are particularly sensitive to technological position factors, while complete industrial products operate in more open situations, where their overall marketability has a decisive influence. While a price advantage and assurance of continuity of supply of consumable components offer tangible benefits to the chief buyer, these factors are of limited direct interest to the designer or chief engineer. The performance of a power unit and its ease of installation will appeal to the designer, the chief designer and perhaps even to the service manager if approached. When the product has to satisfy intermediate buyers, and only by proxy the end-user, the allocation of benefits to the recipients is more difficult. An analysis of the primary functions of a measuring instrument or gauge indicates its several application areas, while its capacity to operate satisfactorily in a hostile environment may point to a niche in the market hitherto not fully exploited.

Hence the need for a technical audit of the functions, applications, operational environments and the state of art position of current company products. The essence of a technical audit is that it should be conducted with total objectivity and professional skill. The required calibre of technological competence depends on the nature and complexity of the product, and if this competence is accompanied by productive imagination the insights gained can point to new opportunities for marketing initiatives. If the audit is conducted from within the organization, the 'auditor' must have no line management responsibility while undertaking the audit.

The technical audit of current products should be a sober and dispassionate assessment of their merits and demerits so as to provide a realistic background for all subsequent evaluations of marketing strengths and weaknesses.

Cardinal attributes of an industrial product are:

(a) functions;
(b) applications;
(c) operational environments;
(d) state of art position.

Simple examples of matrices which can be used for assessing the merits of cardinal attributes are shown in Fig. 11.3. The product profile based on cardinal attributes determines its suitability for a target market. The evaluation of the merits of cardinal attributes of current products when related to market demand requirements can reveal the need for changes and indicate demands for products new to the company or to the market.

Subsidiary attributes supplementary to the cardinal ones, also require formulation adapted to the characteristics of investigated products. Examples of subsidiary attributes and merit factors are shown in Table 11.1. If a product profile based on the merits of its cardinal attributes reveals only a near-marginal suitability for a market, subsidiary attributes can strengthen its otherwise indifferent position, or at least enable it to find a special niche in the market.

The marketing audit

The merits of the cardinal and subsidiary attributes of company products which were examined and evaluated in the technical audit provide the background for the search routes of the SOS study.

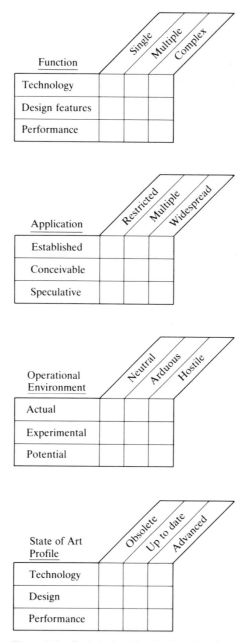

Figure 11.3 Technical Audit—Cardinal Attributes

The product route (Fig. 11.1) A first-line selection of company products based on favourable technical profiles is subjected to an examination of their marketing merits (Table 11.2). For a product with good technical merits a combination of favourable marketing attributes can be crucial for the penetration of a market sector; their weakness in a market with a strong presence of competitors can reduce or even destroy the product's chances. For products, like fasteners, which rely on a network of distributors and wholesalers, strong marketing attributes are decisive.

Table 11.1 Technical audit—subsidiary attributes

Subsidiary technical attributes	Operation Installation Energy	Cost saving/time saving
	Safety Non-pollution	Favourable/unfavourable
	Versatility Serviceability	Very good/good/indifferent
	Weight Bulk Appearance	Favourable/unfavourable

Table 11.2 Marketing audit—marketing merits

Marketing	Company's presence in market Salesforce/distribution Service/spares availability Established contacts Special relations Company's reputation Publicity, PR	Strong/good/moderate/inadequate
Response capability	Production facilities Production capacity Availability of materials Timescale of operations	Ample/reasonable/restricted
Attractiveness of marketing initiative	Complexity of marketing operations Marketability of product Size/durability of demand Growth potential Effect on sales of other products Beneficial synergism (between marketing initiative and other company activities) Benefits for company's image	Considerable/moderate/negligible

The suitability of a selected company product for an identified market demand is assessed in relation to the company's capability to respond to that demand generally and to stated product requirements specifically. The marketing attractiveness of selected products is tested from the point of view of company policy and marketing aims (Table 11.2) and finally the receptiveness of the market (Table 11.3) to a notionally formulated marketing initiative is evaluated. This brings the search to a point where the existence or absence of the coincidence of a market demand pull and a marketing push can be clearly discerned. The final action of the Strategic Opportunities Search is the selection of the most viable marketing initiatives for actual implementation.

The market route (Fig. 11.1) The adoption of the second route of the search is usually based on a special knowledge of a market or initiated by motives of improving an existing position, maintaining a threatened or recovering a lost position in the market.

Table 11.3 Marketing audit—market structure

Market	Large/medium/small	Complex/simple/singular
Product demand	Current/future/latent	Substantial/moderate/small
Product demand requirements	Specification Performance Compatibility Price Quantity/delivery Service/spares Distribution	Very strict/well defined/liberal/vague
	New development Improvement Added complexity Addition to range	Radical/significant/minor
	Competition	Strong/moderate/weak
Market receptiveness	Company's presence	Substantial/moderate/weak
	Restraints	Technical/commercial/legal

Relevant markets require an evaluation of their attributes and their merits of:

(a) market structure;
(b) product demand;
(c) product demand requirements;
(d) market receptiveness.

Examples of main market attributes and their qualifying merit elements are shown in Table 11.3. Market structure and product demand indicate the direction of the first-line search for company products. Product demand requirements disclose the availability of suitable products, reveal the need for improvements and innovations and perhaps point to the need for products new to the company. The last four stages of the search are common to both routes.

ENGINEERS AND INTERNATIONAL MARKETING[1]

In most industries several kinds of engineering such as mechanical, electrical, chemical and lately, of course, electronics operate in active partnership. Engineering enters industries in their embryonic state when they emerge from the phase of scientific or inventive concepts, it then has an all-pervading presence in their manufacturing stage and is still with them in the shape of operational, maintenance and service activities when the products are in the hands of customers and users.

Engineering is, therefore, deeply involved in the industrial marketing system and so are engineers irrespective of whether they are aware of the involvement in a marketing sense or not.

If international marketing of industrial products is to succeed in its task, if its efforts are to produce the right response in the market, it is just as important for those practising marketing to know about engineering and engineers, as it is for engineers to understand marketing and those practising it, and for both parties it is imperative that they should continue to enlarge their mutual understanding with an open mind.

Buyers in industrial markets, the decision-making unit and the buying process are thoroughly discussed in Chapter 2. In the context of international marketing operations and their varied, sometimes complex, situations and encounters, two more factors play an important role: technical competence and language.

Observation and experience over many years of negotiating with top- and middle-level executives of European industries revealed the comparatively high percentage of professional engineers in their ranks, an observation confirmed by numerous surveys, reports, seminars and statistics. Their presence is also manifest at all levels of decision-making units of buyers of industrial products and is further strengthened by the higher status enjoyed by engineers both in corporate as well as social terms.

For the international marketing of industrial products the implications are clear. Unless the technical competence and status of the seller can match that of the buyer, the inherently weaker position of a seller, who needs the buyer's approval, is still further eroded. On the other hand expertise in the subject not only strengthens the seller's position but also builds a competent 'problem-solving' stance so important in industrial marketing. An added advantage is that feedback to the seller's organization is based on a technically realistic assessment of the buyer's needs.

To use a foreign customer's language is a matter of courtesy and also good marketing practice. However, a poor command of it not only devalues the courtesy but as a business practice can do more harm than good. The best knowledge of a foreign language is an asset of limited value unless it is backed by thorough competence in the subject and by a full awareness of the customer's technical needs. Knowledge of a customer's language is also most helpful in informal personal contacts and at sensitive negotiations when the presence of an interpreter could be restraining, perhaps even embarrassing or unpolitic and when the task is not only a matter of reacting to factual statements but also of registering shades of meaning and interpreting understatements and exaggerations.

Engineers—communications—publicity

In the effective performance of his task, in the solution of his problems, in the acquisition of knowledge, the engineer relies on communications with his technological environment from which he obtains information about materials, products, processes and services directly connected with his field of operation and about new discoveries, innovations and improvements in his immediate and related spheres of interest. At the same time the engineer is, directly or indirectly, deliberately or intentionally, the source of similar information for other engineers, buyers, decision makers. Much of that information is given and received as overt publicity, but other information in the form of specifications, test certificates, instructions of use, service manuals, contains at least some elements of allusive or inferential publicity.

The engineer very seldom recognizes that almost all direct and indirect communications between him and his environment contain elements of publicity. A well conceived house style and an effective trade-mark can be very good publicity and are designed for that purpose. An evasive reply to a complaint, a badly printed drawing, inadequate technical details of a specification, all these can be very bad publicity—although not intended to be any publicity at all. A speedily dispatched additional instruction sheet, a clearly detailed installation drawing, a polite and explicit letter can be very good publicity actions, even if not consciously executed with a publicity effect in mind. Packaging which not only contains the industrial goods dispatched, but also protects them from damage, eases recognition on store shelves and encourages proper treatment, produces just as good publicity as an efficient, polite and well-informed telephone operator generates good public relations.

The ultimate success of publicity is determined by the soundness of the marketing concepts on which it is based and by the expertise with which the publicity effort is executed. But in one important aspect publicity differs from other marketing functions. In performing its allocated role it proclaims loudly and publicly, to all it can reach, what the industrial product is and how it functions. At the same time, even when it assumes the most factual and authoritative form, publicity is no more than a promise. Quality, performance, accuracy, endurance, cheapness, ease of use, good service, even prestige by association, is promised by publicity on behalf of the engineer. The effectiveness of publicity depends in no small measure on the engineer honouring the promises given.

The conflicts arising from that situation are numerous. Publicity will try to see in the industrial product attributes which the engineer considers as greatly exaggerated, the engineer will emphasize factors which to publicity have no publicity value. They both use the term 'commercial' to criticize each other. The engineer reproaches publicity for being too commercial, publicity throw up their hands in horror at the utter non-commercialism of the engineer.

A plea is made on behalf of industrial products destined for international markets. Industrial products are fortunate in that they can use a universally understandable ideographic language for the presentation of their functions and shapes. It is the language of sketches, technical drawings, diagrams, photographs, videos. The use of expressive drawings, application photographs, sectioned or exploded views in catalogues and service manuals not only dispenses with costly and often faulty translations but also creates goodwill.

The format of service manuals is also important, it should be adapted to standards existing in the country of destination and enable most convenient use, whether in laboratory, workshop or in the field. It is important to realize that sales literature, drawings, specifications, plans, schemes, are on many occasions the first items customers or prospective customers receive. They are in a way a company's ambassadors and it is enough to compare the reactions to receiving a well printed and well designed letterhead, or a badly reproduced, smudged and difficult to read drawing, to appreciate the implications.

Guarantees of performance or quality may need a last check in new territories, price lists and quotations may require an update check of the currency conversion rate. Literature or special items for public relations functions may need a last minute assessment of the economic or political situation.

EXHIBITIONS

Industrial exhibitions or rather exhibitions serving industrial markets have suffered a long time, and still do, from a misunderstanding and misinterpretation of their capabilities.

A review of the totality of precepts, functions and activities required for the achievement of an effective marketing effort generally, and of an international marketing effort particularly, justifies the assertions that:

- Exhibitions are excellent universal marketing tools for a great majority of industrial products.
- Most normal and many special international marketing operations can be put into practice at exhibitions in an unequalled concentration of space and time.

The marketing capabilities of industrial exhibitions serve the great range of industrial products from one extreme of miniature components to the other of giant machines and structures; they also serve scientific disciplines and technologies. They were in the past and they still are the showrooms for new developments, new services and new concepts. They enable, develop and on occasions restore contacts between people with different national, social, educational or professional backgrounds.

For exhibitors an exhibition is, without doubt, a very public manifestation of their products and their marketing capability, it openly projects their corporate image, it enables visitors—customers, prospects and competitors alike—to assess the competence and manners of their staff.

At an exhibition, the exhibitor can carry out the main marketing functions of selling, advertising, international PR. An exhibition is a very effective medium for launching improved or new products and demonstrating solutions to persistent or new problems.

For visitors, an exhibition which was well selected for the purpose provides a rich field of information, an opportunity to make new contacts, to maintain, renew, improve existing contacts, to make contacts which are normally elusive.

Participating in exhibitions

In simplified terms the intention to participate in an exhibition requires answers to the following questions:

Why do we want to exhibit?
What do we want to exhibit?
Where do we want to exhibit?

In terms of the marketing concept the reply to the first question requires a definition of the business, of the markets and the company's position in them, of the marketing mix and of the range of marketing media employed.

The reply to the second question requires a selection of offerings (products, services, etc.) chosen in the context of the objectives defined in the reply to the first question. The reply to the third question requires a review of exhibitions serving the company's markets and objectives, as defined in the replies to the first two questions.

Organizations with a full awareness of their corporate marketing aims and of their position in the market in which they operate will find no difficulty in replying to the first and second question. This may apply equally well to large corporations as to medium and small companies, even if the latter do not always express their marketing orientation in a currently fashionable jargon. But there are exceptions in both camps. It may seem presumptuous to demand a corporate heart-searching exercise before embarking on such a simple undertaking as participating in an exhibition, but the demand becomes fully justified if only some thought is given to the potential marketing impact of exhibitions, to the great rewards which can be gained, to the danger of substantial losses which can be sustained, and most of all to the opportunities which could be missed.

The selection of exhibitions suitable for a particular set of marketing objectives is a matter of individual assessments, of a search for optimum solutions and of judgement. In times of tight budgets it appears easier and safer summarily to curtail exhibition activities on the grounds of their excessive budgetary and manpower demands, than to undertake a tiresome selection of the few exhibitions which deserve participation, from the many which clamour for it.

Marketing motives for participating in exhibitions range over a wide spectrum of principal and subordinate features illustrated in an abbreviated checklist (Table 11.4). A careful merit rating of the relevant combination of motives produces a 'participation profile' which is in turn examined in relation to the quality of a particular exhibition and its capability to serve the aims expressed by that 'participation profile'.

Visiting exhibitions

The decision to visit an exhibition can be prompted by a casual sightseeing interest, by an optimistic hope that something useful will be discovered or—as it should be—by a well founded assessment of what that particular exhibition can offer.

Table 11.4 Exhibitions—marketing motives

Market share	Increasing, maintaining, recovering
Market penetration	New applications, new industries, vertical, horizontal
New market development	Exploration, probing, infiltration
Sales promotion	Products: established, modified, improved
Marketing of innovations	Products: in new applications, with new features
	New products: new to market, new to industry
Marketing of pioneering	Prototypes of pioneering products, pioneering technologies inter-technology combinations, 'ahead of time' products
Marketing strategy	Contacting elusive influences: operators, service, end-users
	Challenging: monopolies, competitors' 'product arrogance'
Marketing techniques	Inviting interest of potential agents, distributors, wholesalers
	Exploring opportunities for franchises, licences, joint ventures
	Support of parent company for foreign branch, subsidiary, agent
Public relations	Presenting image of expansion, internationalization, capabilities
	Counteracting prejudices, antagonisms, hostility
	Redeeming tarnished image

The need for the systematic planning of the participation in exhibitions is generally recognized but the visiting of exhibitions is unfortunately often left to *ad hoc* arrangements. The securing of an air ticket and hotel reservation is regarded as a sufficiently important organizational achievement needing no further elaboration.

Rational motives for visiting exhibitions usually represent one or more of four main categories of interest: suppliers, customers, competitors, intelligence. The tasks required to satisfy these interests and the addition of other optional interests depend on the scope of the exhibition and the diversity of exhibitors.

Present, new, potential and lapsed suppliers and customers can be contacted—for these contacts an exhibition offers substantial advantages. Information can be obtained from contacts with otherwise elusive executives and technical personnel about future developments, and about competitors' activities.

The hospitable background of an exhibition offers excellent opportunities to repair damaged relations in cases where it would be difficult to re-establish normal contacts without some real or imagined loss of prestige or pride.

Intelligence is usually an integral part of buying, customer and marketing interests, even if not declared as such. The visiting of information centres, trade associations, official or semi-official representations or bureaux can be a special feature in the programme of an intelligence task. Genuine intelligence interests are usually generated by market and marketing research activities and the tasks are sometimes entrusted to visitors to exhibitions engaged in other tasks. In such cases there is a great risk that unless the intelligence task briefing is very explicit and an adequate time allocation is made for it, a systematic intelligence task can degenerate into a superficial reconnaissance exercise. A special intelligence task is the evaluation of the merits of an exhibition. This can be a general assessment made for record purposes or an investigation for a specific objective of marketing or future participation.

INFORMATION

The importance of information and the internal and external sources from which it can be obtained are dealt with in Chapters 3 and 5.

In an ideal world a company's information system should provide all background data and information required for international marketing operations generally and for the search for opportunities specifically. However, experience has shown that while a vast store of information may be available internally, it is perhaps not effectively digested or classified because the current problem was not previously identified or foreseen.

Information systems are usually judged by the effectiveness with which they cope with five main aspects of their activity:

1. Classification and accessibility of existing information.
2. Acquisition and sources of new information.
3. Retrieval and response to requests for information.
4. Initiative and active dissemination of information.
5. Feedback from sources and recipients of information.

All marketing activities rely on information and in turn generate information which apart from numerical and factual data also contains a considerable amount of value judgements. Acquisition of information will run parallel to all market research, product and market audits and opportunities search activities, and it is essential that all received information is suitably recorded, importance-rated and classified to enable its effective use in future studies. In some foreign markets the acquisition of information is fraught with danger of being regarded as industrial espionage or design stealing and a careful examination of legal restraints and pitfalls is of the greatest importance.

Feedback from internal sources is a very important part of a viable information system but often it is difficult to ensure such a feedback from the field. Parting with information, sometimes acquired as a result of special efforts and 'very personal' contacts, is regarded as weakening one's position or sapping one's strength. One of the most frequent complaints of information officers is that they seldom know how useful their bulletins and information sheets are to recipients, to what extent they supply what is actually required, how much of it is superfluous and what is lacking. A useful yield from information depends as much on its quantity and quality as on the purposeful formulation of the requests made for it.

The development of computerized data processing in macro, medium and micro systems has led to a proliferation of equipment which requires a veritable research effort on its own for locating the best choice for a given task. Traditional sales analysis by product, territory and salesman still has its use, but strategic marketing decisions are seldom clear-cut and considerable skill is required in the formation of programmes which, apart from providing specific data, can also monitor unusual signals. Side tables in an executive office piled high with confidential dust-gathering printouts, bear witness to programmes under-researched or unperceptive of the needs of marketing operations.

A survey of the internal information system, its sources and methods of retrieval and dissemination could disclose gaps and deficiencies which need to be remedied to satisfy the demands for specific information profiles. Among the many possibilities, the profiles of products, markets, marketing techniques and competitors are the most frequently demanded. One information system may require only systemization and adaptation to parameters dictated by international marketing operations, another may need substantial augmentation or acquisition of data, location of alternative sources and revision of methods of dissemination.

REFERENCE

1. The sections 'Engineers and international marketing' and 'Exhibitions' are based on Alfred Alles, *Exhibitions, Universal Marketing Tools*, Cassel/Associated Business Programmes, London 1973 (now Associated Business Press).

TWELVE

FINANCIAL CONTROL OF THE MARKETING FUNCTION

Richard M. S. Wilson

INTRODUCTION

The need for financial control

No matter how great his abilities may be in other directions, if the marketing manager lacks an understanding of financial concepts he will be unable to appreciate fully the end results of his planning, and the actions that must be taken to bring these about. In other words, these actions will be beyond his control.

The financial skill required is largely that of being able to compare the financial outcomes of different courses of action, and appreciating the significance of cost–volume–profit interrelationships.

A firm's financial progress is typically measured in terms of profit (preferably related to a capital base), but profits can only arise if the marketing function is successful in selling the firm's goods or services. All the functions of the firm incur costs, but only the marketing function generates revenue.

However, marketing management cannot plan its product strategies, means of distribution, pricing policies, and other marketing activities in isolation of the other functions of the firm. Each marketing manager must be aware of manufacturing costs and their derivation in order to plan his own best course of action. But it must not be overlooked that, while an understanding of financial information and techniques is a necessary prerequisite for marketing analysis, this is insufficient in itself. It must be complemented by competent managerial judgement, and the ability to influence human behaviour in the desired direction.

Any marketing control system should aim to ensure that sales during the period in question are sufficient to achieve the target rate of profit, but be within the capabilities of the enterprise—both physically and economically. This will involve planning to buffer the flow of production with inventory, and will certainly require that a given number of satisfied customers be maintained by the rendering of service factors not directly related to quantities of products, but more concerned with the security of the enterprise (i.e., its continued profitable operation in the long-term future).

THE IDEA OF CONTROL

Management control

If one views financial control as a servant of management, a helpful starting point in developing a perspective for improving one's understanding of it is to consider the nature of management control.

Control should not be thought of as a narrow notion, but as an extremely broad one. It exists to ensure that what ought to be done is done, and to detect when it is not done. Control thus brings about intended or desirable conditions by exercising a positive influence on events, and leaving as little as possible to chance. It involves the use of a reliable, readily understood and sensitive system of information and standards that ensures resources are obtained and used effectively and efficiently in the accomplishment of the firm's objectives. In this setting, a management control system can be defined as a set of policies, procedures and associated information processing designed to give direction to corporate activities in the following ways:

1. By clearly establishing objectives.
2. By devising strategies for the attainment of objectives.
3. By measuring progress in achieving objectives.
4. By indicating the need for corrective action.

This shows that 'historical control' (which is exercised by comparing performance at one point in time with performance in previous periods) is inadequate: control must be oriented towards the future, in line with that which is desired, and not the accidents of the past. Similarly, 'current control' (by which actual results are considered by themselves) is inadequate since it not only fails to adopt a future perspective, it also fails by the absence of a standard of desired performance. Inevitably, **management by hunch** must follow from historical and current 'control'. To be effective, control must be based on planning, scheduling, directing, manipulating, supervising and reporting on goal-striving behaviour—but above all it needs to anticipate change in order to respond to it.

In so far as control reports are composed of past information it is not the intention that one tries to undo such events that have already occurred; the aim should be to use the experience of the past to aid in achieving future objectives. The desired time dimension is clearly the future, as management can only influence events of the future.

Taking the future as the appropriate time dimension, clear distinctions can be drawn among the following:

1. Strategic planning and control—being concerned with overall policies and objectives in the longer term.
2. Management control—as discussed above.
3. Operational control—relating to day-to-day tasks.

All three forms of control are relevant in the context of financial control. For example, the setting of financial policies is a strategic planning activity, whereas planning and reporting on working capital requirements is a management control matter, and, at a more detailed level, the controlling of credit extensions is within the sphere of operational control.

However, management control is the principal focus of attention in financial systems, with a month-to-month span, or even a week-to-week span. Some significant characteristics of management control are:

1. It is complex because it is concerned with the total organization.
2. The information within it tends to be accurate, integrated and developed within a prescribed set of procedures.
3. Although communication is difficult, it aims to lead to desired results by catering for the information needs of many personnel—especially line and senior management.
4. It has its roots in social psychology, and the mental activities involved are essentially those of persuasion and motivation.

The full scope of control can be seen in the cycle of control of Fig. 12.1.

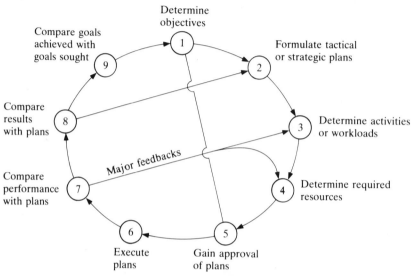

Figure 12.1   The Cycle of Control

This framework accords the necessary company-wide perspective to control by including pre-action (feedforward), during-action, and after-action (feedback) control via:

(a) means of establishing and communicating the objectives that the system is to serve (step 1);
(b) means of adding the additional detail to complete the planning phases (steps 2, 3, 4 and 5);
(c) means of communicating with the performance group (step 7);
(d) methods of reporting on accomplishments (step 8);
(e) methods of comparing performance with plan and identifying significant variations (step 8); and
(f) identification of the variety of corrective actions that may be taken, and the means of taking them (steps 8 and 9).

The control cycle by itself produces nothing of value. Its sole purpose is to facilitate the achievement of the objectives of the enterprise. Inadequate control, which allows chaos or misdirection to substitute for purposive action, is to be avoided; so is over-control, which constrains performance beyond the point of economic return on the control effort.

Financial controllership

Accounting, being neither restricted to one particular area of business nor to a specific industry, was one of the first general management methodologies. As a quantitative method, its underlying problems are those of observation, measurement, systems analysis, model construction and decision theory.

The economic objectives of a business in any given period of time may be diverse and perhaps unique to that firm. But in so far as any such objectives are relevant to accounting, they can be listed as follows:

1. To achieve the target revenues and costs—the income problem.
2. To achieve the target figure of available money at all times during the period—the financial or liquidity problem.
3. To achieve the target pattern of resources, other than money, at all times during the period— the asset structure problem.

To facilitate the accounting control function—with its many dimensions—there is not one single accounting system, but rather several acceptable and complementary systems, each capable of contributing significantly to our understanding of economic events as they affect business firms.

The orthodox approach to accounting simply divides its functions into two basic categories:

1. The stewardship function, involving the maintenance of records for asset control, with particular reference to the function of responsibility to the absent owners.
2. The service function, which treats accounting as a tool for managerial decision making via planning and control systems.

This latter function has greatly increased in importance in recent years, while the record-keeping function has been relegated to the background.

Financial accounting is essentially of a stewardship nature, reporting to outsiders *on* management, rather than *to* management. The traditionally aggregated figures must meet the criterion of **objectivity**, but this often conflicts with the more important control criterion of **usefulness**.

While financial accounting reports focus on the whole business, they must be compiled in accordance with rigid statutory and professional standards. Being historical in perspective, it will be evident that financial accounting is of little value in striving for control.

In contrast, **cost** accounting is concerned with specific segments of the business—relating costs and revenues (hence profits) to products, processes and divisions. Operational control is made effective via variances from standard, but cost accounting is essentially concerned with planning and controlling costs in great detail—too great for top management.

The development of **management** accounting has been based on the criterion of usefulness— the main consideration being *why* rather than *how* in designing reporting systems. The objectivity criterion of financial accounting is largely irrelevant, and the approach of management accounting differs from that of cost accounting in being problem oriented and geared to management control.

Stepping back from the context of information for control from accounting systems to that of the **management of finance**, one can argue that good financial management guides investment where opportunity is greatest, produces relatively uniform yardsticks for judging most of a firm's operations and projects, and is continually concerned with achieving an adequate rate of return on investment (ROI) as this is necessary to survival and the attracting of new capital. It is essential to effective top management, and can be broken down into two major areas:

1. **Financial decision making** This is closely involved with corporate policy formulation via capital budgeting, long-range planning, the evaluation of alternative uses of funds, and the establishing of measurable standards of performance.

2. **Financial planning** This deals with both sources and uses of funds, emphasizing the optimal use of funds. The importance of the fund-raising process is thereby diminished, since management is rightly more concerned with using funds and measuring performance than with how to acquire funds.

The immediate objectives of financial management are to maintain liquidity and aid in improving profitability. These can be achieved by adopting a systems approach in integrating activities into a profit-making pattern so that:

(a) operating functions mesh in such a way that purchases move through a coordinated processing scheme into eventual sales;
(b) the cash flow is timed to eliminate excesses or shortages, and to reduce borrowing needs;
(c) production costs are held to efficient standards;
(d) overhead expenses are limited and controlled; and
(e) current budgetary procedures are related to long-range forecasts.

Profitability will be discussed in more detail later, but at this point let us pay a little attention to **liquidity**. This term refers to a firm's ability to pay its debts as they fall due: if a firm cannot manage to do this, it may have to go into liquidation and close down (which may be on either a voluntary or on a compulsory basis).

Liquidity can be measured in a very narrow way by looking solely at a firm's cash balance. However, many near-cash items (such as debtors' and creditors' balances) are usually included in measures of liquidity since they will enter into (or leave) the firm's cash account within the short term. Perhaps the most widely used measure of liquidity is **working capital** (which is the difference between the value of current assets—which include cash, short-term investments, debtors, and stocks—and current liabilities—which essentially consist of creditors). Figure 12.2 reflects the relationships between working capital, trading activities, and the non-current assets of, and claims on, the firm.

Within the box marked 'Operations' is included a variety of activities—marketing, production, and distribution among others. Sales on credit lead to debtors' balances, which, in turn, produce cash. In due course cash is paid to creditors who supply stock, and so the trading cycle in the lower part of Fig. 12.2 goes round. These activities have a profound effect on the firm's liquidity (as reflected in the working capital position), and all managers should have some appreciation of these basic relationships.

Guidance can come from an enlightened financial controller. He is responsible for the designing and operating of information and control systems, but *not* for the exercising of control—this is the prerogative of the management. The controller is responsible for the normal range of financial and management accounting services, but in addition he must measure and report on the attainment of corporate objectives, and assess the validity of these objectives, along with the general effectiveness of business policy, organizational structure and procedures for attaining objectives.

In order to fulfil his responsibilities, the financial controller must work with all levels of management in all functional areas, interpreting and reporting on the effect of external as well as internal influences on the attainment of objectives. Involved in this is a widening of interest from traditional accounting to applied economic analysis.

In summary, the controller's responsibilities are:

1. To aid in selecting corporate objectives that are capable of being measured.
2. To assist in establishing, coordinating and administering, as an integral part of management, an adequate plan covering all aspects of corporate activities.

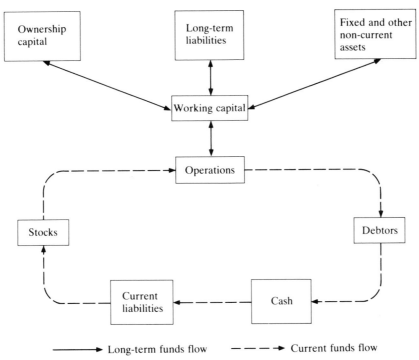

Figure 12.2   The Flow of Funds Through Working Capital

3. To compare performance with plans and standards, and report to all levels of management accordingly.
4. To develop suitable information and control systems, in line with company policy.
5. To consult with all segments of management responsible for policy or action in connection with objectives, adequacy of policies, organization structure and procedures.
6. To administer tax policies and procedures.
7. To analyse and interpret the implications of the economic situation, government policies and social pressures.
8. To negotiate acquisitions and mergers.
9. To maintain credit lines with banks.
10. To ensure that the business assets are protected by adequate insurance and systems of internal control.
11. To establish and maintain good relationships with investment analysts, financial journalists and the investing public.
12. To formulate accounting and financial policy, and maintain an adequately staffed, well managed finance department.

It is evident from the above summary that financial control is not apart from management. Financial control is an integral part of management control of interest to every responsible individual in the firm, be he foreman or managing director. The functional manager can only be fully effective if the financial controller is both able *and* permitted to contribute to the planning and control effort along the lines indicated above.

A system for control

The various inputs (such as money, materials and manpower) into a corporate system, resulting in the production of outputs (such as market share, return on investment and so forth) give a basis for considering systems for control. This is developed via Fig. 12.3 which can be seen to consist of three major inputs: objectives (or desired ends); policies (or prescribed constraints); and plans (or means to ends within constraints). The planning phase takes the various resources that are available to the company (salesforce, plant and equipment, materials and so on) and allocates these in the best available way in line with requirements for the attainment of objectives. Detailed workloads must be established and standards must be set for comparative purposes. This is followed by the execution stage: the plan is put into effect. The major output in this simple framework is an observed level of performance. This we can refer to as feedforward control.

Measures of performance are fed back to the decision maker and compared with the desired levels of performance. This can take place at various levels: for example, an individual sales executive may have been expected to sell 500 units in a given period which would have been the contribution to the brand's market share result which, in turn, would have played its part in striving for an overall rate of return on investment (ROI). Thus there can be a series of comparisons: one at the level of sales person performance; one at the level of the results of the brand; and one at the level of objective attainment.

In measuring output it must be realized that performance measurement has more than one dimension. Consequently, in relation to inputs and the efficiency of their conversion into outputs, it is appropriate to ask:

1. How much was achieved?
2. How good was this achievement?
3. How much did it cost?

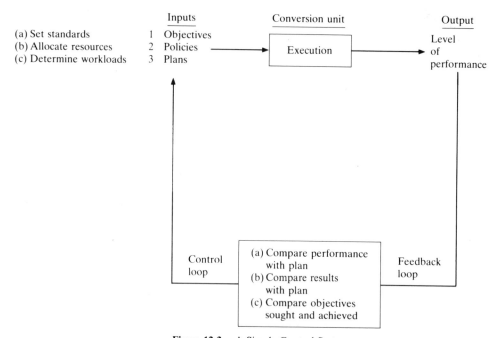

Figure 12.3. A Simple Control System

The need for quantitative, qualitative and financial evaluation of performance becomes clear if one imagines a production unit that operates an incentive scheme related only to the number of items manufactured. High quantity will tend to be at the expense of quality, and this will tend to mean a high rate of rejects resulting in high rectification or scrap costs. A more suitable approach would be to reduce costs by constraining quantity by a specified level of quality.

Following the performance measurement step in the cycle it remains to correct deviations from plan (or to modify the plan to accommodate the deviations). This completes the **feedback control** loop, which is, of course, a continuing feature of the company's existence (see Fig. 12.3).

FEEDFORWARD CONTROL—PLANNING

The role of accounting information

Although the firm consists of the sub-systems of production, marketing, R & D, personnel, administration, etc., the controller, by the very nature of his duties, is able to see the total spectrum of corporate activities in an integrated manner. In the final analysis, money becomes the only common yardstick for planning and gauging performance; this is the controller's domain.

By emphasizing his service (as opposed to stewardship) function, and by having a complete grasp of the company's activities, the controller can lead the way in developing appropriate information and control systems. In fact, he or she can only adequately discharge this responsibility if the types of decisions made and the nature of the activities to be controlled are appreciated.

Complete control can never be achieved purely on the strength of quantitative information. However, management accounting does provide a suitable quantitative base, to which the manager can add both qualitative data and other quantitative factors to balance control action.

Accounting is useful in the control process in three major ways:

1. As a means of **communicating** information on what management wants done.
2. As a means of **motivating** the organization to act in ways most likely to attain the objectives of the business.
3. As a means of **appraising performance** and **reporting** on performance to those concerned.

Information is the medium of control: it is the flow of measurement information, and later the flow of corrective information, that allows an item to be controlled. Information-manipulative company operations such as accounting and marketing research highlight the heavy costs of collecting, processing, storing and transmitting information. The aim, therefore, should be to build an information system that provides that amount of control information which maximizes its value for a given cost, or alternatively minimizes cost for a given mix of information.

Control has two essential elements—information (to relate the objective, plan and performance) and action (to modify performance in accordance with plans and objectives). Information without action is curiosity—not control.

In helping to establish, coordinate and administer a control system, the controller will focus his attention towards devising, compiling and constantly improving an adequate and up-to-date system of reports. In so far as these reports are in the form of **plans** they represent the essence of **feedforward control**. (In other words, the specification of what one seeks to achieve is the starting point for moving forward to achieve it.)

The planning function

The typical manager, although theoretically concerned with both day-to-day operations and planning, tends to pay more attention to operations. This emphasis inevitably leads to sub-optimization, since any company can only have limited resources and should take as few unnecessary risks as possible. This is only feasible if the utilization and allocation of its resources are planned. Any firm that does not look ahead and make plans for the future is clearly courting disaster, and any manager who does not plan ahead is not performing one of his major functions.

Planning is the continuous process of making current decisions systematically, with the best possible knowledge of the future, and organizing the efforts necessary to carrying out these decisions. Although the idea of planning, as an integral part of management, is not new, it is vitally important in that it forms the basis for subsequent control—without planning, control cannot be effective in any meaningful sense. The real gain from planning—when done over a sufficiently long time period—is to provide management with an opportunity to anticipate future problems, thereby permitting itself greater freedom of action to resolve them in a systematic manner en route to the desired goals.

The creation of a plan is expensive, and should, therefore, be done correctly. The only justification for the expense involved is the use of the plan as an effective instrument of control. To achieve this end three conditions must be fulfilled:

1. The plan must be flexible in the face of changing conditions.
2. The plan must be subject to specific review on a regular basis to permit the inclusion of up-to-date information.
3. The plan should be communicated to all concerned if company-wide motivation is to be encouraged.

Before planning can become effective the various elemental parts of a master plan (e.g., product development plan, market development plan, and so forth) must be prepared along a common time dimension, and integrated. Until the master plan is fully integrated it will be impossible for the board to see the full picture and thereby determine whether or not it is desirable. It is at the integration stage that errors, omissions and inconsistencies should be noted and amended. Conformity with objectives should also be ensured at this stage. All is wasted unless the blueprint is actually implemented with each manager being committed to its attainment. At all times, of course, successful planning will be associated with the thinking and aspirations of top management.

In any planning efforts, the financial controller must be aware of all the company's activities and policies. Total financial planning can then follow, involving the developing of financial plans and their integration with operating plans. More specifically, the steps in financial planning are:

1. To determine the financial resources needed to meet the company's operating programme.
2. To forecast how much of the required resources can be met by the internal generation of funds, and how much must be raised externally.
3. To determine the best means of obtaining the required funds.
4. To establish and maintain systems of control over the allocation and use of funds.
5. To formulate programmes to provide the most effective cost–volume–profit relationships.
6. To analyse the financial results of operations, report them, and make recommendations concerning future operations.

The controller, in essence, is thus responsible for ensuring the financial viability and stability of the company, and for monitoring the company's progress in following established plans.

Information for planning

Effective planning can only be based upon a foundation of information, both internal and external, that possesses depth and quality. Furthermore, this information must be both qualitative and quantitative if values are to be established before decisions are made. The basic information flows that are necessary for planning are:

1. Environmental information, relating to social, political, economic and general business conditions.
2. Competitive information, provided by marketing research and intelligence.
3. Internal operating information, consisting of all the measureable information arising from the operational divisions of the firm.

Apart from the fundamental importance of a well designed intelligence system in supplying external information, accounting data form the obvious basis for quantitative planning. This enables management to determine a desirable rate of return on investment, and the means of achieving this by the appropriate acquisition, allocation and utilization of required resources.

Some specific items of information necessary for effective planning will include:

1. The profitability, expressed as either contribution or gross margin, of products and markets. ('Contribution' is revenue minus direct costs, whereas 'gross margin' is revenue minus *full* product cost.)
2. The relationship of volume and profitability of products over their life-cycles (i.e., product history as a basis for projection).
3. The impact of competitive activities and products on volume and profitability.
4. The impact of environmental factors, such as technology, on potential demand and profitability (bearing in mind the elasticity of demand at varying prices, and the variability of market share).
5. The general effectiveness of the marketing (e.g., promotion) and organizational (e.g., administration) backing in optimizing market share, capacity utilization and profitability.

A thorough knowledge of cost behaviour, such as the fixed–variable split, is a basic prerequisite to successful financial planning. Cost analysis (as one element in financial planning) is necessary since all costs do not vary with the level of productive or sales activity, hence it is necessary to know which do, and in what manner, if management is to specify what its costs should be at any anticipated volume (or what its costs should have been for a particular achieved volume of business).

Although every cost-incurring activity involves sacrifice, and this is the only common factor in the various types of cost, cost itself is not a single—or even homogeneous—concept: costs can be defined and measured in many ways. It should be emphasized that it is better to use a rough approximation of the concept of cost that is correct for a particular decision than to have an accurate estimate of an irrelevant concept. The controller, therefore, must carefully consider (in conjunction with those who will use any reports) the types of costs to include in any financial system. The reporting of wrong cost information may be harmful, rather than merely useless, in the decision-making process.

Once the behaviour of *all* costs is understood, these behaviour patterns should be related to the operating conditions at various levels of activity. The actual level that will be experienced will depend on the usual variables—consumer attitudes, competition, economic conditions and so forth. The effect these variables have on sales is reflected in the level of productive activity, and hence costs.

Perhaps the most important distinction in studying cost behaviour is that between fixed and variable costs. This classification is essential to flexible budgeting and cost–volume–profit analysis as well as being the basis of 'relevant costing' for decision making.

A cost will be classified as fixed or variable in relation to the volume of business (i.e., the level of activity), and can only be so classified when the time period has been specified. In the long term, all costs are variable as a result of changes in the scale of the firm's activities. Furthermore, assumptions must be made about the availability of capacity, as this is determined for a given period by the fixed costs. However, volume will tend to move within a range that extends on either side of 'normal' capacity without being accompanied by changes in fixed costs. This range is sometimes termed the 'relevant range'. This highlights the fact that the distinction between fixed and variable costs is valid for a limited period of time, under the assumptions made.

In making decisions, management pays a great deal of attention to the profit opportunities of alternative courses of action. However, in the case of alternatives that involve changes in the level of business, profit does not usually vary in direct proportion to these changes in volume. Consequently, managers must realize that better evaluations can be made to profit opportunities by studying the relationships among costs, volume and profits. Such studies lead to better decisions.

Profit is clearly a function of sales volume, selling prices and costs (see Fig. 12.7). The non-uniform response of certain costs to changes in the volume of business can have a serious impact upon profit. For example, in a firm having a high proportion of fixed costs, a seemingly insignificant decline in sales volume from the expected level may be accompanied by a major drop in expected profit.

In many industries, it is difficult for the individual firm to predict accurately the volume of business that may be expected in the forthcoming planning period. As a result, a wise policy is to consider, for all likely levels of business, the cost, revenue and profit picture.

While the fixed/variable split is probably the most important, the following types of costs should also be understood.

Direct costs These are the costs that can be *specifically* related to particular objectives of interest: for example, the costs of salesmen and other marketing costs of a regional nature can be considered to be direct costs of a particular sales territory.

Indirect costs Indirect (or overhead) costs are those incurred to facilitate various aspects of the business process, but cannot be related directly to any specific unit of output. Examples include administration costs, depreciation, management salaries and R & D expenditure. The majority of overheads are fixed or semi-fixed.

Controllable/uncontrollable costs Controllable costs are those that can be directly regulated at a given level of managerial authority, within a given time period. In other words, they are the costs that are defined as being within an individual's responsibility.

Uncontrollable costs are the opposite of controllable costs—given both the level of management authority and the time period. Thus a salesman cannot control the chairman's remuneration.

In the longer term, all costs are controllable to some degree by someone.

Common (joint) costs Most firms market several products that share common marketing/distribution facilities. The costs that are incurred for general benefit are common or joint costs. These may be fixed or variable, depending on their exact nature.

Sunk costs Once funds have been committed to a particular purpose—especially in the case of capital expenditure—the chances of recovering them depend on how much can be obtained from either disposing of the asset, or selling the output of the asset. The funds so committed are termed **sunk** costs, and are irrelevant in deciding whether to abandon or continue operations, or to replace an old asset with a new one. This is so because no present or future action can alter them.

Programmed costs These costs can be whatever management wants them to be. There is no clear means of determining R & D, advertising, public relations and similar appropriations, so management must specify what it feels is a sufficient amount to achieve stated objectives. When this is done, the cost is fixed for the duration of the 'programme'.

Programmed costs should be distinguished from **committed costs**, which are also fixed but of a different nature. Depreciation, rates, rent and insurances are typical committed costs. The distinction is that programmed costs are discretionary, whereas committed costs are not.

Differential cost Alternatively known as **incremental** or **marginal** cost, differential cost is the change in total cost under each alternative in a choice situation. As such it is an important measure, since the process of decision making is essentially one of choosing among alternatives.

Differential costs can also be described as **relevant** costs. This emphasizes the importance of being able to distinguish among the many different types of cost to solve the problem at hand.

Typical decisions requiring relevant cost information are those relating to make or buy, adding or dropping product lines, replacement of equipment, lease or buy, etc. They relate to the future, and only those costs that differ between alternatives are relevant. Consequently, past (or sunk) costs should be ignored as they are not future oriented.

It must be emphasized that **relevance** is more important than **precision** in the majority of decision making, especially in the light of the uncertainties of the future that render precision difficult to achieve. It follows that the decision maker should refrain from over-reliance on the accuracy of accounting information, as this is frequently spurious.

Responsibility accounting

Responsibility accounting is the approach whereby costs, revenues, etc., are planned and accumulated in accordance with organizational responsibilities, and communicated to and from the individuals responsible for their incurrence.

The need for responsibility accounting follows from certain well established principles of control. To be held responsible for any results, the individual manager should:

(a) know what he is expected to achieve;
(b) know what he is actually achieving; and
(c) have the power to regulate what is happening (i.e., to bring (a) and (b) together).

When all these conditions do not exist simultaneously, it may be unjust and ineffective to hold an individual responsible for the level of costs or profit realized, and the desired control will not be achieved.

From a planning point of view, responsibility accounting is important because, being based on clearly defined areas of responsibility, it enables responsible individuals to play the major role in planning. Regardless of size, planning only makes sense if all levels of management are involved. Thus the managers who are held responsible for performance have a right to participate in setting the goals and levels of performance that they must achieve as part of the overall corporate effort. In this way, human relations should be improved through greater involvement, more job satisfaction, and the avoidance of duplicated effort—hence clashes.

A **responsibility centre** is essentially a personalized concept and represents the sphere of influence of a specific manager.

By compiling plans from responsibility centres, and considering results attributable to the controllable costs at each level of authority, financial control crosses the threshold into behavioural science, especially in the area of motivation.

Once the manager has submitted the plans, it is imperative that he or she be informed of any modification, and the reasoning behind it. If this is not done, the manager may lose confidence in the attainability of the plan (no matter how specific it may be), and fail to see how it fits into the overall corporate pattern. The guiding principle is that those held responsible should be consulted on all matters appertaining to that responsibility.

In summary, the implications of fixing responsibility are as follows:

1. The organizational structure must be clearly defined, and responsibility delegated so that each person knows his or her role.
2. The extent and limits of functional control must be determined.
3. The responsible individuals should be fully involved in preparing plans if they are to be held responsible for results.
4. Responsible individuals must be serviced with regular performance reports.
5. Means must be established to enable plans to be revised in line with actual performance in such a way that responsible individuals are involved.
6. Every item should be the responsibility of some individual within the organization.

The ability to delegate is a sign of a good manager, and responsibility accounting facilitates this. Specifically charging managers with responsibility for a segment of the business is the best known way of ensuring that they perform satisfactorily.

Planning versus forecasting

Planning should be distinguished from the integral aspects of the planning process. This applies in particular to **forecasting**. A forecast is *not* a plan; it is a projection from which plans are developed. For example, a cash forecast might indicate how much cash the company will have on various dates in a future period, and this may show that excessive cash is idle at certain times, and that there is insufficient cash at others. A **plan** would specify what is to be done when there is excessive cash on hand, or a cash shortage.

However, the financial plan should allow for the maximum flexibility consistent with the attainment of objectives. If this condition is not observed, changing parameters may render a rigid plan invalid. Consequently, planning must cater for the dynamics of the real world. For example, should conditions change when the original plan has only partly run its course, the necessary information must be fed back to the decision makers so that the remainder of the programme can be adjusted. The more rapidly the firm can react to a dynamic environment, the greater will be its competitive advantage.

Single-figure estimates are not the best elements of plans, even if they do make specific allowance for the contingencies of an uncertain future. Cognizance should be taken of uncertainty by developing plans for the **range** of possible outcomes. Thus, the most likely level of activity (i.e., sales) may be 1000 units during the forthcoming period, but it could happen that only 800, 900, or as many as 1200 may be sold, depending on competitive activity. Whatever the outcome, the firm should be prepared by planning ahead for a variety of eventualities.

If these matters are borne in mind by the planners, then they can expect:

(a) clearer understanding of the likely future impacts of present decisions;
(b) to be able to anticipate areas requiring future decisions; and
(c) faster and less disruptive implementation of future decisions.

Efficient management should not be satisfied with anything less.

Budgetary planning

A comprehensive budget is the formal expression of management's master plan, as it specifies the firm's objectives and their means of attainment.

Although it can be applied to a single unit (or department) of a business, budgetary planning is much more effective when it consists of a complete and integrated plan for the entire organization. Planning itself should be seen as the predetermination of a course of action in such detail that every responsible unit in the firm may be guided thereby. As such, it involves: sales forecasting; production scheduling; expense budgeting; the planning of inventory levels; the estimating of manufacturing expenses; the making of decisions *ahead of time* concerning such matters as new products and purchasing requirements; and a wide range of other factors.

Some cynical managers may argue that a budgetary plan is of little help in guiding the firm towards its objectives. The reason for this would be given as the firm's inability to control its environment, and hence to predict its future development.

However, this is a weak argument, since *all* planners are aware that the future cannot be predicted with complete accuracy or the environment controlled to any major extent by any one firm. But neither is it to be left to chance—the future presents risk *and* opportunity. By taking the initiative, and exploiting the potential opportunities of the future environment, the firm should be able to ensure an acceptable ROI. The alternative will be merely to accept what happens.

The actual building up of a budgetary plan requires that those items to be planned be specified, the units of measurement determined, and the desired level of performance established. The budget should reflect *expected* (i.e., reasonably attainable) performance, and not be too tight or too slack. (This corresponds with the procedure for setting standards which is considered below.)

Standards

The ultimate test of efficiency is the relationship of profit to capital invested, rather than such measures as the ratio of profit to sales.

Standard ROI targets can be set to form the foundations for managerial planning, policy making and special decision making. Furthermore, ROI permits both internal and external comparisons that lead to the best employment of capital (see Fig. 12.4).

However, problems arise over the definition of both the measure of profit and the measure of the investment base. Figure 12.4 shows the ROI calculation, from which the basic equation relating profit to the investment can be extracted:

$$\frac{\text{Sales}}{\text{Capital employed}} \times \frac{\text{Profit}}{\text{Sales}} = \frac{\text{Profit}}{\text{Capital employed}}$$

or

$$\text{Capital turnover} \times \text{Margin on sales} = \text{ROI}$$

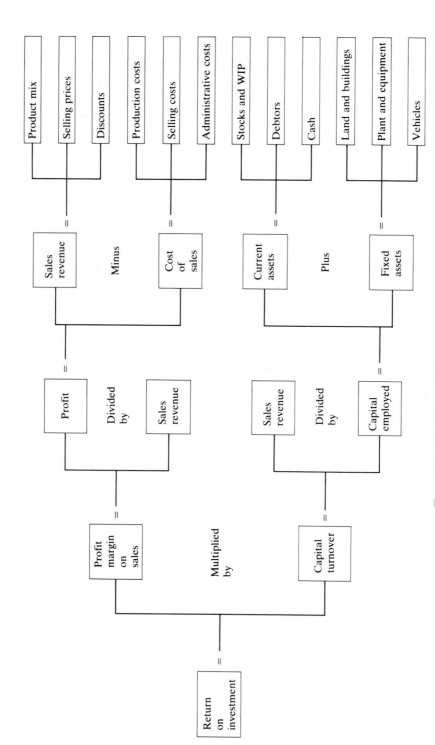

Figure 12.4 Constituents of Return on Investment

It is clear from these relationships that, other things being equal, an increase in sales, a reduction in capital employed, or a reduction in costs will all result in an improved ROI. Management is at times so preoccupied with cost reduction and control that it ignores the need to keep the capital employed down to the minimum level that is consistent with effective performance, or increasing sales from a given capital base.

Whether one is focusing on the setting of ROI targets, or the establishing of less general standards, this task can be seen as part of the larger problem of motivating individuals towards goal-striving behaviour. The standards and plans are *not* the goals—they are the agreed means by which the goals may be achieved. The ideal situation is that in which a control system is so designed that it leads people to take actions that are not only in their own self-interests, but also in the interests of the company.

This process is facilitated by considering the **aspiration levels** of the firm's decision makers. The relationship between motivation and levels of aspiration is fairly clear, and revolves around past success/failures and future hopes. Sufficient flexibility should, therefore, be built into the setting of standards to improve motivation by either upwards or downwards movements of targets in order to achieve continuous improvements in performance.

For example, a manager may fail to reach the established plan for reasons beyond his control. As a result, the level of aspiration will tend to fall, and motivation will drop accordingly. If this process is to be reversed, a new standard should be set that is attainable (while maintaining an efficient level of performance). If this is done realistically, it should improve the manager's motivation by equating a reasonable standard with the aspiration level.

In essence, the standard should specify what the performance should be under prevailing conditions. For deriving company-wide ROI standards, the emphasis should be on *external* parameters, taking account of:

(a) the achieved ROI of successful competitors in the same industry;
(b) the ROI of other leading companies, operating under similar risk and skill circumstances;
(c) the position of the company in its own industry, bearing in mind the degree of competitiveness;
(d) the level of risk faced, with higher risk usually requiring a higher ROI from the investor's point of view; and
(e) the 'expected' ROI—as seen by such groups as trade unions, the financial establishment, creditors, etc.

In connection with more detailed standards of performance, the bases should emphasize *internal* parameters. If this is not so, the standards will not reflect the firm's particular operating circumstances.

Past performance may be thought a useful basis for determining operating standards, but the danger is that it includes inefficiencies that should not be perpetuated. Current conditions and future expectations are of great relevance, since an attainable level of efficiency can be incorporated into the standards as these conditions dictate.

Attainability is an important dimension of any realistic standard. If standards do not reflect both current and efficient levels of performance, as well as individual aspiration levels, they are not likely to be attainable or to motivate.

The 'ideal' standard of the industrial engineer is not a reasonably attainable level of performance, as it describes a perfect situation. Real-life business conditions are anything but perfect, requiring that the ideal gives way to built-in flexibility to accommodate varying circumstances.

In summary, detailed standards for performance measurement should be internally derived, currently attainable, flexible and agreed with those who are to be held responsible for their attainment.

FEEDBACK CONTROL—PERFORMANCE MEASUREMENT

Appraisal

Performance measurement is concerned with the efficiency of converting inputs into outputs and the effectiveness of the actual outputs. This can be considered from two points of view:

(a) the firm as a whole; and
(b) the sub-systems of the firm.

Factors to consider are: what was achieved; how well it was achieved; and the profit or cost of the achievement. Although both quantitative and qualitative measures of success exist, the present concern is with the former, based on the setting of some standard of desired performance for purposes of comparison with the actual level of performance.

It is perhaps paradoxical that performance can only be appraised *after* the event, as this means that nothing can be done to change what has happened, or, in most instances, what is currently happening.

None the less, we have seen that control involves guiding current and future operations in the light of the experience of the past, in accordance with a plan. The plan enables the individual to know in advance what is expected, and how it will be assessed. As a result, every attempt should be made to achieve the plan.

The reaction of individuals to control will vary, depending upon:

(a) the type of individuals and tasks involved;
(b) the environment in which operations are conducted; and
(c) the means and timing of the control effort.

However, feedback control only takes place after actual results have deviated from planned results, hence the effectiveness of control hinges critically upon the setting of plans and standards that are to be achieved, as well as the follow-up response.

It cannot be expected that standards will be met perfectly, so some measure of the significance of results *via-à-vis* standards must be developed. This involves the setting of tolerance limits, with results falling beyond these limits being the subject of control and investigation, while those falling within the limits are accepted as being satisfactory.

The tolerance range should not be so broad as to excuse all levels of performance, nor so narrow as to cause control action to be instigated too frequently.

The basic instrument of control in this respect is the statistical control chart (see Fig. 12.5). This allows successive levels of performance for a particular factor to be observed in relation to standards and to tolerance limits. The example given in Fig. 12.5 illustrates the control of advertising expenditure. As a percentage of sales revenue, this is allowed to fluctuate around a standard of 10 per cent, but as soon as it exceeds a tolerance of 2 per cent *either* way, it is investigated to identify the cause. The reason may be, in this example, the entry into the market of a new competitor, causing an increase in advertising effort on the part of the company to regain lost sales. (The ratio can vary, of course, through either constant sales levels with varying advertising expenditure, or constant advertising with changing sales.) A change in prevailing conditions should result in a reassessment of the standard, and a modification of the levels of tolerance.

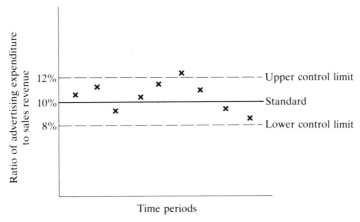

Figure 12.5 Statistical Control Chart

The statistical control chart is based on the well known statistical principle that *significant* variances are those that do not arise purely through chance circumstances. Consequently, the tolerance range should be sufficiently wide to accommodate variations from standard that are purely due to chance. The assumption is that results falling beyond the tolerance limits are attributable to controllable causes and *not* to chance, and are, therefore, worthy of investigation.

This discussion is concerned with the approach known as **management by exception**. A control system operated on this principle is one in which management's attention is drawn to the relatively small number of items having significant variances from plan. Consequently, little attention needs to be paid to the relatively large number of items conforming to plan. This permits managers to focus their attention on planning for the future, instead of becoming submerged in day-to-day trivia. Past events cannot be altered—only their impact on the future can be affected by management action. Management by exception is the means to optimizing future operations on the basis of knowledge from the past.

Ratio analysis

Whenever standards are expressed in ratio form it is possible to compare actual results with target ratios and seek to modify one's activities as necessary to bring about greater conformity. Caution must be exercised when using ratios, however, since they may cover the events they are helping to control with a blanket of averages which is likely to detract from the establishing of causes for the values of particular ratios. Only by ascertaining the causes of outcomes can one seek to put matters right if they have gone out of control.

A systematic approach—such as that offered by ratio analysis—can facilitate the pinpointing of issues in need of managerial attention. One proceeds by working down a **ratio pyramid**: at the apex is the ROI, known as the **primary** ratio. This can be decomposed into two **secondary** ratios (capital turnover and margin on sales), which in turn can be broken down into **tertiary** ratios, and so on. If the value of any particular ratio is not what one expected it to be, it is possible to identify the reasons for this within the structure of the ratio pyramid.

Figure 12.6 illustrates a ratio pyramid that has been developed specifically for use in controlling marketing operations.

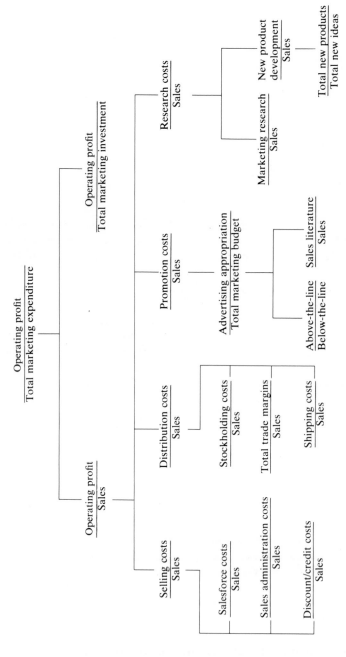

Figure 12.6 Marketing Ratio Pyramid

MARKETING APPLICATIONS

Characteristics of marketing costs

It is invariably found that the costs stemming from marketing activities are difficult to plan and control. The lowest costs are not necessarily to be preferred, since these may not result in the effective attainment of the desired sales volume and profit. Most order-getting costs are programmed rather than variable, and tend to influence the volume of sales rather than being influenced by it. Consequently, the budgeting of order-getting costs should be directly related to sales forecasts.

The characteristics of marketing costs lead to problems in analysis. Such characteristics include:

1. Long-run effects (e.g., the effect of an advertising campaign lasts longer than the campaign, and is usually lagged).
2. The difficulty in measuring productivity, since standards are not easily determined. (Standards can be set for sales activities, e.g., cost to create £1 of sales, average cost of each unit sold, cost to generate £1 of profit, cost per transaction, cost per customer serviced. However, in product decisions, levels of performance may be expressed in terms of the minimum required level of sales per product, or the minimum profit contribution required.)
3. The non-symmetrical nature of costs. (For example, costs increase more in changing from regional to national distribution than would be saved by changing from national to regional distribution.)
4. Costs are frequently indivisible or joint costs, often intended to support a product group.
5. Some costs have discontinuities, or a stepped character shape.

Planning in the light of these characteristics must be based to a significant extent on past experience, competitive activities, test marketing exercises and the estimated expenditure that desired profits at various levels of activity will permit.

Accounting data in the more conventional form provide a point of departure for marketing cost analyses, but these data must be reworked on the basis of units that are subject to management control. (The relevant control unit will depend on the purpose of the analysis, but may be a product, product line, sales territory, marketing division, customer group, etc.)

The part that the financial controller can play in helping to control the marketing function is only gradually being accepted. The controller has, in fact, been looked upon either with suspicion or doubt as someone who only considered figures when marketing executives were convinced that people were more important. At best this made the controller a mere recorder of history—at worst, a positive barrier to progress.

Enlightenment will increase as the profit awareness of marketing management increases further, accompanied by an emphasis on the controller's service function. This service aspect of the controller's work requires that there should be a complete awareness of the firm's products, its markets, the marketing organization, and the particular problems that marketing management faces. Only armed with this knowledge can the financial controller begin to develop the appropriate control and information systems.

Financial control in marketing

The three major variables with which the marketng manager and the financial controller are concerned are marketing expenditure, market share and profitability. These variables can be displayed graphically to show their interrelationships, as in Fig. 12.7.

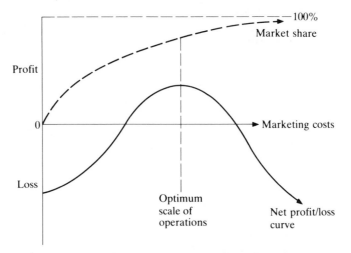

Figure 12.7 Marketing Costs, Profits and Penetration

This graph shows the important point that increasing profitability is not necessarily a function of an increasing market share. A frequently met obsession with sales managers is that of maximizing **sales volume**, whereas the action they should be recommending is to optimize **profit**. The relationship between sales and profitability should follow one of the following patterns:

1. Increasing sales with a proportionately lower increase in costs improves profitability.
2. Increasing sales with constant costs improves profitability.
3. Increasing sales and decreasing costs improves profitability.
4. Maintaining sales at a constant level but decreasing costs improves profitability.
5. Decreasing sales with a proportionately greater decrease in costs improves profitability.

The financial outcome, in terms of the profitability of sales, is reflected in the profit and loss account. This summary statement should be oriented towards the marketing function, avoiding full-cost allocations in the valuation of products. This is shown in Fig. 12.8.

All proposed control reports should be evaluated prior to general use to ensure that they are relevant, useful and as simple as possible. If intended for planning purposes, the controller's reports should highlight cost data related to:

(a) the products to be offered, and their profitability;
(b) the marketing mix and allocation of effort to individual product lines; and
(c) the geographic territories or customer groups requiring varied intensities of effort.

Proposals relating to changes in either the products offered or the marketing mix should be evaluated through cost–volume–profit studies.

The whole reporting system can be strengthened by the existence of cost analysts within the marketing department. They would be responsible for preparing analyses for decision making, such as associating costs with physical units rather than with the value of sales. This automatically eliminates any distortions arising from price variations.

Moreover, these analysts could secure uniformity in the measures used by marketing management and the controller's department—especially in relation to salesforce activities. Such measures might well include: cost per call; cost per customer; cost per order; break-even order size;

```
GROSS SALES                              XXXX
    Less: Cash discount                    XX
NET SALES                                             XXXX
    Less: Cost of Sales                                XXX
    (valued at direct standard cost)                  ____
GROSS CONTRIBUTION                                    XXXX
    Less:  Marketing costs
           Advertising             XX
           Promotion               XX
           Field selling           XX
           Distribution            XX
           Product management      XX
           Marketing administration XX
           Marketing research      XX
           Total                                       XXX
MERCHANDISING PROFIT                                   XXX
    Less:  Manufacturing overhead   XX
           Administrative overhead  XX
           R & D expenditure        XX
           TOTAL                                        XX
NET PROFIT BEFORE TAX                                 £XXX
```

Figure 12.8 Marketing-Oriented Profit Statement

sales per call, etc. These measures could then shed light on profitability, workloads, sales quotas and compensation problems.

This is one means of securing closer coordination of the finance and marketing functions which is so obviously desirable. The marketing manager's responsibility for profitability demands that there is a concern with costs and budgetary methods employed within the firm. Also an understanding of the way in which costs are built up and allocated to individual products; how budgets are arrived at; and how the services of the financial controller can best be employed to secure effective control and effective forward planning. Additionally, the marketing manager must appreciate the effect on profit of changes in the volume of production and should know the marginal earnings of each product (within the existing limits of production and organization). However, very few instances have been found in which the financial controller has combined the variable costs of both marketing *and* production at various volume levels for the use of the marketing people.

Marketing cost analysis

Marketing cost analysis fulfils various managerial needs by its use in:

(a) analysing marketing costs so that they can be combined with production cost data to determine overall profitability;
(b) analysing the marketing costs of individual products to determine their profitability;
(c) analysing the costs required to serve different classes of customer and different territories or areas;
(d) computing such figures as cost per call, cost per order, cost to put a new customer on the books, or cost to hold £1 worth of inventory for a year;
(e) evaluating alternative strategies by indicating their cost implications; and
(f) evaluating managers according to their actual controllable cost responsibilities.

A fundamental objective of marketing cost analysis is to increase the efficiency of marketing expenditures, which does not necessarily mean reducing these expenditures. The basic marketing cost analysis procedure involves reclassifying *natural* expenses (e.g., salaries, travelling expenses, promotional costs) as *functional* costs (i.e., advertising costs, research costs, product management costs, etc., or one functional classification for each element of the marketing mix).

These functional expenses are then allocated to the control unit—such as selling expenses to customer groups on the basis of sales calls made; and advertising outlays to products on a 'unitized' basis. The allocations must be based on some causal relationships. It can then be seen that cost control in marketing depends on the generation of information to attach costs realistically to the activities they support, and that this, in turn, constitutes the basis on which the contribution is calculated—the size of which determines the efficiency of the activity.

It was observed earlier that marketing outlays influence the level of sales, so it is wrong to relate costs to sales value, since the costs of marketing efforts are independent of the results obtained: management, not sales, determines these costs.

Further to this possible malpractice, it is dangerous to break costs down too far. Every *direct* relationship should result in an allocation, but unitizing every indirect cost—be it variable or fixed—to the control unit (channel of distribution, sales territory, product line, salesman, customer group, size of order, etc.) can be misleading. Data relating to costs and units should be examined separately before they are expressed as cost per unit. This highlights the nature of cost behaviour patterns, and whether or not these costs are direct or indirect and variable or fixed.

CONCLUSIONS

Within the constraints of available space it is hardly possible to cover more than a few of the issues underlying the effective financial control of the marketing function. Nevertheless, it is hoped that some flavour has been given of the basis for an enlightened approach to the application of financial control.

Of the more conspicuous omissions are coverage of pricing, on the one hand, and physical distribution on the other. But any attempt to do justice to either of these key elements of the marketing mix would require a much fuller exposition of cost analysis techniques than it has been feasible to include in this volume.

If the reader, after studying this chapter, is able to establish a new dialogue with financial colleagues that might lead to the design of financial control **to accommodate the problems of industrial marketing as seen by the marketer**, then its purpose will have been served. Accounting is, after all, a service function: if it cannot offer a service to its customers that helps in resolving their problems, it is not justifying its existence. The marketing concept has a relevance in many settings, including the provision of financial control.

FURTHER READING

Among the relatively modest number of books covering the subject matter of this chapter, the following may be helpful in giving further (and fuller) guidance. Wilson (1981) includes an exhaustive, classified bibliography.

Goodman, S. R. *Techniques of Profitability Analysis*, Wiley, New York 1970.

Mossman, F. H., W. J. E. Crissy, and P. M. Fischer. *Financial Dimensions of Marketing Management*, Ronald Press, New York 1978.

National Association of Accountants. *Information for Marketing Management* (NAA Research Studies in Planning and Control—No. 3), NAA, New York 1971.

Ratnatunga, J. T. D. *Financial Controls in Marketing: The Accounting–Marketing Interface* (Canberra Series in Administrative Studies—Monograph 6), Canberra CAE, Canberra 1983.

Ray, D. L., J. L. Gattorna, and M. Allen. *Handbook of Distribution Costing and Control* (*IJPDMM*, Vol. 10, Nos 5/6), MCB Publications, Bradford 1980.

Schiff, M. and M. Mellman. *The Financial Management of the Marketing Function*, FERF, New York 1962.

Sevin, C. H. *Marketing Productivity Analysis*, McGraw-Hill, New York 1965.

Wilson, R. M. S. *Management Controls and Marketing Planning*, Heinemann (on behalf of the Institute of Marketing and the CAM Foundation), London 1979.

Wilson, R. M. S. (compiler). *Financial Dimensions of Marketing* (2 volumes), Macmillan (in association with the Institute of Cost and Management Accountants), London 1981.

Wilson, R. M. S. *Cost Control Handbook*, 2nd edn, Gower, Aldershot 1983. (See especially Chapter 17, pp. 493–545, 'Marketing-order getting'; and Chapter 18, pp. 547–78, 'Distribution-order filling'.)

CHAPTER
THIRTEEN

MANAGING MARKETING

E. John Davis

If the concept of marketing is accepted by an organization, then it is logical that the management of the marketing function within it should be based on a proper appreciation of the needs of both the customers and of the organization itself. Since these needs will tend to vary widely each organization should develop its own, often unique, solution to the problems of marketing management, rather than simply follow some pattern or chart developed for use in other situations. The aim of this chapter then is to provide some basis for assessing the needs of the organization and its customers, and to outline some of the main forms which the management of marketing may take.

Marketing management performs the same four basic functions as other management— analysis, planning, execution and control. Perhaps more than most managers, marketing managers must face outwards to know and appreciate what is happening and what might happen in the world outside, and inwards to know and appreciate what is happening and what might happen within the organization.

In looking at any existing marketing department or organization, functions are far more important than titles. Many truly marketing oriented companies have no title of marketing director at all, and the marketing function is coordinated by the managing director. In other companies, regrettably, there is little evidence of a true marketing function even though one of the board members may have the title of marketing director. There are perhaps a few companies where there may be little to be achieved by marketing, and the appointment of a sales director may give a better link between function and title. In some companies there is such a close and fundamental link between the marketing and production functions, through design, delivery schedules and so on, that it is logical to have one person as director of marketing and production to ensure a fully coordinated response to customer needs.

ROLE OF MARKETING DEPARTMENT

The first stage in developing or reviewing a marketing department should be a study to assess what role a marketing department might usefully play in the company. This needs to take account of internal factors and functions, and outside needs both of the company and its customers in order to provide a sound base for any action. The study should also extend to examine the functions of other departments in respect of client contact, new product design or development, servicing and maintenance, which might fall within the scope of a marketing department.

The objective of such a study will be to provide information on where the company is now with regard to the need for marketing functions, the extent to which they are currently provided and the allocation of current responsibilities. Given this information it should then be possible to formulate plans for the future development of a structure for marketing management which will meet those needs in the future.

At board level someone needs to take responsibility for discussions, decisions and the general formulation of marketing policy. This may be through a specific marketing director, or with responsibility resting with other board members, but there needs to be a marketing policy, and one which is compatible with other aspects of company policy. Many of these other aspects have already been discussed in this book and the links will not be elaborated here. Suffice it to say that the marketing policy for a company whose other policies include technological leadership, designing up to standards and investment in new plant should be somewhat different from that of a company committed to 'me-too' products, designed down to a price and with a minimum of new investment. Of course, many of these other aspects of company policy will have been developed in the light of market structures, competitors' activities and so forth, but it will depend on whoever is responsible for marketing policy to ensure that marketing considerations are given proper weight in the development of these related policies as well as ensuring the coherent development of the marketing policy itself.

FORMS OF MARKETING ORGANIZATION

Marketing management, usually led by the marketing director now in his executive or managerial role, has to implement marketing policies with regard to the company's offerings in its markets. Problems then arise about the most useful form of organization for the marketing department or the marketing function, in the light of company needs and market conditions. With a company offering only one product for one end-use in one country, then there may be little problem, and a simple structure allowing for the marketing functions needed by the company to be carried out by managers under the control of the head of the marketing operation will suffice. At the extreme one person may cover all the functions from market analysis and research, through planning, promotion, the sales office and the salesforce, to budgeting and control.

In larger organizations, which are still operating in an uncomplicated marketing or product environment, these functions may be split among several people, but with no further problems other than maintaining communication between them and coordinating the work they do. Hence while there may be some proliferation of managers—sales managers, advertising/promotion managers, distribution managers, and so on—the basic structure of the marketing operation remains simple, monolithic and unified.

Where an organization is in a more complex situation and has a range of products or end-uses or geographic areas to cover there are options open about the form of marketing structure to be adopted. Some organizations have deliberately hived off those parts responsible for different products, as companies or divisions or whatever, so that the management functions, including marketing, are kept simple within each unit. While this may provide some advantages there may be disadvantages as well, and it is interesting to note that while some companies are decentralizing in this way, others may be pulling such operations back into a more centralized structure. Certainly some thought should be given to whether, in the light of market structures, competition and so forth, this degree of fragmentation is advantageous from the marketing or any other point of view. If there is little commonality between product offerings, between markets and users, in communication with customers, deliveries, servicing and other points of contact, then there may be some benefit in adopting or retaining these dispersed simple systems, not least because easily visible profit centres can be established linking production, marketing and all other functions connected with a particular product/market nexus. In most cases, however, and particularly where the products offered by a company have grown from a common base in technology, end-uses, or markets, then the opportunities for taking learning and experience from one area of operations to another, and for achieving economies in common operations, lead to more complex patterns of marketing management.

Where the simple structure of a marketing department is not appropriate, more complex management structures may be linked to three major approaches to the division of tasks and responsibilities within the department. The markets for which the department is responsible may be divided according to the products offered by the company; by the user industries supplied or the end-uses to which the products are put; or by geographic areas, particularly where the company is operating in a number of different countries; and the marketing function may be organized along whichever line appears most appropriate.

Factors related to products

Considerations which might lead a company to organize its marketing on a product-related basis are the extent to which the products differ from each other, or at least fall into a number of distinct groups. Where there are many products, some form of taxonomy is required, taking account of the normal factors of product form and design, the technology involved in production or in use, price and pricing, and presentation. If distinct groups of products emerge in such a taxonomy, then different marketing tactics and strategies may be needed, calling for different approaches to marketing management. For example, if within a single product field some part of the market is concerned with standard products quoted from list prices, packaged in hundreds, and delivered to a specific schedule, but another part is concerned with products of similar form but produced to individual specifications, at negotiated prices, in small lots at random times, then different marketing and sales problems may indicate a need for a marketing organization differentiated by product. If all products involve similar levels of complexity or technology, are all priced according to the same system and all involve similar knowledge and training for effective use by customers, no such differentiation may be needed from a product aspect.

Where it is logical to organize marketing management on a product basis then the managers responsible for marketing individual brands or product groups may well be known as product or brand managers. The use of brand managers originated in consumer marketing, but the logic applies equally to industrial markets where there is a need to have one manager responsible for all aspects of marketing relating to a brand or product group. Such a manager may then answer to the general manager responsible for any profit centre containing the brand, as well as to the marketing director.

Factors related to end-use

If products are highly differentiated then it is not unusual to find the end-uses or end-users highly differentiated, although some multi-product companies have developed their range of products specifically to meet the needs of particular groups of users. However, even with homogeneous products the end-uses may differ to a sufficient extent to regard them as indicative of different markets, with potentially different structures, needs, competitive situations, or customs and practices. Many industrial components are, for example, sold into three different end-use situations: to original equipment manufacturers, to trade repair and service establishments and to DIY enthusiasts. Similar components may be supplied by a single company to firms making cars, coaches and buses, vans and trucks, or boats and light aircraft. Here it is likely that the different requirements of the differing types of customers on quantities, packaging, pricing, delivery and so on will be so diverse that meeting those needs, and keeping track of the different market sectors, will best be carried out by different marketing and sales organizations. With high technology products, where there may be a strong element of expert communication in the relationship between the company and its markets, different sets of personnel operating in different ways, specifically geared to the different sets of end-uses, may provide the most effective marketing organization.

In this context the term market manager may be applied to the person charged with specific responsibility for the application of the company's marketing policy in a defined market or segment, again probably linking to general management in one direction and to the marketing director in another.

Factors relating to geography

The main consideration here is whether any export markets need treating in ways which differ from those used in the home market. Management of overseas markets frequently involves working through factors, agents or other channels not used at home; working within different systems of law or regulation; working to meet differing customer needs in different climates and with different workforces; working in different languages and using different media to communicate; and so on. Hence there may be logic in organizing the marketing management of these activities on a separate and different basis, with different marketing managers appointed with responsibilities for specific territories. Such territorial marketing managers may then find a need to organize their own activities along product or market segment lines, selecting appropriate staff or distribution channels to meet local product or segment needs.

Customer needs and perceptions

The discussion so far has looked at the problems of managing marketing from the company's angle, and its own assessment of what form of marketing organization might best suit its own perceived needs. There is, of course, the alternative dimension, and an important aspect of the company–customer relationship, which may affect either how the whole company and its marketing are organized or how marketing management of a product or segment is developed, concerns the way in which customers perceive an organization. This, of course, includes the overall image of the company, but alongside, or within this, there are questions of how a customer perceives the ideal supplier company in the market, and the perception of an individual supplier. For example, do customers in a market expect one contact to be able to handle all quotations, all orders, all technical queries, all complaints? Or is the ideal supplier organization seen as one in which there is access to staff at various levels and with various backgrounds and disciplines, so that contact can easily be made with whoever the customer regards as the appropriate person?

In a similar dimension, which of the customer's personnel expect to be in touch with a supplier? Is contact in a particular market seen simply as involving the buying department and the supplier's representative, or is the pattern of contact in a market more diverse, with R & D, production, planning and other departments in the customer's organization expecting some contact as well. If so then the levels of expertise, the levels of management or seniority involved at the customer end will have some bearing not only on the effective organization of a company's representatives but also on the whole range of client contact. This in turn may revolve around the way in which the marketing function and the marketing department are organized generally, in this case backing up the salesforce as well as carrying out their own more strategic functions.

MANAGEMENT OF SPECIFIC MARKETING FUNCTIONS

In the light of these and similar considerations, relating not only to marketing activities but also to other areas such as procurement, production, or finance, a company may already have decided that it will organize itself by divisions or subdivisions anyway. Then it would be logical for marketing functions to be located within these divisions, but, beyond that, marketing factors should have played some part in determining that such a policy should be adopted at all, and where the lines should be drawn in terms of products, end-uses, regions and so forth.

The marketing functions required by a company normally involve the use of specialist knowledge or skills possessed by marketing staff or outside organizations such as market research companies, advertising agencies, exhibition contractors and so on. The functions to which those skills are applied range from initial investigation and continuing analyses of markets and trends within them, through forecasting, product and market development, the development of company and brand images, and all the other functions that may be encompassed in marketing planning and control. This normally calls for some degree of functional specialization even in a single product/market company; and as the complexity of the marketing function increases so the scope for, and the benefits from, specialization also increase. Problems may, however, begin to arise where there are conflicts of interest between brand or market management intent on furthering its own sectional interests, and corporate or head office management seeking coordination of effort to further corporate goals.

Simple examples illustrate some of the problems that may arise. Central management may believe that greater consistency may be engendered in the company's advertising if it is all handled by the same agency, apart from any spin-off in company–agency relationships. However, a divisional marketing manager or a brand/market manager may well believe that a different agency has the knowledge, skills or whatever, to produce better results for his brand. Some organizations will insist on the company line being followed, others may make it more or less easy for variations in policy to take place, almost to the extent that the central policy itself becomes badly eroded.

Pricing policies can be a cause of friction, and this apart from any effects of pricing decisions on the bottom line. Head office concerned with overall images, effects and profitability may decide on a particular policy which, while producing generally beneficial results, may be less advantageous for certain products or in certain markets. Again, depending on the balance between forces of centralization and devolution, local departures from central policy may be permitted, ranging from the exceptional to the frequent.

In the area of market forecasting some organizations locate this function centrally, even working down to fine detail. Others merely work on global or industry forecasts at the centre, leaving specific market forecasts to operating units. It would, however, be logical to expect those developing brand or market forecasts to start with an acceptance of the forecasts and underlying assumptions developed by the centre; but in some cases local knowledge would indicate different starting assumptions or different conclusions. Clearly discussion is needed, and although such differences may generally be hidden within the company—rather than made public by changes in agencies or pricing policies—many decisions arising from forecasts will result in actions evident to those outside.

One functional area where there is increasing awareness of a need for consistency and coherence between the parts of an organization is in the area of external relations. This tends to go beyond the simple and local public or press relations operations linked to new developments, new products, promotions and so forth, and becomes of vital importance for some industries in sensitive areas—the extractive industries, nuclear power, computing to some extent, some chemicals, among others. Here strong central policies may be needed, backed by firm and strictly applied procedures to ensure that all potentially sensitive issues are quickly channelled to experts at high levels in head office before any local, and potentially damaging, action is initiated. However much local management, marketing or otherwise, may wish to spring to the defence of its brand or market, action here needs to be fully coordinated if exploitation by skilled manipulators of external pressure groups is to be avoided or at least minimized.

As a result of these and similar problems the structure of marketing management differs widely between organizations, not only with regard to the formal pattern and organizational chart, but also with regard to the balance of power between the brand marketing functions and the central or corporate functions. The balance is probably most critical in companies involved in dynamic and highly competitive markets, where constraints imposed from the centre can severely hamper the development of market potential. It is not unusual to find that the balance varies between markets, and a company may well appreciate the need to give more freedom to those endeavouring to break into new or more dynamic markets, compared with the freedom allowed to managers responsible for existing and more static products in developed markets. In some cases this is recognized by the specific development of forms of management in new or dynamic areas under such names as venture or project groups. Some major organizations have gone so far as to set up subsidiary companies specifically to develop new products or new markets, free from the established procedures of the main part of the company.

Venture group management

The essence of this form of management is that a team of people is brought together from different disciplines to manage the development of a product and its market, and is given much more latitude and discretion than is usually given to managers of established products. Part of the philosophy is the acceptance that the operations covered by such groups involve abnormally high risks compared with other company activities; and that timing and the speed with which decisions can be taken are important factors. Hence the establishment of small groups of dynamic executives with the technical capability of seeing a project through with a minimum of external interference. Within such a group there would probably be marketing personnel as well as those from R & D, production, procurement, finance and so on.

There can be a corollary to the idea of venture groups which is not always recognized by management—that is that a great deal of frustration can be developed among some marketing managers if personal characteristics are not considered in relation to the role they are asked to fulfil. Posting a mature manager somewhat set in his ways to a venture group may be recognized as a source of potential trouble; but posting a young eager executive as marketing manager of a mature or even declining product or market can be damaging to that market as well as frustrating to the manager who tries to introduce change where change may be counter-productive. However, matching a manager to the degree of maturity or dynamism in a market is not the only basis for selection.

Selection of marketing personnel

Many senior marketing managers in industrial markets gained their initial marketing experience in consumer markets, where development of the marketing function was generally earlier and faster than in industrial markets. Many others have developed their marketing experience and knowledge having first been involved in the engineering, production or other technical sides of their companies. In large departments it may be possible and advantageous to develop a mix of managers with a range of marketing and industrial experience, but in many small companies this will not be possible. Given that any marketing manager must have a deep knowledge and understanding of his product and his market, then if this has to be contained within one person, that person will probably be someone from the industry who has developed marketing skills, rather than someone with marketing skills coming into the industry. Hence, while large organizations may employ a few marketing specialists as such within the context of a large department, smaller organizations will probably take industry people and convert them to marketing managers via practical experience and possibly some of the training courses available (see also Chapter 16).

Where there is a need for marketing personnel to have specialist knowledge of the products and their uses, there is always a risk that after some time in a marketing post problems arise with keeping up to date and general product involvement. Hence there may be a case for periodic rotation of personnel into and out of marketing. Provided such rotation is not too rapid then there can be considerable benefits for the people involved, and for the organization. Managers whose careers subsequently develop in other directions should benefit if they have spent some time working on the analysis, forecasting and planning problems in marketing, in carrying through marketing plans to meet particular forecasts or objectives, and controlling expenditure on promotions, publicity, exhibitions and so on. The marketing effort of the company should benefit, first because of the presence in the marketing department of direct experience and knowledge of the processes of research and development, production, servicing and so on; but also because in time there will exist throughout the company an awareness and experience of what the marketing department is and does, and through that an enhanced appreciation of the importance of the customer to the business.

CONCLUSIONS

The form and structure which marketing management is to take in an organization must be developed in the light of the specific conditions being faced or expected, whether they arise from direct product or market considerations, customer expectations, competitive activity, or extraneous factors. In a successful operation the needs generated by different products in different markets will be met, often in different ways, as well as the need for cohesive and integrated marketing policies and strategies at corporate level.

Within industrial companies generally, marketing activity tends to be more closely linked to other functions, even to the extent of being subsumed within them in some cases. Hence there is a need to define carefully the role of the marketing department itself without inhibiting the multi-faceted approach to both product and market development needed in most situations.

Both the management of marketing and the integration of marketing effort with other company effort tend to call for high levels of technical and product expertise among marketing personnel in companies supplying industrial goods and services. The balance within a department between personnel with marketing backgrounds and product/technical backgrounds is again a matter for the individual company, but some rotation of technical staff from their own departments into a marketing department can prove beneficial both for them and for the department.

In the end the shape of marketing management in an organization, whether simple or complex, must be governed by basic marketing principles—what form of marketing organization will provide a satisfactory service to the company itself and its customers.

FOURTEEN

MARKETING WITHIN THE TOTAL CORPORATE COMPLEX

Christopher J. West

One school of marketing theorists maintains that companies are in a constant state of hostilities. Customers are the principal territory over which the campaigns are waged and competitors are the opposing forces. All divisions of the company are engaged in the struggle but the front line strategic and tactical responsibility lies with the marketing department. In well organized companies the marketing director is the commander in chief reporting directly to the chief executive. Decisions on the major strategic objectives are made at the top of the company. So too are decisions on the allocations of resources and as the major *corporate* purpose is gaining and maintaining customers it is imperative that *all* resources, within and outside the marketing unit, are harnessed to that end. Wars are won not only by the troops in the field but also by the ability of the military commander to control the production resources required to feed them with supplies and the finance to pay for the war effort. These are the hawks of marketing and there is no denying that there is merit in their approach.

Marketing doves take a 'softer' line. They perceive marketing as an important but distinctly separate activity within the corporate framework. They do not see it as an assertive function attempting to discipline other staff members to the requirements of customers, but more as part of the management college in which customers' requirements are balanced against engineering, production, financial and personnel considerations. The marketing dove accepts that the customer is not *always* right and that there are occasions when the sales and marketing task is to gain acceptance for a product and service which the company wishes to supply.

Hawks and doves have common ground in the fact that they both see marketing as an important component of the management structure. In this they differ from the traditional organization in which marketing, or more commonly selling, was assigned the relatively lowly task of disposing of the output of the company at a price which would yield an acceptable profit.

In fact none of the above viewpoints, hawks, doves or traditionalists, describes the ideal role and position of marketing in a corporate organization. They are either pragmatic responses in a situation where marketing is introduced to an existing corporate structure or a reflection of the missionary zeal of a dominant marketing personality. Very few companies have the opportunity to retreat to the organizational drawing board in order to inject marketing into their structures and the reshaping of territorial boundaries tends, therefore, to be evolutionary rather than dramatic. The result will depend entirely on the strength of the personalities involved, the degree of resistance encountered and sales and profit performance. Hopefully it will also take account of the environment in which the company operates.

The birth pangs of a marketing unit are often severe. Conception may arise because of the need to fill a vacuum or a perceived need to inject the customer perspective into a corporate structure which was previously wholly egocentric. In either case there is likely to be conflict since many of the tasks prescribed for marketing could be fulfilled by other departments and there is no doubt that to perform adequately marketing must encroach on to the previously unchallenged domains of others in the company. The marketing unit that has evolved out of a sales department, like a butterfly from the chrysalis, will inevitably encounter hostility and rejection. Many in industrial companies will see little use, within their restricted and serious worlds, for a flamboyant extrovert activity closely associated with the promotion of baked beans, cosmetics or toilet tissue.

However painful, the establishment of a marketing department is no more a sign that the organization is marketing orientated than weekly church attendance is of Christianity. The outward sign does not mean that all the principles are rigidly adhered to nor does it provide any meaningful guidance to corporate destiny. To many the trappings of marketing are sufficient in themselves, providing they do not interfere too much with older and more hallowed practices.

To say that marketing is a business philosophy is now something of a cliché, but observation of corporate structures indicates that many suppress or ignore the essence of marketing in favour of the more obviously profitable daily marketing actions that are designed to separate the customer from his cash. To them marketing is 'souped-up' selling, a collection of promotional aids designed to make the salesforce's life a lot easier and more effective. To an extent it is, but there is a lot more to marketing and for any hope of success the basic philosophy has to be incorporated in the organizational framework.

There is a Chinese saying to the effect that 'even the longest of journeys commences with the first step'. The first step in marketing is to recognize that the discipline consists of a basic philosophy and a set of techniques which can help to implement the philosophy. The philosophy is fundamental but the techniques will change to suit the type, size, location, customer base and staffing of the company together with a host of other criteria. History, which ensures that some of the marketing techniques, such as selling, are in place before any conversion to marketing occurs, results in the cart invariably being put before the horse. Organizational rigidity maintains the *status quo*. To break out from this pattern it must be agreed *throughout the company* that customers' current and future requirements will make a major contribution to all strategic and tactical decision making. Without customers the company will fail and actions which do not satisfy customers will lead to their choosing alternative sources of supply.

Some have interpreted this as meaning that to be successful companies should be controlled by marketing personnel. Evidence from successful companies shows this to be nonsense. Good marketing cannot override or replace sound financial controls, effective production management, good design and efficient purchasing. Nevertheless the marketing unit must be more than the interface between the company and its customers, it must also ensure that other parts of the company perform according to what is acceptable to the customer. Customer satisfaction (at a profit) is an objective for everyone in the company and the marketing unit's task is to ensure that this is achieved. In order to do so a number of distinct and separate tasks have to be undertaken (see Fig. 14.1). These are:

- Injecting the customer perspective into the corporate planning process so that the targets and objectives are realizable and take account of environmental and competitive threats as well as capitalizing on market opportunities.

- Implementing the marketing component of the overall plan.
- Ensuring that *all* staff are aware of customers' requirements and operate in a way which will maximize customer satisfaction.
- Ensuring that the company's owners are sympathetic with overall objectives and are prepared to give the right level of financial and other support.

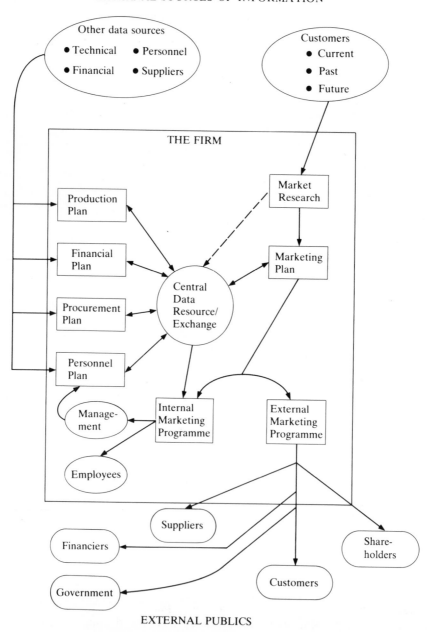

Figure 14.1 Marketing in the Corporate Environment

MARKET-BASED PLANNING

The marketing philosophy states that the customer and customer requirements should lie at the centre of all short-, medium- *and* long-term planning. Thus future product policy, market positioning, pricing strategy, service levels and distribution policy should take account of the market trends and the changing requirements and policies of customers. The marketing philosophy starts from the point that a company has a set of assets and management's task is to maximize the yield that those assets can produce both in the short and long term. At all times, however, the assets must be used to create benefits that customers want. Marketing staff are as intimately concerned with survival and development as the accountant and planner but neither of these has direct access to the source of future revenue—customers.

Once plans have been set the marketing department has the primary responsibility for daily dealing with customers. This includes direct selling, promotional programmes, image development campaigns and the feedback of information for tactical purposes and for further rounds of strategic analysis.

Planning and **implementation** are invariably separate activities but it is through the planning process that marketing feeds most into the overall corporate system. The day-to-day activities of all departments tend to be carried on separately but major dangers arise when company plans are struck without reference to market opportunities and development. Placing the customer in a secondary position at the planning stage invariably wrong-foots any subsequent marketing activity and sets up the tensions that are commonly observed between marketing and other functions within the organization.

To be fully effective marketing needs to play its part at the earliest stage of any planning process and must carry as much weight as financial, engineering and other considerations. It must be said, however, that with a few obvious and notable exceptions companies operating in the industrial sector have exhibited a reluctance to give marketing this degree of prominence in their corporate activities. There are many reasons for this of which the most significant are an unwillingness to break with traditional behavioural patterns, a firmly held belief that marketing is too costly relative to the benefits that it can yield and a complete lack of understanding of the role and objectives of marketing. Smaller organizations are more likely to relegate marketing to a secondary role than large organizations whose greater complexity gives rise to division of labour and specialization. Even so, admitting marketing personnel to the corporate charmed circle does not necessarily mean that they are listened to or given adequate resources to perform their tasks.

Within the company, therefore, it is clear that marketing has two priority tasks. The first is to sell itself into a position from which it can do the most good. The second is to market the company's goods and services to customers. Increasing importance is also being attached to the supplementary tasks which include marketing the company to its workforce and its owners. Both can improve performance and are logical extensions of the marketing function.

MARKETING MARKETING

Awareness of marketing is higher today than ever before. Business courses, seminars, books and even ministerial statements have stressed the role that marketing has to play in corporate development. Many professional courses such as accountancy now include a marketing component so that few business executives are completely ignorant on the subject. However, the evolution of marketing in the corporate environment places it at a disadvantage when it comes to playing a major role in companies. The importance of selling has been recognized since groups of individuals first started to trade with each other. A mechanism for disposing of output was the natural counterpart to the production resource and without it the unit would not survive for long. As competition intensified the need grew for harder and harder selling and the success of many industrial empires was in no small measure due to the power of their salesforces. Nevertheless, very few sales people rose to prominence in the industrial world to gain the levels of recognition accorded to notable engineers or industrial reformers. Indeed the reverse was too often the case. The attributes which made a successful salesman (commitment, ego-drive, sociability) made him suspect as a rounded business person. This view persists. Any simple association test carried out on the word 'salesman' is unlikely to produce many flattering results.

Most marketing departments have evolved out of an existing sales department and in doing so have acquired the image problems associated with selling. In fact some of the other marketing activities, such as advertising and public relations may have exacerbated the problem. It is not uncommon for marketing to be perceived as a flamboyant activity concerned more with the projection of concepts of dubious veracity than with serious day-to-day business life. The very need for an Advertising Standards Association and campaigns for truth in advertising confirms the worst fears of many.

At the same time marketing has a major problem in demonstrating its worth. The designer, the engineer and the accountant have tangible results to point to for their toils. The salesforce can point to sales performance but so much else in marketing is completely intangible. The image of a company takes considerable effort to describe let alone measure. The medium- and long-term positioning of the company in its market place can be made worthless overnight by substantial and unforeseen economic shifts. The very fact that marketing people state that they have to work in conjunction with other departments is seen as an admission that unlike the development of a worldbeating product, marketing cannot solve the company's problems alone and there are all too few examples available to refute the charge.

On the one hand marketing people are seen as so sharp that they might cut themselves; on the other too academic to make a tangible contribution to profits. These are formidable hurdles to overcome and where they exist it is not surprising that the marketing manager has a substantially harder task in convincing colleagues than will ever be the case with customers. Many fail, however, not because they lack the expertise but because they do not attempt the task. Recognition that a problem exists is the key step following which a programme to gain acceptance can be devised.

The objectives of an internal marketing programme are simple, namely obtaining recognition for marketing and access to financial and other resources required to make an adequate contribution to company development. As with all forms of marketing success the success of an internal marketing programme is dependent on the personnel involved, not the least the marketing manager or director. Weak marketing will, of course, be perpetuated by weak marketing staff who are consistently railroaded into submission by other and more powerful departments. The injection of a strong marketing manager into this situation has an element of chance about it unless the owner recognizes the problem and provides a solution. Internal marketing cannot begin in earnest until a manager sufficiently strong to undertake the programme is in place.

To carry out the programme effectively the manager must report directly to the board or to the owner. There should be no filter capable of blunting the message and diluting the perception of marketing's contribution. Once these criteria have been fulfilled the internal marketing programme can be set up and undertaken in the same way as any conventional marketing exercise. The steps are easy to describe but no one should be under the illusion that they are easy to implement or that success will be forthcoming quickly. Internal attitudes are hard to change and the ultimate rewards (status and income) are jealously fought over by others in the organization.

A comprehensive internal marketing programme will consist of the following elements:

- The publication of a policy statement showing the perceived role and objectives of the marketing department, the resources currently at its disposal and the resources required in order to carry out an efficient marketing programme on behalf of the company.
- The identification of the individuals most likely to block the development of a full marketing programme (the target audience).
- Description of the basis of their objections.
- The definition of an educational programme that will reduce, if not eliminate, their hostility.
- Identification of managers supportive of marketing activity and determination of the amount of influence they can exert.
- The use of the most persuasive marketing techniques to import the message that will favourably dispose the target audience towards marketing activity.

The techniques both for researching the situation and implementing the programme will consist largely of personal meetings at all layers of management. As with all services, selling by success story is the most powerful tool available and in this context success elsewhere is useful additional evidence to success within the organization itself. The basic copy for the campaign should be examples of how the marketing department, in concert with others in the company, has or can improve overall performance remembering that hard facts will cut more ice than theoretical statements. Simple things done well are likely to be more persuasive than complicated exercises which sound adventurous but have a high risk of failure.

If the most senior marketing employee is not on the board of the company, gaining a board position must be an important part of the marketing programme. The marketing manager seeking this objective risks being branded as an opportunist, but without a voice at board level there is little chance that any substantial degree of marketing orientation can be achieved.

EXERTING INFLUENCE

The most immediate way in which the marketing department can make its presence and usefulness felt is by providing information. If the company, as opposed to the marketing department alone, is to be customer orientated in its thinking then there must be some formal mechanism whereby information relating to customer requirements is fed to all interested parties within the organization. A key difference between a sales and a marketing organization is that the former regards customer information as useful only for its own proprietary requirements. The marketing organization recognizes that the customer must predominate in everybody's thinking and seeks to ensure not only that this is so but also that the right types and volumes of information are available at the right time.

Most executives will admit that there are many situations in which a lack of information hampers their ability to take decisions. The phrase 'If only we knew . . .' must be one of the most common heard in business environments and the greatest area of unknown is the external market. However, the problem can be so deep rooted that even data which are fairly readily available, such as sales records, are not analysed and circulated.

The establishment of an information system which circulates key data on customers to all interested parties is not only a useful step in demonstrating the utility of the marketing department but also lubricates the marketing process. Information systems at their simplest consist of regular statistics and qualitative information relating to performance, customer acceptance of the product, service requirements, new feature requirements, pricing trends and the competitive situation. The information may be acquired from a variety of sources and by a number of means providing it is accurate or at least that the accuracy limits are clearly stated. Distribution is normally in hard copy form but the electronic revolution is ensuring that both the dissemination and manipulation of information are becoming considerably faster and easier. In-house viewdata and microprocessor-based systems are finding a place even in industrial companies.

A major advantage of an information system is not only that the information is made available but also that all departments work off a common information base. Separately generated information for different purposes may be inconsistent and may also overlap so that at best the company pays twice or more for the same data, and at worst different departments are drawing conclusions from different data bases.

USING INFORMATION INTERNALLY

Although an essential precursor, making data available does not mean that they will be used. It will take time before the design engineer automatically consults sales reports on customers' reaction to the product before committing to design changes, or the accounts clerk consults a status report on a customer before pressing for payment of a previous invoice. This is the point at which the educational programme will be required.

Although a primary task of a good marketing department is to act as the eyes and ears for the company in the outside world it must also have the skills to make sure that the information is used profitably. If this does not happen the costs of information acquisition are wasted. To fulfil the educational need the department must first identify the problems which data can solve and, in addition, must suggest how they can be used. This is best done by means of briefing and workshops during which data are presented, applications for data are described and the problems of the recipient departments discussed. The result will invariably be requests for more information and the establishment of a regular reporting format. The scale and form of the meetings will vary according to whether they are set up for major strategic reviews or for regular operational decision making. Most business executives will know that large meetings are not conducive to achieving results and to be really effective the presenter of market data should work as much as possible on a one-for-one basis with the audience.

COORDINATION

The information system described above will inject marketing considerations into strategy formulation and into tactical decision making but will still not ensure that customer requirements are taken fully into account. As stated previously the marketing department should rank equally with production, purchasing, finance and personnel in order to perform adequately. If this is achieved an extra burden is automatically placed on the chief executive, since there will then be an added set of requirements which may be fundamentally incompatible with those of other departments. The result will be chaos unless there is a formal coordination procedure using the mechanisms of plans and budgets.

The very thought of a formal planning process is likely to be anathema to small organizations that pride themselves on their ability to react quickly to the market environment or any other opportunities that present themselves. But planning and flexibility are not incompatible since the latter can be built into the former. To miss out on an opportunity because it was not included in the plan or the budget would be criminal.

Without some statement of objectives and the means by which they are to be achieved, a company of any size is bound to be aimless. Obviously large organizations will require more complicated statements than small companies, though at divisional level the difference may not be so evident. The harmonizing element of any plan is the sales level that the company can expect to achieve during the planning period and the profits that can be expected to result from those sales. Sales are dependent on:

(a) the size of the market;
(b) the competitive environment;
(c) the ability of the company to produce;
(d) customer acceptance of the products;
(e) the company cost structure;
(f) the ability to offer differentiated advantages.

The above points are as much dependent on production, staffing and financial constraints as on the market place itself. The planning process rationalizes any conflicts and produces a unified statement of intent. If the market contains opportunistic elements an element of flexibility can be built into the plan.

The most important output from the plan is a set of budgets which show what each department is expected to produce and the resources that are to be deployed in that process. The marketing budget will show the sales revenue to be achieved and the personnel, financial and other resources that are to be deployed.

DAY-TO-DAY OPERATIONS

So far we have considered marketing in the context of strategic and tactical decision making but to be really effective the marketing message must penetrate more deeply into the organization than executives taking decisions. When Levitt stated that marketing was concerned with every nook and cranny of the organization he was not making an understatement. Every member of the firm has a marketing role, wittingly or unwittingly, since their performance, actions and statements can affect the ability of the firm to attract and hold customers. The offhand, slow or inarticulate telephonist, the uncooperative maintenance engineer and the van driver who is late can have just as devastating an effect on company performance as a defective or unsuitable product. These points are relatively obvious since each of the individuals mentioned has direct contact with customers, but every other member of the firm takes actions which affect customer satisfaction and many of these could be forgiven for ignoring the customer in their day-to-day activities. Such forgiveness cannot, however, be extended to a management system which fails to make the entire company aware of the importance of the market. The slogan 'customers make pay days possible' has to be extended to everybody.

In pursuing this objective and taking a leaf from Japanese industry, where worker participation in all aspects of management is considerably advanced, an increasing number of organizations are establishing quality control committees charged with the responsibility for ensuring that the importance of satisfying customers' requirements for quality, delivery and service are appreciated from the shop floor upwards. The committees include representatives from all of the major functions in order that a balanced view is projected. The role of the committee is not only to monitor activities and suggest means of improvement but also to consider the vexed question of incentives and motivation which will ensure that the staff always operate in the best interests of the company.

MARKETING TO STAFF

Most companies have progressed beyond the days when the workforce was considered one of the more difficult but versatile types of machine tool. In the more successful and stable organizations the gulf between management and workers has been bridged and cooperation achieved through the development of a strong working relationship. The respect for the manager who rolls up his sleeves and participates on the shop floor is immediately apparent. Unfortunately, although such action may be practical in the small organization, the gulf between workers and managers inevitably widens as companies grow in size. As the span from the top to the bottom of the organization widens personal contact diminishes, and the problem commonly encountered is that little else takes its place, except socially orientated employee relations programmes. The employee's requirement to feel part of the creative force is not diminished in large companies and there is considerable evidence that he or she will perform better if the reasons for doing so are known.

The techniques and skills that have been developed for inducing customers to buy have equal application in inducing employees to develop or maintain a favourable attitude towards the company. The payoff is an improvement in performance and profit which in some companies could well exceed the results derived from any external marketing activity.

To be effective an internal marketing plan must be constructed covering the same ground as an external plan. To do this a thorough understanding of staff attitudes and requirements is needed. Thus the ingredients of an internal marketing plan include research among employees, information requirement specification, the selection of the most effective communications techniques and their implementation. Advertising, direct mail and exhibitions have all been used to great effect in internal marketing campaigns as well as the more conventional techniques such as newsletters and journals.

MARKETING TO OWNERS

Owners represent another specific target audience for corporate messages, and marketing techniques have been increasingly deployed, particularly when the ownership is widely scattered (as in the case of large public companies). The owners' attitude can affect not only the share price and public standing of the company but also their acceptance of development plans, their willingness to provide additional funding or their level of toleration of poor performance.

A QUESTION OF SIZE

As a function marketing is poorly represented among small companies which might indicate that the discipline is the preserve of the large corporation and the conglomerate. Clearly the large company has greater need for specialized functions and division of labour but smaller companies have to compete on equal terms in the market place in order to make headway with customers. The fact that the total industrial universe is heavily biased towards small companies is no consolation since in aggregate they account for only a small proportion of sales.

In organizational terms the small company is better placed to market effectively than its larger competitor. The manager of a small firm is better placed to control what is going on and to ensure that the customer perspective permeates the company. A four-man furniture manufacturing company recently asked about the involvement of staff in marketing stated that everybody lent a hand. If all the staff of the company are involved in some way in directly servicing customers they are unlikely to forget them when they retire behind the scenes.

The problem in small companies is usually one of inadequate resources, a lack of marketing knowledge and insufficient time to plan the company's affairs properly. It is all too easy to ignore the future when there are problems in getting orders out of the factory. Nevertheless, the more limited horizons of smaller companies make their marketing task more manageable and relatively easily undertaken as a part-time function of the chief executive or manager. Lack of specialized knowledge requirement is not a valid excuse for failing to undertake marketing since this can always be obtained from external sources. For small companies there is even a variety of assistance programmes which will part fund the cost of acquiring such expertise.

CONCLUSION

Successful marketing requires that the principles permeate the very fabric of the corporate organization. The stand alone marketing department has a major contribution to make but for the customers' requirements to be taken fully into account all employees, management and operatives, must be aware of the contribution they have to make towards the creation of customer-satisfying benefits. The marketing system must, therefore, incorporate not only the external communication functions but also facilities for communicating market requirements to staff of other departments and the owners. This requirement is particularly prominent during corporate planning programmes but also extends to the normal day-to-day activities of the company.

FIFTEEN

MARKETING MYOPIA*

Theodore Levitt

Every major industry was once a growth industry. But some that are now riding a wave of growth enthusiasm are very much in the shadow of decline. Others which are thought of as seasoned growth industries have actually stopped growing. In every case the reason growth is threatened, slowed or stopped is *not* because the market is saturated. It is because there has been a failure of management.

FATEFUL PURPOSES

The failure is at the top. The executives responsible for it, in the last analysis, are those who deal with broad aims and policies. Thus:

The railroads did not stop growing because the need for passenger and freight transportation declined. That grew. The railroads are in trouble today not because the need was filled by others (cars, trucks, aeroplanes, even telephones), but because it was *not* filled by the railroads themselves. They let others take customers away from them because they assumed themselves to be in the railroad business rather than in the transportation business. The reason they defined their industry incorrectly was because they were railroad oriented instead of transportation oriented; they were product oriented instead of customer oriented.

Hollywood barely escaped being totally ravished by television. Actually, all the established film companies went through drastic reorganizations. Some simply disappeared. All of them got into trouble not because of TV's inroads but because of their own myopia. As with the railroads, Hollywood defined its business incorrectly. It thought it was the movie business. 'Movies' implied a specific, limited product. This produced a fatuous contentment which from the beginning led producers to view TV as a threat. Hollywood scorned and rejected TV when it should have welcomed it as an opportunity—an opportunity to expand the entertainment business.

Today TV is a bigger business than the old narrowly defined movie business ever was. Had Hollywood been customer oriented (providing entertainment), rather than product oriented (making movies), would it have gone through the fiscal purgatory that it did? I doubt it. What ultimately saved Hollywood and accounts for its recent resurgence was the wave of new young

---

* Reprinted by permission of the publishers from the *Harvard Business Review* (Cambridge, Mass., USA, July/August 1960).

writers, producers and directors whose previous successes in television had decimated the old movie companies and toppled the big movie moguls.

There are other less obvious examples of industries that have been and are now endangering their futures by improperly defining their purposes. I shall discuss some in detail later and analyse the kind of policies that lead to trouble. Right now it may help to show what a thoroughly customer-oriented management *can* do to keep a growth industry growing, even after the obvious opportunities have been exhausted; and here there are two examples that have been around for a long time. They are nylon and glass—specifically, E. I. Du Pont de Nemours & Company and Corning Glass Works.

Both companies have great technical competence. Their product orientation is unquestioned. But this alone does not explain their success. After all, who was more product oriented and product conscious than the erstwhile New England textile companies that have been so thoroughly massacred? The Du Ponts and the Cornings have succeeded not primarily because of their product or research orientation but because they have been thoroughly customer oriented also. It is constant watchfulness for opportunities to apply their technical know-how to the creation of customer-satisfying uses which accounts for their prodigious output of successful new products. Without a very sophisticated eye on the customer, most of their new products might have been wrong, their sales methods useless.

Aluminium has also continued to be a growth industry, thanks to the efforts of two wartime-created companies which deliberately set about creating new customer-satisfying uses. Without Kaiser Aluminium & Chemical Corporation and Reynolds Metals Company, the total demand for aluminium today would be vastly less than it is.

ERROR OF ANALYSIS

Some may argue that it is foolish to set the railroads off against aluminium or the movies off against glass. Are not aluminium and glass naturally so versatile that the industries are bound to have more growth opportunities than the railroads and movies? This view commits precisely the error I have been talking about. It defines an industry, or a product, or a cluster of know-how so narrowly as to guarantee its premature senescence. When we mention 'railroads', we should make sure we mean 'transportation'. As transporters, the railroads still have a good chance for very considerable growth. They are not limited to the railroad business as such (though in my opinion rail transportation is potentially a much stronger transportation medium than is generally believed).

What the railroads lack is not opportunity, but some of the same managerial imaginativeness and audacity that made them great. Even an amateur like Jacques Barzun can see what is lacking when he says:

'I grieve to see the most advanced physical and social organization of the last century go down in shabby disgrace for lack of the same comprehensive imagination that built it up. [What is lacking is] the will of the companies to survive and to satisfy the public by inventiveness and skill.'[1]

SHADOW OF OBSOLESCENCE

It is impossible to mention a single major industry that did not at one time qualify for the magic appellation of 'growth industry'. In each case its assumed strength lay in the apparently unchallenged superiority of its product. There appeared to be no effective substitute for it. It was itself a runaway substitute for the product it so triumphantly replaced. Yet one after another of these celebrated industries has come under a shadow. Let us look briefly at a few more of them, this time taking examples that have so far received a little less attention.

Dry cleaning This was once a growth industry with lavish prospects. In an age of wool garments, imagine being finally able to get them safely and easily clean. The boom was on.

Yet here we are thirty years after the boom started and the industry is in trouble. Where has the competition come from? From a better way of cleaning? No. It has come from synthetic fibres and chemical additives that have cut the need for dry cleaning. But this is only the beginning. Lurking in the wings and ready to make chemical dry cleaning totally obsolescent is that powerful magician, ultrasonics.

Electric utilities This is another one of those supposedly 'no-substitute' products that has been enthroned on a pedestal of invincible growth. When the incandescent lamp came along, kerosene lights were finished. Later the water wheel and the steam engine were cut to ribbons by the flexibility, reliability, simplicity and just plain easy availability of electric motors. The prosperity of electric utilities continues to wax extravagant as the home is converted into a museum of electric gadgetry. How can anybody miss by investing in utilities, with no competition, nothing but growth ahead?

But a second look is not quite so comforting. A score of non-utility companies are well advanced towards developing a powerful chemical fuel cell which could sit in some hidden closet of every home silently ticking off electric power. The electric lines that vulgarize so many neighbourhoods will be eliminated. So will the endless demolition of streets and service interruptions during storms. Also on the horizon is solar energy, again pioneered by non-utility companies.

Who says that the utilities have no competition? They may be natural monopolies now, but tomorrow they may be natural deaths. To avoid this prospect, they too will have to develop fuel cells, solar energy and other power sources. To survive, they themselves will have to plot the obsolescence of what now produces their livelihood.

Grocery stores Many people find it hard to realize that there ever was a thriving establishment known as the 'corner grocery store'. The supermarket has taken over with a powerful effectiveness. Yet the big food chains of the 1930s narrowly escaped being completely wiped out by the aggressive expansion of independent supermarkets. The first genuine supermarket was opened in 1930, in Jamaica, Long Island. By 1933 supermarkets were thriving in California Ohio, Pennsylvania, and elsewhere. Yet the established chains pompously ignored them. When they chose to notice them, it was with such derisive descriptions as 'cheapy', 'horse-and-buggy', 'cracker-barrel storekeeping' and 'unethical opportunists'.

The executive of one big chain announced at the time that he found it 'hard to believe that people will drive for miles to shop for foods and sacrifice the personal service chains have perfected and to which Mrs Consumer is accustomed'.[2] As late as 1936 the National Wholesale Grocers convention and the New Jersey Retail Grocers Association said there was nothing to fear. They said that the supers' narrow appeal to the price buyer limited the size of their market. They had to draw from miles around. When imitators came, there would be wholesale liquidations as volume fell. The current high sales of the supers was said to be partly due to their novelty. Basically people wanted convenient neighbourhood grocers. If the neighbourhood stores 'cooperate with their suppliers, pay attention to their costs, and improve their service' they would be able to weather the competition until it blew over.[3]

It never blew over. The chains discovered that survival required going into the supermarket business. This meant the wholesale destruction of their huge investments in corner store sites and in established distribution and merchandising methods. The companies with 'the courage of their convictions' resolutely stuck to the corner store philosophy. They kept their pride but lost their shirts.

SELF-DECEIVING CYCLE

But memories are short. For example, it is hard for people who today confidently hail the twin messiahs of electronics and chemicals to see how things could possibly go wrong with these galloping industries. They probably also cannot see how a reasonably sensible business man could have been as myopic as the famous Boston millionaire who 50 years ago unintentionally sentenced his heirs to poverty by stipulating that his entire estate be for ever invested exclusively in electric streetcar securities. His posthumous declaration, 'There will always be a big demand for efficient urban transportation', is no consolation to his heirs who sustain life by pumping gasoline at automobile filling stations.

Yet, in a causal survey I recently took among a group of intelligent business executives, nearly half agreed that it would be hard to hurt their heirs by tying their estates for ever to the electronics industry. When I then confronted them with the Boston streetcar example, they chorused unanimously, 'That's different!' But is it? Is not the basic situation identical?

In truth *there is no such thing* as a growth industry, I believe. There are only companies organized and operated to create and capitalize on growth opportunities. Industries that assume themselves to be riding some automatic growth escalator invariably descend into stagnation. The history of every dead and dying 'growth' industry shows a self-deceiving cycle of bountiful expansion and undetected decay. There are four conditions which usually guarantee this cycle:

1. The belief that growth is assured by an expanding and more affluent population.
2. The belief that there is no competitive substitute for the industry's major product.
3. Too much faith in mass production and in the advantages of rapidly declining unit costs as output rises.
4. Preoccupation with a product that lends itself to carefully controlled scientific experimentation, improvement and manufacturing cost reduction.

I should like now to begin examining each of these conditions in some detail. To build my case as boldly as possible, I shall illustrate the points with reference to three industries—petroleum, automobiles and electronics—particularly petroleum, because it spans more years and more vicissitudes. Not only do these three have excellent reputations with the general public and also enjoy the confidence of sophisticated investors, but their managements have become known for progressive thinking in areas like financial control, product research, and management training. If obsolescence can cripple even these industries, it can happen anywhere.

POPULATION MYTH

The belief that profits are assured by an expanding and more affluent population is dear to the heart of every industry. It takes the edge off the apprehensions everybody understandably feels about the future. If consumers are multiplying and also buying more of your product or service, you can face the future with considerably more comfort than if the market is shrinking. An expanding market keeps the manufacturer from having to think very hard or imaginatively. If thinking is an intellectual response to a problem, then the absence of a problem leads to the absence of thinking. If your product has an automatically expanding market, then you will not give much thought to how to expand it.

One of the most interesting examples of this is provided by the petroleum industry. Probably our oldest growth industry, it has an enviable record. While there are some current apprehensions about its growth rate, the industry itself tends to be optimistic. But I believe it can be demonstrated that it is undergoing a fundamental yet typical change. It is not only ceasing to be a growth industry, but may actually be a declining one, relative to other business. Although there is widespread unawareness of it, I believe that within twenty-five years the oil industry may find itself in much the same position of retrospective glory that the railroads are now in. Despite its pioneering work in developing and applying the present value method of investment evaluation, in employee relations and in working with backward countries, the petroleum business is a distressing example of how complacency and wrongheadedness can stubbornly convert opportunity into near disaster.

One of the characteristics of this and other industries that have believed very strongly in the beneficial consequences of an expanding population, while at the same time being industries with a generic product for which there has appeared to be no competitive substitute, is that the individual companies have sought to outdo their competitors by improving on what they are already doing. This makes sense, of course, if one assumes that sales are tied to the country's population strings, because the customer can compare products only on a feature-by-feature basis. I believe it is significant, for example, that not since John D. Rockefeller sent free kerosene lamps to China has the oil industry done anything really outstanding to create a demand for its product. Not even in product improvement has it showered itself with eminence. The greatest single improvement, namely, the development of tetraethyl lead, came from outside the industry, specifically from General Motors and Du Pont. The big contributions made by the industry itself are confined to the technology of oil exploration, production and refining.

ASKING FOR TROUBLE

In other words, the industry's efforts have focused on improving the *efficiency* of getting and making its product, not really on improving the generic product or its marketing. Moreover, its chief product has continuously been defined in the narrowest possible terms, namely, gasoline, not energy, fuel or transportation.

This attitude has helped assure that major improvements in gasoline quality tend not to originate in the oil industry. Also, the development of superior alternative fuels comes from outside the oil industry, as will be shown later.

Major innovations in automobile fuel marketing are originated by small new oil companies that are not primarily preoccupied with production or refining. These are the companies that have been responsible for the rapidly expanding multipump gasoline stations, with their successful emphasis on large and clean layouts, rapid and efficient driveway service, and quality gasoline at low prices.

Thus, the oil industry is asking for trouble from outsiders. Sooner or later, in this land of hungry inventors and entrepreneurs, a threat is sure to come. The possibilities of this will become more apparent when we turn to the next dangerous belief of many managements. For the sake of continuity, because this second belief is tied closely to the first, I shall continue with the same example.

IDEA OF INDISPENSABILITY

The petroleum industry is pretty much persuaded that there is no competitive substitute for its major product, gasoline—or if there is, that it will continue to be a derivative of crude oil, such as diesel fuel or kerosene jet fuel.

There is a lot of automatic wishful thinking in this assumption. The trouble is that most refining companies own huge amounts of crude oil reserves. These have value only if there is a market for products into which oil can be converted—hence the tenacious belief in the continuing competitive superiority of automobile fuels made from crude oil.

This idea persists despite all historic evidence against it. The evidence not only shows that oil has never been a superior product for any purpose for very long, but it also shows that the oil industry has never really been a growth industry. It has been a succession of different businesses that have gone through the usual historic cycles of growth, maturity and decay. Its overall survival is owed to a series of miraculous escapes from total obsolescence, of last-minute and unexpected reprieves from total disaster reminiscent of the *Perils of Pauline*.

PERILS OF PETROLEUM

I shall sketch in only the main episodes. First, crude oil was largely a patent medicine. But even before that fad ran out, demand was greatly expanded by the use of oil in kerosene lamps. The prospect of lighting the world's lamps gave rise to an extravagant promise of growth. The prospects were similar to those the industry now holds for gasoline in other parts of the world. It can hardly wait for the underdeveloped nations to get a car in every garage.

In the days of the kerosene lamp, the oil companies competed with each other and against gaslight by trying to improve the illuminating characteristics of kerosene. Then suddenly the impossible happened. Edison invented a light which was totally non-dependent on crude oil. Had it not been for the growing use of kerosene in space heaters, the incandescent lamp would have completely finished oil as a growth industry at that time. Oil would have been good for little else than axle grease.

Then disaster and reprieve struck again. Two great innovations occurred, neither originating in the oil industry. The successful development of coal-burning domestic central-heating systems made the space heater obsolescent. While the industry reeled, along came its most magnificent boost yet—the internal combustion engine, also invented by outsiders. Then when the prodigious expansion for gasoline finally began to level off in the 1920s, along came the miraculous escape of a central oil heater. Once again, the escape was provided by an outsider's invention and development. And when that market weakened, wartime demand for aviation fuel came to the rescue. After the war the expansion of civilian aviation, the dieselization of railroads and the explosive demand for cars and trucks kept the industry's growth in high gear.

Meanwhile centralized oil heating—whose boom potential had only recently been proclaimed—ran into severe competition from natural gas. While the oil companies themselves owned the gas that now competed with their oil, the industry did not originate the natural gas revolution, nor has it to this day greatly profited from its gas ownership. The gas revolution was made by newly formed transmission companies that marketed the product with an aggressive ardour. They started a magnificent new industry, first against the advice and then against the resistance of the oil companies.

By all the logic of the situation, the oil companies themselves should have made the gas revolution. They not only owned the gas; they also were the only people experienced in handling, scrubbing and using it, the only people experienced in pipeline technology and transmission, and they understood heating problems. But, partly because they knew that natural gas would compete with their own sale of heating oil, the oil companies pooh-poohed the potentials of gas.

The revolution was finally started by oil pipeline executives who, unable to persuade their own companies to go into gas, quit and organized the spectacularly successful gas transmission companies. Even after their success became painfully evident to the oil companies, the latter did not go into gas transmission. The multibillion dollar business which should have been theirs went to others. As in the past, the industry was blinded by its narrow preoccupation with a specific product and the value of its reserves. It paid little or no attention to its consumers' basic needs and preferences.

The postwar years have not witnessed any change. Immediately after World War II the oil industry was greatly encouraged about its future by the rapid expansion of demand for its traditional line of products. In 1950 most companies projected annual rates of domestic expansion of around 6 per cent through at least to 1975. Though the ratio of crude oil reserves to demand in the Free World was about 20 to 1, with 10 to 1 being usually considered a reasonable working ratio in the United States, booming demand sent oil men searching for more without sufficient regard to what the future really promised. In 1952 they 'hit' in the Middle East; the ratio skyrocketed to 42 to 1. If gross additions to reserves continue at the average rate of the past five years (thirty-seven billion barrels annually), then by 1970 the reserve ratio will be up to 45 to 1. This abundance of oil has weakened crude and product prices all over the world.

UNCERTAIN FUTURE

Management cannot find much consolation today in the rapidly expanding petrochemical industry, another oil-using idea that did not originate in the leading firms. The total United States' production of petrochemicals is equivalent to about 2 per cent (by volume) of the demand for all petroleum products. Although the petrochemical industry is now expected to grow by about 10 per cent per year, this will not offset other drains on the growth of crude oil consumption. Furthermore, while petrochemical products are many and growing, it is well to remember that there are non-petroleum sources of the basic raw material, such as coal. Besides, a lot of plastics can be produced with relatively little oil. A fifty-thousand-barrel-per-day oil refinery is now considered the absolute minimum size for efficiency. But a five-thousand-barrel-per-day chemical plant is a giant operation.

Oil has never been a continuously strong growth industry. It has grown by fits and starts, always miraculously saved by innovations and developments not of its own making. The reason it has not grown in a smooth progression is that each time it thought it had a superior product safe from the possibility of competitive substitutes, the product turned out to be inferior and notoriously subject to obsolescence. Until now, gasoline (for motor fuel, anyhow) has escaped this fate. But, as we shall see later, it too may be on its last legs.

The point of all this is that there is no guarantee against product obsolescence. If a company's own research does not make it obsolete, another's will. Unless an industry is especially lucky, as oil has been until now, it can easily go down in a sea of red figures—just as the railroads have, as the buggy whip manufacturers have, as the corner grocery chains have, as most of the big movie companies have and indeed as many other industries have.

The best way for a firm to be lucky is to make its own luck. That requires knowing what makes a business successful. One of the greatest enemies of this knowledge is mass production.

PRODUCTION PRESSURES

Mass-production industries are impelled by a great drive to produce all they can. The prospect of steeply declining unit costs as output rises is more than most companies can usually resist. The profit possibilities look spectacular. All effort focuses on production. The result is that marketing gets neglected.

John Kenneth Galbraith contends that just the opposite occurs.[4] Output is so prodigious that all effort concentrates on trying to get rid of it. He says this accounts for singing commercials, desecration of the countryside with advertising signs and other wasteful and vulgar practices. Galbraith has a finger on something real, but he misses the strategic point. Mass production does indeed generate great pressure to 'move' the product. But what usually gets emphasized is selling, not marketing. Marketing, being a more sophisticated and complex process, gets ignored.

The difference between marketing and selling is more than semantic. Selling focuses on the needs of the seller, marketing on the needs of the buyer. Selling is preoccupied with the seller's need to convert his product into cash; marketing with the idea of satisfying the needs of the customer by means of the product and the whole cluster of things associated with creating, delivering, and finally consuming it.

In some industries the enticements of full mass production have been so powerful that for many years top management in effect has told the sales departments, 'You get rid of it; we'll worry about profits'. By contrast a truly marketing-minded firm tries to create value-satisfying goods and services that consumers will want to buy. What it offers for sale includes not only the generic product or service, but also how it is made available to the customer, in what form, when, under what conditions and at what terms of trade. Most important, what it offers for sale is determined not by the seller but by the buyer. The seller takes his cues from the buyer in such a way that the product becomes a consequence of the marketing effort, not vice versa.

LAG IN DETROIT

This may sound like an elementary rule of business, but that does not keep it from being violated wholesale. It is certainly more violated than honoured. Take the automobile industry.

Here mass production is most famous, most honoured and has the greatest impact on the entire society. The industry has hitched its fortune to the relentless requirements of the annual model change, a policy that makes customer orientation an especially urgent necessity. Consequently the auto companies annually spend millions of dollars on consumer research. But the fact that the new compact cars are selling so well in their first year indicates that Detroit's vast researches have for a long time failed to reveal what the customer really wanted. Detroit was not persuaded that he wanted anything different from what he had been getting until it lost millions of customers to other small car manufacturers.

How could this unbelievable lag behind consumer wants have been perpetuated so long? Why did not research reveal consumer preferences before consumers' buying decisions themselves revealed the facts? Is that not what consumer research is for—to find out before the fact what is going to happen? The answer is that Detroit never really researched the customer's wants. It only researched his preferences between the kinds of things which it had already decided to offer him. For Detroit is mainly product oriented, not customer oriented. To the extent that the customer is recognized as having needs that the manufacturer should try to satisfy, Detroit usually acts as if the job can be done entirely by product changes. Occasionally attention gets paid to financing, too, but that is done more in order to sell than to enable the customer to buy.

As for taking care of other customer needs, there is not enough being done to write about.

The areas of the greatest unsatisfied needs are ignored, or at best get stepchild attention. These are at the point of sale and on the matter of automotive repair and maintenance. Detroit views these problem areas as being of secondary importance. That is underscored by the fact that the retailing and servicing ends of this industry are neither owned and operated nor controlled by the manufacturers. Once the car is produced, things are pretty much in the dealer's inadequate hands. Illustrative of Detroit's arm's-length attitude is the fact that, while servicing holds enormous sales-stimulating, profit-building opportunities, only fifty-seven of Chevrolet's seven thousand dealers provide night maintenance service.

Motorists repeatedly express their dissatisfaction with servicing and their apprehensions about buying cars under the present selling setup. The anxieties and problems they encounter during the auto buying and maintenance processes are probably more intense and widespread today than thirty years ago. Yet the automobile companies do not seem to listen to or take their cues from the anguished consumer. If they do listen, it must be through the filter of their own preoccupation with production. The marketing effort is still viewed as a necessary consequence of the product, not vice versa, as it should be. That is the legacy of mass production, with its parochial view that profit resides essentially in low-cost full production.

WHAT FORD PUT FIRST

The profit lure of mass production obviously has a place in the plans and strategy of business management, but it must always *follow* hard thinking about the customer. This is one of the most important lessons that we can learn from the contradictory behaviour of Henry Ford. In a sense Ford was both the most brilliant and the most senseless marketer in American history. He was senseless because he refused to give the customer anything but a black car. He was brilliant because he fashioned a production system designed to fit market needs. We habitually celebrate him for the wrong reason, his production genius. His real genius was marketing. We think he was able to cut his selling price and therefore sell millions of $500 cars because his invention of the assembly line had reduced the costs. Actually he invented the assembly line because he had concluded that at $500 he could sell millions of cars. Mass production was the *result* not the cause of his low prices.

Ford repeatedly emphasized this point, but a nation of production-oriented business managers refuses to hear the great lesson he taught. Here is his operating philosophy as he expressed it succinctly:

'Our policy is to reduce the price, extend the operations and improve the article. You will notice that the reduction of price comes first. We have never considered any costs as fixed. Therefore we first reduce the price to the point where we believe more sales will result. Then we go ahead and try to make the prices. We do not bother about the costs. The new price forces the costs down. The more usual way is to take the costs and then determine the price, and although that method may be scientific in the narrow sense; it is not scientific in the broad sense, because what earthly use is it to know the cost if it tells you that you cannot manufacture at a price at which the article can be sold? But more to the point is the fact that, although one may calculate what a cost is, and of course all of our costs are carefully calculated, no one knows what a cost ought to be. One of the ways of discovering . . . is to name a price so low as to force everybody in the place to the highest point of efficiency. The low price makes everybody dig for profits. We make more discoveries concerning manufacturing and selling under this forced method than by any method of leisurely investigation.'[5]

PRODUCT PROVINCIALISM

The tantalizing profit possibilities of low unit production costs may be the most seriously self-deceiving attitude that can afflict a company, particularly a 'growth' company where an apparently assured expansion of demand already tends to undermine a proper concern for the importance of marketing and the customer.

The usual result of this narrow preoccupation with so-called concrete matters is that instead of growing, the industry declines. It usually means that the product fails to adapt to the constantly changing patterns of consumer needs and tastes, to new and modified marketing institutions and practices or to product developments in competing or complementary industries. The industry has its eyes so firmly on its own specific product that it does not see how it is being made obsolete.

The classical example of this is the buggy whip industry. No amount of product improvement could stave off its death sentence. But had the industry defined itself as being in the transportation business rather than the buggy whip business, it might have survived. It would have done what survival always entails, that is, changing. Even if it had only defined its business as providing a stimulant or catalyst to an energy source, it might have survived by becoming a manufacturer of, say, fanbelts or air cleaners.

What may some day be a still more classical example is, again, the oil industry. Having let others steal marvellous opportunities from it (for example, natural gas, as already mentioned, missile fuels and jet engine lubricants), one would expect it to have taken steps never to let that happen again. But this is not the case. We are now getting extraordinary new developments in fuel systems specifically designed to power automobiles. Not only are these developments concentrated in firms outside the petroleum industry, but petroleum is almost systematically ignoring them, securely content in its wedded bliss to oil. It is the story of the kerosene lamp versus the incandescent lamp all over again. Oil is trying to improve hydrocarbon fuels rather than to develop *any* fuels best suited to the needs of their users, whether or not made in different ways and with different raw materials from oil.

Here are some of the things which non-petroleum companies are working on.

Over a dozen such firms now have advanced working models of energy systems which, when perfected, will replace the internal combustion engine and eliminate the demand for gasoline. The superior merit of each of these systems is their elimination of frequent, time-consuming, and irritating refuelling stops. Most of these systems are fuel cells designed to create electrical energy directly from chemicals without combustion. Most of them use chemicals that are not derived from oil, generally hydrogen and oxygen.

Several other companies have advanced models of electric storage batteries designed to power automobiles. One of these is an aircraft producer that is working jointly with several electric utility companies. The latter hope to use off-peak generating capacity to supply overnight, plug-in battery regeneration. Another company, also using the battery approach, is a medium-size electronics firm with extensive small-battery experience that it developed in connection with its work on hearing aids. It is collaborating with an automobile manufacturer. Recent improvements arising from the need for high-powered miniature power storage plants in rockets have put us within reach of a relatively small battery capable of withstanding great overloads or surges of power. Germanium diode applications and batteries using sintered-plate and nickel–cadmium techniques promise to make a revolution in our energy sources.

Solar energy conversion systems are also getting increasing attention. One usually cautious Detroit auto executive recently ventured that solar-powered cars might be common by 1980.

As for the oil companies, they are more or less 'watching developments', as one research director put it to me. A few are doing a bit of research on fuel cells, but almost always confined to developing cells powered by hydrocarbon chemicals. None of them are enthusiastically researching fuel cells, batteries or solar power plants. None of them are spending a fraction as much on research in these profoundly important areas as they are on the usual run-of-the-mill things like reducing combustion chamber deposit in gasoline engines. One major integrated petroleum company recently took a tentative look at the fuel cell and concluded that although 'the companies actively working on it indicate a belief in ultimate success . . . the timing and magnitude of its impact are too remote to warrant recognition in our forecasts'.

One might, of course, ask: Why should the oil companies do anything different? Would not chemical fuel cells, batteries or solar energy kill the present product lines? The answer is that they would indeed, and that is precisely the reason for the oil firms having to develop these power units before their competitors, so they will not be companies without an industry.

Management might be more likely to do what is needed for its own preservation if it thought of itself as being in the energy business. But even that would not be enough if it persists in imprisoning itself in the narrow grip of its tight product orientation. It has to think of itself as taking care of customer needs, not finding, refining or even selling oil. Once it genuinely thinks of its business as taking care of people's transportation needs, nothing can stop it from creating its own extravagantly profitable growth.

'CREATIVE DESTRUCTION'

Since words are cheap and deeds are dear, it may be appropriate to indicate what this kind of thinking involves and leads to. Let us start at the beginning—the customer. It can be shown that motorists strongly dislike the bother, delay and experience of buying gasoline. People actually do not buy gasoline. They cannot see it, taste it, feel it, appreciate it or really test it. What they buy is the right to continue driving their cars. The gas station is like a tax collector to whom people are compelled to pay a periodic toll as the price of using their cars. This makes the gas station a basically unpopular institution. It can never be made popular or pleasant, only less unpopular, less unpleasant.

To reduce its unpopularity completely means eliminating it. Nobody likes a tax collector, not even a pleasantly cheerful one. Nobody likes to interrupt a trip to buy a phantom product, not even from a handsome Adonis or a seductive Venus. Hence, companies that are working on exotic fuel substitutes which will eliminate the need for frequent refuelling are heading directly into the outstretched arms of the irritated motorist. They are riding a wave of inevitability, not because they are creating something which is technologically superior or more sophisticated, but because they are satisfying a powerful customer need. They are also eliminating noxious odours and air pollution.

Once the petroleum companies recognize the customer-satisfying logic of what another power system can do, they will see that they have no more choice about working on an efficient, long-lasting fuel (or some way of delivering present fuels without bothering the motorist) than the big food chains had a choice about going into the supermarket business, or the vacuum tube companies had a choice about making semiconductors. For their own good the oil firms will have to destroy their own highly profitable assets. No amount of wishful thinking can save them from the necessity of engaging in this form of 'creative destruction'.

I phrase the need as strongly as this because I think management must make quite an effort to break itself loose from conventional ways. It is all too easy in this day and age for a company or industry to let its sense of purpose become dominated by the economies of full production and to develop a dangerously lopsided product orientation. In short, if management lets itself drift, it invariably drifts in the direction of thinking of itself as producing goods and services, not customer satisfaction. While it probably will not descend to the depths of telling its salesmen, 'You get rid of it; we'll worry about profits', it can, without knowing it, be practising precisely that formula for withering decay. The historic fate of one growth industry after another has been its suicidal product provincialism.

DANGERS OF R & D

Another big danger to a firm's continued growth arises when top management is wholly transfixed by the profit possibilities of technical research and development. To illustrate I shall turn first to a new industry—electronics—and then return once more to the oil companies. By comparing a fresh example with a familiar one, I hope to emphasize the prevalence and insidiousness of a hazardous way of thinking.

MARKETING SHORTCHANGED

In the case of electronics, the greatest danger which faces the glamorous new companies in this field is not that they do not pay enough attention to research and development, but that they pay *too much* attention to it. And the fact that the fastest growing electronics firms owe their eminence to their heavy emphasis on technical research is completely beside the point. They have vaulted to affluence on a sudden crest of unusually strong general receptiveness to new technical ideas. Also, their success has been shaped in the virtually guaranteed market of military subsidies and by military orders that in many cases actually preceded the existence of facilities to make the products. Their expansion has, in other words, been almost totally devoid of marketing effort.

Thus, they are growing up under conditions that come dangerously close to creating the illusion that a superior product will sell itself. Having created a successful company by making a superior product, it is not surprising that management continues to be oriented towards the product rather than the people who consume it. It develops the philosophy that continued growth is a matter of continued product innovation and improvement.

A number of other factors tend to strengthen and sustain this belief:

1. Because electronic products are highly complex and sophisticated, managements become top-heavy with engineers and scientists. This creates a selective bias in favour of research and production at the expense of marketing. The organization tends to view itself as making things rather than satisfying customer needs. Marketing gets treated as a residual activity, 'something else' that must be done once the vital job of product creation and production is completed.
2. To this bias in favour of product research, development and production is added the bias in favour of dealing with controllable variables. Engineers and scientists are at home in the world of concrete things like machines, test tubes, production lines, and even balance sheets. The abstractions to which they feel kindly are those which are testable or manipulatable in the laboratory, or, if not testable, then functional, such as Euclid's axioms. In short, the managements of the new glamour-growth companies tend to favour those business activities which lend themselves to careful study, experimentation and control—the hard, practical realities of the lab, the shop, the books.

What gets shortchanged are the realities of the **market**. Consumers are unpredictable, varied, fickle, stupid, shortsighted, stubborn and generally bothersome. This is not what the engineer-managers say, but deep down in their consciousness it is what they believe. And this accounts for their concentrating on what they know and what they can control, namely, product research, engineering and production. The emphasis on production becomes particularly attractive when the product can be made at declining unit costs. There is no more inviting way of making money than by running the plant full blast.

Today the top-heavy science–engineering production orientation of so many electronics companies works reasonably well because they are pushing into new frontiers in which the armed services have pioneered virtually assured markets. The companies are in the felicitous position of having to fill, not find, markets; of not having to discover what the customer needs and wants, but of having the customer voluntarily come forward with specific new product demands. If a team of consultants had been assigned specifically to design a business situation calculated to prevent the emergence and development of a customer-oriented marketing viewpoint, it could not have produced anything better than the conditions just described.

STEPCHILD TREATMENT

The oil industry is a stunning example of how science, technology and mass production can divert an entire group of companies from their main task. To the extent the consumer is studied at all (which is not much), the focus is for ever on getting information which is designed to help the oil companies improve what they are now doing. They try to discover more convincing advertising themes, more effective sales promotional drives, what the market shares of the various companies are, what people like or dislike about service station dealers and oil companies, and so forth. Nobody seems as interested in probing deeply into the basic human needs that the industry might be trying to satisfy as in probing into the basic properties of the raw material that the companies work with in trying to deliver customer satisfactions.

Basic questions about customers and markets seldom get asked. The latter occupy a stepchild status. They are recognized as existing, as having to be taken care of, but not worth very much real thought or dedicated attention. Nobody gets as excited about the customers in his own backyard as about the oil in the Sahara Desert. Nothing illustrates better the neglect of marketing than its treatment in the industry press.

The centennial issue of the *American Petroleum Institute Quarterly*, published in 1959 to celebrate the discovery of oil in Titusville, Pennsylvania, contained twenty-one feature articles proclaiming the industry's greatness. Only one of these talked about its achievements in marketing, and that was only a pictorial record of how service station architecture has changed. The issue also contained a special section on 'New Horizons', which was devoted to showing the magnificent role oil would play in America's future. Every reference was ebulliently optimistic, never implying once that oil might have some hard competition. Even the reference to atomic energy was a cheerful catalogue of how oil would help make atomic energy a success. There was not a single apprehension that the oil industry's affluence might be threatened or a suggestion that one 'new horizon' might include new and better ways of serving oil's present customers.

But the most revealing example of the stepchild treatment that marketing gets was still another special series of short articles on 'The Revolutionary Potential of Electronics'. Under that heading this list of articles appeared in the table of contents: 'In the Search for Oil', 'In Production Operations', 'In Refinery Processes', 'In Pipeline Operations'.

Significantly, every one of the industry's major functional areas is listed, *except* marketing. Why? Either it is believed that electronics holds no revolutionary potential for petroleum marketing (which is palpably wrong), or the editors forgot to discuss marketing (which is more likely, and illustrates its stepchild status).

The order in which the four functional areas are listed also betrays the alienation of the oil industry from the consumer. The industry is implicitly defined as beginning with the search for oil and ending with its distribution from the refinery. But the truth is, it seems to me, that the industry begins with the needs of the customer for its products. From the primal position its definition moves steadily backstream to areas of progressively lesser importance, until it finally comes to rest at the 'search for oil'.

BEGINNING AND END

The view that an industry is a customer-satisfying process, not a goods-producing process, is vital for all business men to understand. An industry begins with the customer and his needs, not with a patent, a raw material or a selling skill. Given the customer's needs, the industry develops backwards, first concerning itself with the physical *delivery* of customer satisfactions. Then it moves back further to *creating* the things by which these satisfactions are in part achieved. How these materials are created is a matter of indifference to the customer, hence the particular form of manufacturing processing or what-have-you cannot be considered as a vital aspect of the industry. Finally, the industry moves back still further to *finding* the raw materials necessary for making its products.

The irony of some industries oriented towards technical research and development is that the scientists who occupy the high executive positions are totally unscientific when it comes to defining their companies' overall needs and purposes. They violate the first two rules of the scientific method—being aware of and defining their companies' problems, and then developing testable hypotheses about solving them. They are scientific only about the convenient things, such as laboratory and product experiments. The reason that the customer (and the satisfaction of his deepest needs) is not considered as being 'the problem' is not because there is any certain belief that no such problem exists, but because an organizational lifetime has conditioned management to look in the opposite direction. Marketing is a stepchild.

I do not mean that selling is ignored. Far from it. But selling, again, is not marketing. As already pointed out, selling concerns itself with the tricks and techniques of getting people to exchange their cash for your product. It is not concerned with the values that the exchange is all about. And it does not, as marketing invariably does, view the entire business process as consisting of a tightly integrated effort to discover, create, arouse and satisfy customer needs. The customer is somebody 'out there' who, with proper cunning, can be separated from his loose change.

Actually, not even selling gets much attention in some technologically minded firms. Because there is a virtually guaranteed market for the abundant flow of their new products, they do not actually know what a real market is. It is as if they lived in a planned economy, moving their products routinely from factory to retail outlet. Their successful concentration on products tends to convince them of the soundness of what they have been doing, and they fail to see the gathering clouds over the market.

CONCLUSIONS

Less than seventy-five years ago American railroads enjoyed a fierce loyalty among astute Wall Streeters. European monarchs invested in them heavily. Eternal wealth was thought to be the benediction for anybody who could scrape a few thousand dollars together to put into rail stocks. No other form of transportation could compete with the railroads in speed, flexibility, durability, economy and growth potentials. As Jacques Barzun put it, 'By the turn of the century it was an institution, an image of man, a tradition, a code of honour, a source of poetry, a nursery of boyhood desires, a sublimest of toys, and the most solemn machine—next to the funeral hearse—that marks the epochs in man's life.'[6]

Even after the advent of automobiles, trucks and aeroplanes, the railroad tycoons remained imperturbably self-confident. If you had told them sixty years ago that in thirty years they would be flat on their backs, broke, and pleading for government subsidies, they would have thought you totally demented. Such a future was simply not considered possible. It was not even a discussible subject, or an askable question, or a matter which any sane person would consider worth speculating about. The very thought was insane. Yet a lot of insane notions now have matter-of-fact acceptance—for example, the idea of 100-ton tubes of metal moving smoothly through the air 20 000 feet above the earth, loaded with 100 sane and solid citizens casually drinking martinis—and they have dealt cruel blows to the railroads.

What specifically must other companies do to avoid this fate? What does customer orientation involve? These questions have in part been answered by the preceding examples and analysis. It would take another article to show in detail what is required for specific industries. In any case, it should be obvious that building an effective customer-oriented company involves far more than good intentions or promotional tricks; it involves profound matters of human organization and leadership. For the present, let me merely suggest what appear to be some general requirements.

VISCERAL FEEL OF GREATNESS

Obviously the company has to do what survival demands. It has to adapt to the requirements of the market, and it has to do it sooner rather than later. But mere survival is a so-so aspiration. Anybody can survive in some way or other, even the skid-row bum. The trick is to survive gallantly, to feel the surging impulse of commercial mastery; not just to experience the sweet smell of success, but to have the visceral feel of entrepreneurial greatness.

No organization can achieve greatness without a vigorous leader who is driven onward by his own pulsating **will to succeed**. He has to have a vision of grandeur, a vision that can produce eager followers in vast numbers. In business, the followers are the customers. To produce these customers, the entire corporation must be viewed as a customer-creating and customer-satisfying organism. Management must think of itself not as producing products but as providing customer-creating value satisfactions. It must push this idea (and everything it means and requires) into every nook and cranny of the organization. It has to do this continuously and with the kind of flair that excites and stimulates the people in it. Otherwise, the company will be merely a series of pigeonholed parts, with no consolidating sense of purpose or direction.

In short, the organization must learn to think of itself not as producing goods or services but as **buying customers**, as doing the things that will make people *want* to do business with it. And the chief executive himself has the inescapable responsibility for creating this environment, this viewpoint, this attitude, this aspiration. He himself must set the company's style, its direction and its goals. This means he has to know precisely where he himself wants to go, and to make sure the whole organization is enthusiastically aware of where that is. This is a first requisite of leadership, for **unless he knows where he is going, any road will take him there**.

If any road is okay, the chief executive might as well pack his attaché case and go fishing. If an organization does not know or care where it is going, it does not need to advertise that fact with a ceremonial figurehead. Everybody will notice it soon enough.

REFERENCES

1. Barzun, Jacques. 'Trains and the mind of man', *Holiday*, Curtiss Publishing Co., Philadelphia 1960, p. 21.
2. Zimmerman, M. M. *The Super Market: A Revolution in Distribution*, McGraw-Hill, New York 1955, p. 48.
3. Ibid., pp. 45–47.
4. Galbraith, J. K. *The Affluent Society*, Houghton Mifflin, Boston 1958, pp. 152–60.
5. Ford, Henry. *My Life and Work*, Doubleday, Page & Co., New York 1923, pp. 146–47.
6. Barzun, Jacques. Op. cit., p. 20.

MARKETING MANAGERS AND THEIR DEVELOPMENT

Norman A. Hart

The time has gone when marketing managers were no more than sales managers who had changed the titles on their doors, and then continued to do precisely the same job as before.

The function of marketing management is now firmly established alongside finance, R & D, production, personnel and purchasing. It is, however, the youngest of the major management functions and its recognition is less among industrial product and service companies than it is in the general consumer field. There still exist then companies having a sales director and no marketing director, and even more difficult to understand, a few with both a sales director and a marketing director.

Turning to the 'development' of such managers there is nothing fundamentally different here from any other function. The starting point then is with management in general, and here a recent comment on future needs makes relevant points.

> The first is that the job of managing is going to be even more difficult in the future than in the past, and this applies to all sectors and all sizes of enterprise, public or private. The second is that successful management in the long term will demand higher standards of knowledge, understanding and general culture than ever before.[1]

The report goes on to define management as 'the creation and maintenance of an environment for effective and efficient operation of individuals working in groups'.

There are numerous reasons why management will become more and more demanding and these include the growing sizes of organizations, the increased rate of change due to new technologies, the increased competition both nationally and internationally, greater involvement of the state in business matters, and changing political and cultural factors.

For existing managers there is an obvious need for 'development' in the widest sense, and for potential managers there is emerging a new level of professional competence, evidenced largely by the increasing output of young people with relevant qualifications at degree level, sub-degree, and postgraduate. Indeed it is this younger element which is giving added impetus to the need for established managers to be developed as they have to face up to the personal challenge of people better qualified and trained than themselves.

MANAGEMENT QUALIFICATIONS

There has been a dramatic increase in the number of people qualifying in management and business studies. These range from national certificates to first degrees and on to postgraduate studies at master's and doctoral level as well as the diploma in management studies.

The very variety of courses makes the output difficult to quantify but some very approximate figures indicate the magnitude of change which is likely to hit British industry over the next decade or so. The outcome, as yet unrecognized, is likely to change the nature of management from a traditional British base of the talented amateur to the well qualified professional.

At first degree level alone the current output (1984) is of the order of 3000 graduates per annum from some 80 universities and polytechnics, to which can be added at least the same number of sub- and post-graduate qualifications. Thus 6000 people a year with relevant qualifications might well lead to an input to British industry within a decade of 60 000 potential managers who arguably are better trained than their predecessors. This in no way diminishes the primary requirements of personal characteristics of initiative and entrepreneurial ability, but it does provide an important technical overlay of knowledge which is going to be required for the success of future managers. As an example of this phenomenon it is interesting to look at a typical 'business qualification'. An example has been taken from Bradford Management Centre of their part-time MBA programme (Table 16.1).

Table 16.1

Year	Autumn school	Term 1	Term 2	Term 3
1	Days 1, 2 Introduction 3 Finance 4 Managerial economics 5 Marketing	Managerial economics Statistics 1	Marketing 1 Statistics 2 (including computer programming)	Organizational behaviour Financial management 1
2	Production management	Marketing 2 Financial management 2	Personnel and industrial relations management Management science	Business policy International business
3	Days 1, 2, 3 Dissertation workshop 4, 5 Society and management	Dissertation Society and management		

It can be seen that the people on such a course as well as gaining experience from their respective full-time jobs are gaining what has been termed 'accelerated experience' over the full range of organizational management.

PROFESSIONAL QUALIFICATIONS

In addition to the academic qualifications outlined above, increasing numbers of young managers are studying for certificates and diplomas in marketing and related subjects. These range from the introduction levels of RSA and LCCI to the Institute of Marketing, the CAM Foundation and the Market Research Society. The numbers currently studying are well over 10 000 and while the qualifications are not universally recognized this is likely to change rapidly as more and more senior management is qualified.

The subjects covered are broad with the intention that for any one person in the first five years of working, first-hand experience will be gained in just one or two of the specialized marketing functions: the studies will make good the inevitable gaps. And so aspiring managers will move towards their goal with a full working knowledge gained partly from experience and in a large measure from vocational studies.

The following example comes from the CAM Foundation which offers a Certificate in Communication Studies followed by a modular diploma which enables a student to choose precisely a particular field of specialization.

A number of basic business courses—national certificates and diplomas—include marketing in their syllabuses, and, increasingly, secretarial courses touch upon it as do completely diverse subject areas such as home economics, banking, engineering, design, distribution and so on.

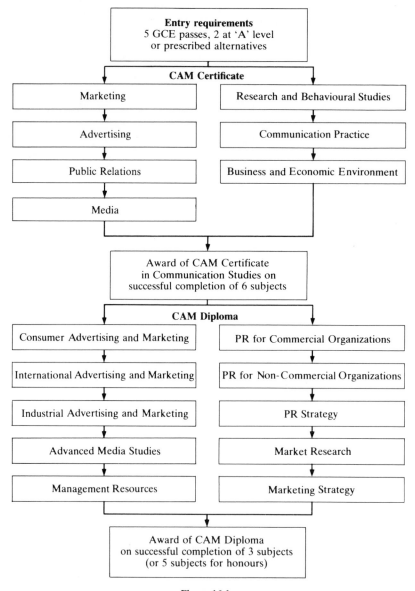

Figure 16.1

Professional marketing education

The Institute of Marketing can justifiably claim to have pioneered professional or vocational education first in sales management and now in marketing. Its courses are taught all over the world and its standards are high and increasing. The teaching base rests largely with evening classes at colleges of further education and polytechnics but it is backed by other alternatives such as correspondance courses.

For most students a course of study leading to the Institute's Diploma covers a period of three years part-time study and Table 16.2 indicates the range of subjects in which a student is required to demonstrate competence.

Table 16.2

Year	Subjects
1	Fundamentals of marketing
1	Economics of marketing
1	Business organization
1	Elements of statistics
2	Practice of marketing
2	Legal aspects of marketing
2	Behavioural aspects of marketing
2	Financial management accounting
3	International aspects of marketing
3	Marketing management—planning and control
3	Marketing management—analysis and decision
3	Marketing communication

ROUTES TO MARKETING MANAGEMENT

A marketing manager is likely to have come through any of the following routes:

- Salesman/manager
- Brand manager
- Sales office manager
- Advertising manager
- Product development
- Customer service
- Market research and information.

There are others, for example consultancy, advertising agency or any of the 'marketing services'.

The primary task, given that the individuals concerned will already have an 'industrial' bias, is to change a thoroughly competent executive to an effective and efficient manager. The added dimensions are in two areas, the management of people and the management of money. And to this must be added a general awareness of the working of all the specializations which go to make up the complete marketing activity.

So marketing managers come from all directions, and their development has an initial induction component, followed by the need to be kept abreast of a fast changing management activity.

THE MARKETING MANAGER'S JOB

Wide variations can be expected from company to company, but a good example of the marketing manager's job is given in *Training for Marketing*[2] from which the following extract is taken.

Example job descriptions

JOB DESCRIPTION

Date:	1 October 19—
Job title:	Marketing Manager
Reports to:	Chief Executive
Job location:	Head Office
Controls:	Sales Manager Advertising and Public Relations Manager Product Managers Market Research Manager
Objectives:	To formulate marketing and profit objectives from company objectives and to develop and implement a marketing plan to reach these objectives.
Authorities and responsibilities:	1 To estimate the share of the market that can be achieved in terms of sales and profit forecasts and the cost of achieving these figures through the marketing plan, making the most effective use of market research, product development, distribution, advertising, selling, sales promotion and servicing. 2 To prepare strategic long and short term marketing plans based on realistic sales and gross profit targets. 3 To determine objectives of advertising, market research, product research and consumer research. 4 To determine product priority, range and presentation; anticipate market changes and evaluate alternative marketing techniques to achieve defined objectives. 5 To determine pricing policy and to keep price levels of company products under continuous review to ensure that they are profitable and competitive. 6 To define the jobs of his subordinates in such a way that standards can be set and performance measured against these and training directed at systematically improving performance.
Appraisal:	Performance against these objectives, and specified targets, will be appraised at least twice per year and promotion and annual salary increases given against these appraisals.
Standards to be derived from:	1 Sales targets by volume, revenue and mix. 2 Profit targets by product and market share. 3 New product development programme. 4 Total marketing expenditure v. budget.

JOB DESCRIPTION

Date:	1 October 19—
Job title:	Sales Manager
Reports to:	Marketing Manager
Job location:	Head Office
Controls:	Salesmen Area Managers 3 Sales Office Staff
Objectives	To achieve the agreed sales and profit targets through the sales of the company's products.
Authorities and resposibilities:	1 To establish the product's sales potential and its characteristics and draw up sales forecasts based on these. 2 To prepare annual budgets and control company's selling activities within the agreed sales budget. 3 To recruit, select, train, appraise and develop field sales and sales office staff. 4 To set targets, both financial and by products, for field staff to meet sales budget. 5 To determine salesmen's geographical territories and the number of calls per journey cycle, eliminating unprofitable calls. 6 To arrange and conduct field staff meetings, ensuring that staff are aware of company's sales policy, advertising and promotion activities. Encouraging suggestions from salesmen and informing them of current sales situation. 7 To promote sales in conjunction with marketing and advertising managers, through exhibitions, advertising, display and general promotional activities. 8 To co-operate with marketing manager deciding pricing strategy and to be responsible for issuing price lists and conditions of sale. 9 To be responsible for the administration of the sales office, ensuring acceptable cash flow from debtors. 10 To give immediate attention to any complaint and decide on action to be taken according to company policy.
Appraisal:	Performance against these objectives, and specified targets, will be appraised annually and promotion and salary increases given against these appraisals.
Standards to be derived from:	1 Territory performance in terms of sales target. 2 Key account performance as percentage of territory target. 3 Development of sales staff.

From the same publication comes a description of the skills and knowledge required other than the specific components of marketing.

Firstly he needs to know about the general functions of management such as the setting of objectives, planning, organisation, staffing, motivation and control.

Secondly, the marketing manager must also be informed in the other fields of company operation in order to be able to integrate the marketing function within them.... In the field of finance the marketing manager should be familiar with budgeting, costing, break-even analysis, management ratios and investment analysis. Under production the essential topics are: capacities, factory limitations and opportunities, productive capabilities, product service requirements and production lead times. Under the heading of research and development, he should be aware of technological developments, technical possibilities, testing procedures and research and development lead times.

QUALITIES OF A MARKETING MANAGER

For a manager to be successful there must be the right combination of three factors:

- Personal qualities
- Knowledge
- Luck.

The matter of knowledge has already been discussed, though future knowledge requirements will be dealt with later. On luck there is nothing useful that one can say. And it is personal qualities which now need to be examined.

The qualities needed by managers at all levels in the future will be those which have made successful managers in the past. Shorn of jargon, they are intelligence, adaptability, an ability to get along with people of all kinds, strength of character or toughness, good health and abundant energy, physical and intellectual. It would be nice to be able to say that they should be scrupulously honest in their dealings with everyone but there have been many successful managers who have not been—and got away with it. These qualities can be developed and strengthened through increased knowledge and by being placed in situations where they have to be exercised.

SELECTION

With large organizations it is often the policy to promote from within, in which case the selection of people for a position of new responsibility is at least accompanied by a proven track record and a good deal of data from internal sources.

Most appointments, however, are from outside and here the selection is probably as difficult or more difficult due perhaps to the importance of personal qualities.

The first step is to convert the job specification into a man (or woman) profile. This is simply a matter of writing down all the desirable attributes that would go to make up the ideal person to fit the job description. This then becomes the basis of the advertising campaign to attract applicants, and in expanded form it is the basis of a checklist which helps to build in a structure and perhaps some objectivity at the subsequent interviewing.

The following example is of an animal feeds salesman and is taken from *Training for Marketing*.

MAN PROFILE: Animal feeds salesman

1. ATTAINMENTS
   (What educational levels are needed? What sort of experience is required?)

   3 'O' levels inc. maths. 'A' levels including a science preferred. Some veterinary or agricultural experience; ideally 1 year selling in an agricultural environment.

2. PHYSICAL MAKE-UP
   (What physique/health factors are important, e.g., to lift, use equipment, concentrate, work outdoors, etc.?)

   Fit enough to drive 30 000 miles p.a.; to lift products up to 1 cwt; to work erratic hours; to withstand outdoor working conditions.

3. GENERAL INTELLIGENCE
(What intelligence level is sufficient?)

Average.

4. SPECIAL APTITUDES
(What aptitudes are required to relate with people; for manual dexterity; to be able to calculate?)

Car driver (clean licence); must get on with others, especially at professional and social level; communication skills.

5. INTERESTS
(What special interests are required to create rapport with customer?)

Interest in agricultural topics; some participation in local social activities.

6. DISPOSITION
(What attitudes are required towards self-motivation, decision taking, leadership, etc.?)

Willing to work hard to build territory; 'self-starter' must accept responsibility (little direct supervision); absolute integrity (dealing with cash, veterinary advice).

7. CIRCUMSTANCES
(What background considerations are important, e.g., age, home location?)

Ideally 28–35; male, preferably married resident in area (ideally with local connections); able to start within a month.

A TRAINING CHECKLIST

Training is an activity which suffers from two severe limitations: it can always be put off until tomorrow, and no one is really interested. In the face of this it is useful to carry out a periodical training audit, and the following is a typical checklist to facilitate this.[3]

Organizations employing managers should take the following steps:

1. Review regularly whatever systems they have for formulating management training objectives, for determining training needs, for selecting external or providing internal training courses, and for evaluating the effects of management training.
2. Seek to clarify their training objectives.
3. Involve managers as directly as possible in the appraisal of their performance and potential, preferably by discussion.
4. Involve managers as directly as possible in the diagnosis of their training needs, preferably by discussion.
5. Consider whether what may at first sight appear to be a 'training need' may in reality be a need for organizational restructuring or new recruitment or transfer policies.
6. Wherever possible to seek collaboration with external educators/trainers (whether colleges or universities, consultants, or industrial training boards) in developing training that is tailored to their own identified needs and interests.
7. In the case of small companies, to explore the possibilities of collaborating with neighbouring small companies in developing joint management training programmes.
8. Establish procedures for vetting the range of external courses.
9. Provide advice and consultation for managers about alternative training possibilities and especially about external course selection.
10. Attempt to evaluate both the benefits that managers derive from management training, internal or external, and the overall worth of the management training effort.

TYPES OF TRAINING

The development of marketing managers is, of course, a great deal more than the provision of a few courses and the sending of some up-and-coming managers on to outside seminars. It is rather a way of life, a business philosophy in which a company sets out openly to encourage and facilitate the movement of its staff into new and challenging positions until they reach an optimum level of ability and job satisfaction. To this extent the role of annual staff reviews is important as an opportunity for discussing personal strengths and weaknesses, and reaching a joint view on action to be taken.

Movement of staff into different job functions in order to broaden their experience base is probably more important than any number of courses though there are severe limits on the number of such moves within any given time.

Similarly most courses have little to do in the way of developing personal characteristics. Motivation for instance cannot be taught though it can certainly be strengthened by suitable encouragement by senior management. Equally so confidence, enthusiasm, self-criticism and discipline.

That said, the fact is that there is considerable scope for pure training and education, all with a view to imparting new and relevant knowledge both to up-and-coming managers and to those who are already in post.

There are broadly eight categories under which types of training can be examined. These are:

1. Full-time courses
2. Part-time courses
3. Evening classes
4. Correspondence courses
5. Executive programmes
6. Seminars
7. Conferences
8. In-company courses

Full-time courses

This is a major exercise since it involves giving a member of staff at least an academic year's absence.

The first course to consider is the Diploma in Management Studies (DMS). This is called 'postgraduate' though in fact a university degree is not always necessary for admission. Quality varies from one institution to another, and the amount of marketing studies is another variable. An alternative here for the specialist is to enrol for a postgraduate Diploma in Marketing. This might be an internal college qualification or it might be validated by the CNAA.

The MBA is probably the most prestigious course and qualification, having inherited a high reputation initially from the American management schools. Many British institutions now offer this qualification, some one year, some two, and all with a greater or lesser degree of marketing. There is also an opportunity at master's level to go for a specialized marketing degree either as a taught course or by research.

Part-time courses

These are mostly for people at the beginning of their careers and start maybe with Higher National Certificates in Business Studies, some of which have a good proportion of marketing subjects. These will be two or three years and are very practical relevant courses.

There are also a number of first degrees in business studies on a part-time basis, and a growing number of master's programmes. Additionally, the professional qualification of CAM and the Institute of Marketing mentioned earlier are almost all part-time or evening.

Evening classes

Almost every town of any size will have a local college where an evening class in marketing can be discovered. This may be 'non-qualification', at an elementary level, or sometimes over a period of time quite advanced. The pros and cons of evening study have been debated over the years, and things are no different with classes in marketing. Students are tired, and sometimes so are the lecturers; student numbers decline by 50 per cent after Christmas; homework is not done or not even set and so on. Yet for some this remains the most important source of gaining new knowledge. Certainly anyone gaining a qualification, particularly an advanced one, after a series of evening sessions, can be accepted as well motivated.

Correspondence courses

There are a good number of worthwhile, if expensive correspondence courses in every specialized subject imaginable and for some they are the only way of filling in the knowledge gaps left by experience alone and where a person is determined to enhance his or her career prospects.

Executive programmes

There are a number of management colleges dependent or independent of universities where one- to four-week courses are provided on marketing and related subjects. They are very expensive and the quality of tuition is usually very high. Compared with in-company work they are immediately less relevant and at the same time provide a much wider perspective. The intermingling of course members from all disciplines and types of organization is in itself a valuable by-product.

Perhaps the greatest criticism is that for a week or two the people concerned can find a kind of theoretical business fantasy only to lose it completely upon return to base. This can be overcome by requiring a report not only on the course itself but also on the specific new actions which are proposed arising out of this course of study.

Seminars

These are usually of shorter duration, one or two days, and deal more likely with a subject which is either current (e.g., new satellite media) or highly specialized (e.g., PR in marketing). They are also expensive. Notwithstanding the shortcomings, they can play a very valuable role providing they are accurately tailored to an individual's needs. Beware here of what might be termed the commercial operators who are only in it for a 'fast buck'. Safer to stick with the more reputable and responsible sponsoring organizations.

Conferences

Look with great caution at conferences. There are obviously some excellent ones but perhaps the majority are benefit matches for the organizers, and as the attenders so often put it 'the real value is in the personal contacts in between formal sessions'.

In-company courses

For any company of any size these must surely form the backbone of any long-term management development programme.

In-house tutors will, of course, be biased and introverted but they might be very good tutors for all that. Many organizations deliberately tackle that problem by having a number of outside specialists and this can work very well providing they are adequately briefed. The absence of mixing with people from other organizations is made good by mixing with people from the same organization, but maybe from all parts of the business, thus providing a different but valuable broadening of perspective.

THE FUTURE

The rate of change in business activities coupled with increasing competition from home and abroad will mean that companies must take training seriously if they are to survive. The very least it will do is to give 'added value' to your product. The most you can expect is to increase progressively the efficiency and effectiveness of the whole organization, with a more satisfied workforce leading to higher financial returns.

REFERENCES

1. *Management Education: a world view of experience and needs*, BIM, London 1981.
2. *Training for Marketing*, HM Stationery Office, London 1972.
3. *The Training of British Managers*, HM Stationery Office, London 1972.

SEVENTEEN

INDUSTRIAL MARKETING—A JANUS-LIKE APPROACH, RETROSPECT AND PREDICTION

Aubrey Wilson

It is a sobering activity for anyone attempting to predict the future to return to an old forecast to establish how far past prognostications align with the reality of the history of the period. The temptation to exaggerate the successful guesses, for that is what all forecasting is, and to bury the unsuccessful ones, is enormous. Alternatively, if an explanation for a poor forecast is called for, then there are 1000 excuses to justify the variation from the actuality.

The pleasure of being able to say 'I told you so' is more than counterbalanced by the risks of embarrassment which wild inaccuracies engender. It is to be wondered, therefore, that anyone not forced to do so should want to rush into print with their very personal views on what the future holds.

But forecasting or prediction is as old as man himself. Prophesy, witchcraft, necromancy, sorcery, were the trading skills of the Sybils, Old Testament prophets, Merlins, Lilith and Nostradamus; philtres, fire and the entrails of freshly killed pigeons were their materials. The desire to peer into the future is as fundamental to man's nature as is his need for personal acceptance and recognition and his overwhelming desire to know, but at the same time to fear, what tomorrow holds. It is this atavistic urge to pull back the curtain which tempts the forecaster to risk the public scrutiny of a claimed wisdom and insight.

It takes a man of the stature of the late Herman Kahn, to risk a 200 year forecast[1] when with all the science, hardware, skills and recorded historical data meteorologists will only anticipate the month ahead in the loosest terms. Kahn's Hudson Institute's[2] anticipation of Britain in the 1980s has an almost uncanny accuracy. The decline of the steel industry, the decimation of the consumer domestic appliance manufacturing industry and of the Midlands prosperity, booming at the time of the forecast, and even a decline in the world price of oil, were all predicted.

Such 10-year accuracy encourages a re-examination of scenarios and others, like myself, lacking the prescience of Kahn find the usual mixture of success and failure. Thus to return to 'Marketing in the next decade' which concluded the 1963 version of this book it can be seen that:

- It has certainly become possible, as it was not two decades ago, to test many propositions that had then only been treated as academic before there was, as now, ubiquitous access to data processing even in one-man businesses. The new generation of small and cheap computers may not have emerged in the decade for which their appearance was forecast, but certainly they were not all that far behind the timescale. Inevitably in marketing the computer has had a pervasive impact.

- The most important prognosis concerning the achievement of a far deeper understanding of the dynamics of individual buying situations was accurate. Today there can be few involved in industrial marketing who have not rejected the simplistic approach of the 1960s and exploited the extensive knowledge which now exists.
- The service economy for industry was stated in 1963 to be 'just around the corner'. This is another expectation which has been fulfilled as all those involved in marketing non-consumer goods and services are well aware with the array of services which have become available to them.
- Industrial distribution supply lines have grown shorter and infinitely more efficient.
- The enhancement of those three vital skills—technical, human and conceptual—is obvious to see.

So much for success. What about the failed forecasts?

- Long-range planning was held out in 1963 as one of the key advances and looked well placed to fill the important role anticipated for it. But the turbulent and highly disturbed conditions which emerged at the end of the first decade of the forecast, and the aftermath of the 1973 Middle East war, reduced the timescale of business thinking, and with it market planning, from the usual 5 and 10 years to the more immediate. Survival became the name of the game.
- The new generation of marketing managers which it was suggested would have line and staff experience and thus remove unnatural barriers, have not emerged. While managers may be more knowledgeable and more skilled in many marketing activities, they remain as parochial as they have always been. 'Common training for line and staff' is still uncommon.
- Despite the vast improvement in information flow and accessibility there is little evidence that the marketing aspects of business are managed with anything approaching the same precision as is production.

These somewhat chastening reminders of the fallibility of the forecaster do serve to ensure that in re-indulging in a prediction exercise, the wilder flights of fancy are constrained. A Janus-like view has its value since a consideration of the past will give better judgement in the future, even if it is perhaps historians rather than history who repeat themselves.

A LINNAEUS APPROACH

'The past is a foreign country, they do things differently there' wrote J. P. Hartley. In industrial marketing it is perhaps appropriate to bemoan that the past is still pervasive and things are not done as differently as all that or as is desirable if business is to come to terms with the new ethos.

Looking back now it can be seen that in marketing there have been 'eras' or phases rather than decades, which can be as neatly labelled as Paine's 'Age of Reason' or Galbraith's 'Age of Uncertainty' even if not so closely related to their subject. Not surprisingly most of these designations come from the USA.

In America the 1950s were perceived as the 'product' era when all the attention was directed to product features and benefits. The 1960s were named the 'image' era when companies found that their image was more important to sell the product than specific features of the product. The 1970s were described as the 'positioning' era which was defined as the ranking a product commands in the buyer's mind, related to the leader's position.

In industrial marketing in the United Kingdom and in the rest of Europe it is also possible to discern eras or phases which can be neatly classified. The 1960s were seen to have been the decade of 'experimentation'. Indeed they were. Industry crawled out of the Palaeozoic ooze of being product centred on to the dry land of marketing orientation. The marketing concept for many industrial firms was accepted perhaps two or three decades after its implications and practice had penetrated large parts of the consumer goods industry. If there was one lesson sentient industry learned in the 1960s, it was that if you do not market, something terrible happens—nothing! This period was perhaps the equivalent of the American 'product' era.

By 1970 the fact that industrial firms, products and services had images and their buyers' choice was influenced by their perceptions of them had penetrated large segments of industry. Firms became 'image sensitive' and set themselves sensible image targets. These had the inestimable advantage to the industrial customer of the reality being moved towards the image objective. The multiple image concept, although first promulgated as early as 1960, only came to substantial acceptance in industrial marketing in the 1970s. The 'image' era of 1960 in the USA became the 'image decade' in Europe in the 1970s.

Thus using the USA as a guideline it might well be prognosticated that Europe will now enter its own 'positioning' era. This may be so, but an examination of more fundamental advances over the last 20 to 30 years suggests that the changes between now and the end of the century will be even more important and significant. Interesting and indeed perhaps even useful as they are, these taxonomies in fact obscure the really important breakthroughs in industrial marketing if only because changes obstinately refuse to fall into decade categorizations, although as generalizations they are useful.

For the 1960s the key advance in fact was the final, if grudging, acceptance that industrial buying was anything but a simple moment of truth activity. The subsequent 'features and benefits' approach to marketing and image sensitivity was made infinitely more practical and useful by the knowledge obtained of how buying units and power centres were composed, how the purchasing process itself divided into its various phases and classes and then, of course, the decision-forming factors. A number of proving research studies added final confirmation to the body of theoretical and empiric knowledge achieved during the 1960s.

Alongside these developments there was much new thinking on the problem of the non-differentiated industrial product where previously the major response in these markets had been price cutting—a technique described as slitting someone else's throat and bleeding to death yourself. New thinking and new approaches brought about significant changes for manufacturers of standard products and which, perhaps more interestingly, led to another major breakthrough at the end of the decade which is referred to later.

An achievement of the 1970s was the long awaited and much needed closer integration of selling and marketing although some firms continue and will continue obstinately to regard them as separate and indeed almost unconnected activities. Marketing men's significant failure to 'sell' marketing to other parts of the company was at last being remedied.

Again failing to fit into the decade classification two other major innovations in marketing thinking and practice can be seen. First, at last, a unifying theory that explained a large number of marketing disasters, some on a vast scale. These markets, referred to in a *Harvard Business Review* as 'Ghost'[3] markets, were ascribed to the enhanced ability of researchers to measure non-existent markets ranging from high technology to basic products. Greater sensitivity to the likelihood of a market which appears to have substance but which is pure ectoplasm would have unquestionably prevented many marketing disasters.

As the 1970s ended Du Pont revealed its approach to the question of price cutting which links with the earlier features and benefits approach of the 1960s and the marketing problems of non-differentiated products. The Du Pont method was to research product attributes most valued (by a system of testing the effect of the removal of different attributes and by price increments) and to promote the product in those segments where the attributes were most valued.

It thus enabled anyone using the approach to assess accurately how far prices could be increased and which attributes could be dropped or reduced to make a price reduction equally profitable. It also has the inestimable advantages of highlighting the promotional message which would have most meaning to the customer, indicating product changes or new products needed, and identifying where perceptions of the firm or product were incorrect or unformed. The technique was and is of very considerable value in bringing into sharp focus the marketing message and the methods to be used. Also it avoided the pitfalls of price-sensitive markets.

But overlying these time distinctions were pervasive economic and social changes. If the 1960s were a period of experimentation then the 1970s can be seen in retrospect to be the 'survival' era. A plethora of books on surviving under conditions of inflation, operating in a market bedevilled by shortages, politically and industrially induced restrictions and marketing on small budgets all evidence the problems encountered. Advances in industrial marketing there were, as has been shown, but whether firms besieged now by conditions undreamed of in the happier days of the 1950s and 1960s will risk experimentation, large investments on irrecoverable marketing costs, is a matter for conjecture.

WHAT'S NEW ABOUT THE FUTURE?

And so to the remaining years of this century. Will industrial marketing be more sophisticated and complex or will economic turmoil and social change mean a return to perhaps simpler and more primitive approaches?

Perhaps the most thoughtful and provoking study of marketing's future has been undertaken by William Waters[4] who has expressed the era concept as a basis for forecasting in an alternative scenario. Although related to consumer goods it is easily translatable to industrial goods if a time shift is made. Instead of periods of 'product', 'image' and 'positioning' emphasis, he has identified a marketing cycle. The first phase started with 'scarcity' when the marketing function was simply to sell what was produced. Marketing was a subsidiary to production because rapidly growing demand tended to exceed supply. This was the era of the product. Stage II he identified as occurring about the turn of the century. When mass production became a reality, sales 'push' was required with its panoply of supporting activities—advertising, distribution, branding. Abundance in relative terms replaced scarcity for much of the period. Market saturation occurred but customers' interests were still subordinate to the product and to the producer's need.

Stage III emerged following the cataclysms of the Second World War. Self-service, mass advertising, most particularly television, moved the emphasis from the management of selling to the management of consumer behaviour. This at last was the marketing concept in action.

And the future begins here. The fourth phase of marketing is already upon us and will rise to dominate in the next 10 years.

Waters's best judgement of marketing's changing priorities and activities is summarized in Table 17.1 where he compares Stage III marketing (marketing concept) through its transitional period into the brave new world of Stage IV marketing. It will be seen at once that the rise and fall of unit volume as a measure of performance, the fall and fall of 'market share' and 'gross revenues' as indicators and the rise and rise of 'return on investment', 'number of distribution outlets', 'traceable sales' and the 'timeliness of research' are of prior importance.

MARKETING'S RESPONSIBILITIES

Waters's scenario predicates major adjustments in management attitudes and thus the seminal changes which will occur between now and the end of the century will almost certainly stem from

Table 17.1 Marketing's shifting priorities (source: SRI, Calfornia)

Marketing consideration	Relative importance of marketing consideration		
	Marketing III	Transition period	Marketing IV
Sales performance			
Unit volume (sales)	xx	xxx	x
Unit volume (orders)	x	x	xx
Share of market	xxx	xx	xx
Quality of sales mix	x	x	x
Repeat purchase ratio	x	x	x
Financial performance			
Gross revenues	xx	xx	x
Net revenues	—	x	xx
Profit per unit	—	x	x
Cash flow	—	xxx	xx
Return on investment	x	x	xxx
Distribution			
Number of outlets	x	x	xx
Quality of outlets	x	x	x
Advertising performance			
Brand recognition	x	x	x
Advertising recall	x	x	x
Traceable sales	x	x	xx
Advertising costs	x	x	x
Consumer-government affairs management			
Incidence of complaints	—	x	xx
Lawsuit dispositions	—	—	x
Government regulation problems	—	x	xx
Level of recall activity	—	x	x
Associated costs	—	—	xx
Service performance			
Incidence of complaints	x	x	x
Associated costs	—	x	xx
Company reputation			
Company name (logo) recognition	x	x	x
Favourable versus unfavourable opinions	—	—	x
Company name (logo) and brand association	—	—	x
Sales forecasting			
Overall accuracy	—	—	x
Production scheduling accuracy (short term)	x	x	x
Production planning accuracy (long term)	—	x	x
Marketing information and research			
Coverage	x	x	x
Accuracy	x	x	x
Quality	x	x	x
Timeliness	x	x	xx

Key: xxx = Primary importance; xx = Secondary importance; x = Others; — = Not important.

Note The above ratings represent the author's best judgement. A comprehensive survey of a representative sample of US companies would probably result in somewhat different ratings for some items; however, it is unlikely that such a survey would reflect a significantly different overall pattern of change.

a new way of thinking about the role and function of marketing and with this will come resultant changes in the way marketing is undertaken. The disruption in world economies which began in the early 1970s is still regarded as a temporary phenomenon despite the fact that 10 years have demonstrated an ever increasing turbulence. Accepting that calmer times are unlikely to return for very many years, if at all, must be the first step in coming to terms with highly volatile situations and markets. Thus the need for surveillance, flexibility, speed of decision and a willingness to abandon no longer relevant techniques and ideas as well as no longer acceptable products and services will typify the successful marketing manager.

The marketing concept, important and successful in its time, was devised on the basis of market 'pull', that is influencing users by marketing to 'pull' products through the system. Its viability has, however, been seriously reduced because of the severe distortions and the faltering expansion, and in many instances decline of economies. Moreover, changing social values, consumerism and attitudes to business are having their impact on industrial marketing.

It has been argued that no amount of excellent marketing or excellent selling will persuade an industrial buyer to purchase goods and services he does not want. This is in contradistinction to the consumer buyer. Both propositions are dubious and industrial marketers of all goods and services will have to think again about their role. This piece of introspection will undoubtedly bring about changes in every aspect of industrial marketing.

Just as business devised the marketing concept to exploit expansion, it will in the future have to develop new approaches to deal with societal issues which are intruding into markets. Unsafe materials may be acceptable to original equipment manufacturers but their customers and their customers' customers increasingly will bring pressure on their own immediate suppliers as society protests with increasing vigour at the supply of dangerous products, useless products or undesirable products.[5] Nothing which is sold to industry, no matter how far removed from the ultimate consumer, commands any demand that does not itself derive from a consumer demand. This lesson was taught many years ago and today is even more pertinent.

The manufacturer of industrial products may believe he is remote from the pressures of society but he is not insulated from them. The link between the ultimate consumer and the most remote supplier has always and will always exist and Fig. 17.1 exemplifies this. The connection which appears more tenuous the further the distance of the supplier from the ultimate consumer, will become far more important and sensitive as an increasingly vocal market makes its views

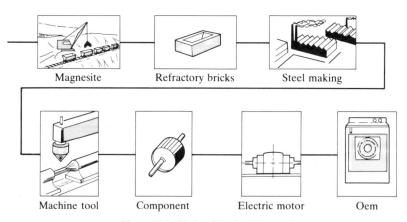

| Magnesite | Refractory bricks | Steel making |

| Machine tool | Component | Electric motor | Oem |

Figure 17.1 Chain of Derived Demand

known and will, when necessary, back such views with the strongest action available to any customer—the freedom not to purchase.

Over the next decade, therefore, one of the most significant changes will be an acceptance that marketing's responsibilities, goals and priorities are now different. The primary task will continue to be the anticipation and satisfaction of a user's needs but many marketing activities will alter in method and content.

The important concomitant of this adjustment will be the quality and type of leadership which will emerge. The individuals who will be the pace-setters in marketing in the future will almost certainly have qualities very different from marketing leaders of the past and of today. Tomorrow's marketing chiefs will be the product of the increasing complexity of business caused by a far greater regulatory environment and a vocal, well represented and militant customer group. None of this implies that the humanistic side of marketing will be any less important only that the intuitive characteristics of today's marketing managers will be of a different nature. Tomorrow, top marketing leaders will be business statesmen aware of the critical distinction between profit taking and profiteering, resource utilization and resource exploitation and honest and technically legal, but nevertheless misleading messages.

MARKET INTELLIGENCE

While long-range planning has had its horizons severely circumscribed by the inability to forecast, with any certainty, the course of world events, marketing planning will take on a new importance if only because the margin of acceptable error is narrowing. Far more variables will be considered and it will be practical to do so given the great advances which will continue to occur in data collection, processing and interpretation.

Industrial marketing research has made an immense contribution to the discipline of marketing, but has still failed to develop to its full potential and to provide management with the strategic assistance it requires. The link between research and the development of the strategies inherent in applying the marketing concept has never been firmly established and researchers have viewed their own function far too narrowly.

The role of researchers will in future be very different to that which they have adopted in the past or into which they have been forced. It will be imperative to identify management's substantive problems rather than to offer a mechanics service of simply providing information management *thinks* it needs instead of seeking to understand the problem which the information is meant to resolve.

Measuring a market is not the same as knowing it, a fact which has not yet penetrated the corporate psyche of many firms. An 'intention to purchase' expressed against an innovative concept or product even today, let alone in the 1990s, is about as believable as Hitler's claim on 26 September 1938: 'It is [Sudetenland] the last territorial claim which I have to make in Europe.'

The history of marketing is littered with corpses of brilliantly researched situations with wildly inaccurate interpretations of the results which pre-empted the development of suitable strategies for the profitable exploitation of the innovative products.[6] Moreover, an innovative product can succeed in one ethos and fail in another. Compare the market for Citizen Band Radio in the USA and the UK to witness a difference between the same product in two countries. Similarly, a total misconception of user preference could not be better illustrated than by the relative failure of the laser disc video system as compared to the cartridge. Certainly users wanted better quality pictures as was claimed for the disc, but they wanted 'time shift' far more. No one will ever know whether the researchers asked the wrong questions or got the wrong answers. Failure of these sorts in future will be more difficult to explain and excuse. The examples are both substantially, but not wholly, consumer products but the implication of the failures for manufacturers of components, for example, for these original equipments is obvious and is direct.

Today's situation is that those who contribute market intelligence and judgement on market reactions usually command only one discipline—marketing research. The day of economic paeon tilling the soil under instructions is nearing its end. The new management ethos which will emerge demands a far wider knowledge than just of research techniques; wider indeed than just marketing itself. The successful marketing managers of industrial firms by the year 2000 may well be those whose basic training is finance or law, as much as marketing. More importantly the individuals will combine a strong entrepreneurial drive, with innovative and creative flair all of which are at least equal to the complementary characteristics of the engineers and scientists.

Thus for the future, the marketing researcher, to perform adequately to meet the demands of the new style marketing managers, will have to be competent in the whole of marketing, not just one narrow segment—research. He will be creative in devising and introducing innovative strategies. His role will change significantly. It will be widened and he will be accepted as an integral part of marketing management, not simply a service to it. The new marketing approaches and the new attitude to marketing will be successfully adopted with the benefit of the undoubted and previously underexploited skills of the marketing researcher.

SERVICES TO THE RESCUE

It was suggested earlier that in marketing terms, decades or eras can be identified by the dominant characteristics of activities in that period. If the next decade is to be named then the evidence points to the service industries. The marketing of all services, but most particularly professional services, has been neglected by academics and practitioners alike; a neglect encouraged by the mandatory restrictions imposed by some professions on their members. Now there is a noticeable reaction against such restraints. Practice development techniques, which in some respects are very different in content and emphasis from product marketing, are being increasingly used and more importantly approved by the collegial and other organizations which control service activities.

That Britain should be in the forefront of service marketing is both understandable and sensible. British financial services of all types, engineering and management consultancy, marketing research, architecture, publishing, entertainment, R & D, training and education, all have world markets and stature. Services have much to commend them. They are labour intensive at a time when industry is increasingly capital intensive; in recession services employment declines less quickly than manufacturing employment; the types of demand which initiate general fluctuations in the economy are precisely those which affect goods production to a far greater degree than the supply of services.

Because in marketing intangibles either surrogates for the 'product' must be used or some techniques totally abandoned—media advertising, sampling, demonstration, exhibitions for example—new sensitivities as well as new techniques will be developed which will take the marketing of services well beyond their present crude levels.

Given the erosion of Britain's manufacturing base, a fate other developed countries might well anticipate, there is every reason to suppose that economic necessity will push marketing in the United Kingdom towards an as yet barely studied and practised area of activity—service marketing—that holds considerable promise and rewards out of all proportion to the investment and effort.

NEW PRODUCT DEVELOPMENT

It is part of the polemics of industrial marketing as to whether product strategy is included in marketing strategy or whether it is separate but parallel to it. By the end of the century the argument will appear about as useful and practical as a medieval disputation as to how many angels can dance on the head of a pin. Product development will be part of marketing—a vital part.

It is now an accepted fact that there are no Western type economies which can meet competition in their domestic or export markets for low and in many cases medium technology goods manufactured in developing countries. Textiles and many consumer electronic products are perfect examples. In many cases the markets of the industrialized nations have been completely eroded and increasingly more complex products, previously beyond the capabilities of the low cost producing countries, are coming under the same pressure.

Price has become the main competitive medium. There are two ways of defending a price-sensitive market. These are, improvements in product quality through technological innovation as basic source of comparative advantage (in reality renewal) or else totally innovative products. In either circumstance price can be superseded by a preference for product values—real or perceptual. This in turn implies a knowledge of just what the buyer—intermediate or final—values. What has been considered a philosophic verity since Plato first enunciated it nearly 2500 years ago, 'The true creator is necessity who is the mother of invention', has become decreasingly applicable.

While it is undeniable that 'necessity' has led to many, if not most innovations up to the turn of the century, subsequently the mother of invention has been 'desire' rather than 'need'. These 'desires' are and will continue to be generated by cultural and social pressures, not just affecting people in their private lives, but also their business, scientific or academic pursuits. R & D it is said is 'seeds' orientated, marketing 'needs' orientated. 'Desire' led demand when compared with the deprivation of the Third World may well be seen as 'greed'. Pejorative or not 'desire' led demand will continue to be a feature of many markets. 'Seed', 'need' and 'greed' will culminate in the different approaches to innovation for the closing years of the century.

It can be deduced with little risk of argument that innovation to be commercially successful has to meet a need or a desire that may be only latent and that it requires the skills of the communicators to raise it to conscious level, and beyond that to comprehension and belief and then to those actions that lead to the exchange of values. But in relating these marketing objectives to the new ethos in industrial markets, it can be seen that marketing in future will require not just skill and aggressiveness but also grace and sophistication.

Increasingly, the processes of innovation will be conducted in parallel with a deeper and consistent study of the target for the innovative concept or product (or service)—the customer. There is already *prima facie* evidence to show what can only be termed 'national attitudes' to involving the customer at the optimum moment do affect innovative performance.

A comparative study of the UK and West German machine tool industries,[7] while not conclusive is most certainly indicative of the impact of attitudinal factors on performance. Britain once dominated world markets for machine tools but has lost heavily to West Germany, USA, Japan and more recently to such countries as Korea. A study has been conducted of the unsuccessful (UK) and successful (German) producer countries in product innovation and development and their attitudes to customer involvement in the innovative process were based on research among both manufacturers and their customers. In summary, British companies appeared to have more of the trappings and less of the substance of marketing than the West German ones.

British companies were more likely to have market research managers or marketing directors and were more likely to do specific market research work for new products . . . but they had less direct involvement with the customer. In West Germany . . . customer involvement in the innovative products development process was seen as axiomatic if the company wanted to be successful. In contrast British suppliers' prevalent attitudes were not to involve the customer in the innovation process until the product was put on the market.

The research went on to show that customers of West German firms tended to value technical attributes and were more likely to suggest ideas for product developments or new products than were the customers of British firms. It was concluded that, given that customers of West German firms have a more positive attitude to new technology, it is clear that their role may be crucial in the new product development efforts. **An active user creates an active supplier**. Is this perhaps the maxim for the 1990s?

It is, of course, specious to suggest that it is only the customer–supplier interaction which encourages successful innovation. There are other elements: research institutions, universities, trade associations and the financial community, but unquestionably there is a strong, indeed overwhelming, case for involving the customer early in the innovative processes. Firms to be successful in the future will have to set aside the fears of disclosures, risking this against the rewards of rapid market acceptance.

Evangelism for improved and earlier supplier–customer interaction will only provide the motivation not the mechanism for achieving it. Opportunity search which is one polarity of the innovative process—that is 'market push' as opposed to 'technology push'—is currently all too often delegated at too great a distance from the action. R & D has often become isolated from the realities not just of the market place but of the firm's own strategists who have felt it sufficient to set the parameters and wait for results. Moreover too many technical and scientific executives have a preference for action rather than conceptualization which after all is why they have opted for business rather than, say, an academic life. But this desire for action is unfortunately all too often exhibited as a disdain and dislike for the market place. In future the gap between the engineer and the scientist and the market will be narrowed and closed—a metamorphosis emerging from the qualities of managers and the climate of management already referred to.[8]

Current management training and management approval encourage decision making and problem solving and this in turn leads to coping, not innovation. Add to this a lack of focus on opportunity search and the combination, while it may not be toxic (although a comparison of the 'top 500' firms a decade ago and today suggests it might well be), is certainly debilitating. It is a very safe prediction that the list of top 500 firms in every Western country by the end of the century will differ by as much as 60–70 per cent from today's list. In short, if the personality, culture and job satisfaction of personnel are in elegant problem solutions and their implementations not exploiting a market potential, then the development of innovative cures to which there are no known diseases is likely to be the dominant pattern of results. The future will not support such attitudes.

The encouragement of successful innovation is, and will continue to be, undeniably a team process but the question to be asked is whether personnel who are market sensitive (not just the commercially sensitive which is quite a different thing) are to be part of that team.

Perhaps closer links between manufacturers and their customers will not be the panacea that will lead to a high rate of successful exploitation of innovative and renewed products, but it can be said with certainty that without such working liaisons the present depressing rate of failure and the aggravating rate of success of competitive countries will continue.

No organization has prospered for any length of time by standing still. They thrive primarily because they change and change means the incorporation of creative activities into ongoing programmes. The type and direction of such activities can be led by the market if suppliers will change their cavalier attitudes to users and consult earlier, more closely and more frequently. There is a whole battery of research and information techniques which enables a flow of useful, relevant information to pass between the manufacturers and the ultimate users. It does not require high cost, esoteric methods to achieve the desideratum, which is yet another reason why the failure of innovative ideas is to be deplored. It is as expensive as it is unnecessary.

The job of management should not be about administrating the *status quo*; its primary role is to bring about change—to manage innovation at all levels and in all the business activities. But technical innovation without the involvement of the user, encourages only small incremental and safe changes which often can be tested tentatively, rather than major breakthroughs.

Not all innovation can be market proved and the chances of failure must inevitably be high, and will become even greater in the future. As an analogy it can be seen that perhaps not one out of the five new theatrical productions succeeds, but the ones that do, provide a return many thousand per cent more than the investment. It is little consolation to know that while 80 per cent or more of innovations will fail, someone somewhere is going to succeed spectacularly. In the world of the theatre the rewards of success may well cover the losses of failure. In an executive career or in corporate survival, such a comforting back-up situation does not exist even remotely. Thus the need for all innovation to achieve a higher success striking rate is personal, corporate and dominant. The results of failure can be and usually are catastrophic for the individual in both a career and social sense and for the corporation in terms of survival.

There is no theory, no system, no hardware, no definable single characteristic or combination of characteristics which now or in the future will guarantee success in exploiting invention. The grosser errors can, however, be avoided if the market is probed and interrogated in a sensible way. Just as critically and as importantly, if the results must be interpreted in the form of creative marketing strategies and action. Only this way can the project be brought from concept to commercial success. This will undoubtedly occur with greater frequency in the years to come.

The closer relationship of user and innovator must be the desideratum for all businesses which make any claim to be innovative and which are determined to be successfully innovative— successful by whatever criteria they choose to select.

'For the next ten years, the most important and far reaching of all developments will be neither methods nor skills but the changes in men's minds and their attitudes towards business and marketing.' This was how the chapter 'Marketing in the next decade' in the 1963 version of this book ended. Some 20 years later nothing has changed this desideratum. If the much needed changes in attitude did not occur on the scale or wholly in the way which had been anticipated and hoped for, there is still every reason to assume that the metamorphosis will yet occur. Perhaps it will be encouraged this time, as it was not before, by the volatility of economies, a different, questioning attitude of customers, their expanding aspirations, the increasing blurring of conventional boundaries between products and services and the need to demonstrate, that with all its unquestioned faults, the infinite superiority of a free society in providing for its citizens over that of the strictly planned economies where market forces are not allowed to fulfil the aspirations of the people. The industrialized societies of the West are far from being a cornucopia of plenty for everyone but they do not create the dreary low quality uniformity or the endemic shortages which typify the alternative form of political structures. Marketing is not a tool for the ruthless exploitation of the capitalist ethic; it is the means for providing, at the very least, the hope and possibility of far higher standards of living and greatly improved quality of life for everyone.

REFERENCES

1. Kahn, Herman. *The Next 200 Years*, Associated Business Programmes, London 1976.
2. Hudson Institute. *The United Kingdom 1980*, Associated Business Programmes, London 1974.
3. Wilson, Aubrey and Bryan Atkin. 'Exorcising ghosts in marketing', *Harvard Business Review* (Cambridge, Mass.), September/October 1976.
4. Waters, William. 'Consumer marketing in a period of change', *Business Intelligence Programme Guidelines*, No. 1009 (SRI Menlo Park, California), November 1976.
5. Wilson, Aubrey and Christopher West. 'The marketing of unmentionables', *Harvard Business Review* (Cambridge, Mass.), January/February 1981.
6. 'Exorcising ghosts in marketing', op. cit.
7. Parkinson, Steve. 'Successful new product development—an international comparative study', *The Business Graduator*, Business Graduate Association, London, Spring 1982.
8. Wilson, Aubrey. 'Innovation in the market place', *Management Today*, June 1984.

INDEX